300 to 1
(My 52-year Journey with St. Louis Hockey and a Championship for the Ages)

By Mark Sophir

Copyright Mark Sophir (2019)

This book is not affiliated with or authorized, sponsored, or endorsed by the St. Louis Blues or the National Hockey League. All trademarks are the properties of their respective owners.

Dedication

This book is dedicated to my soon-to-be 90-year old Dad who took me to my first Blues hockey game. We fell in love with the sport together and went to literally hundreds of games in the first ten years of the team's existence, before he moved away to Florida and I went off to college.

In retrospect, I find it hilarious that he *never once* saw the end of a game - he always wanted to "beat the traffic," as if we lived in Los Angeles, Chicago or Austin. But who was I to complain? (Ok, I complained a lot, but I knew how incredibly lucky I was to at least see two and a half periods of nearly every home game for almost a decade).

After returning to St. Louis following law school, I no longer attended as many games, busy with work and raising a family, and the cost of good tickets had skyrocketed from the $6 bargain of that first season. But I have always tried to make several games each year and most playoff games. And when I go now I stay to the end. Under my Dad's rules, I would have missed quite a few Overtime thrillers (like the Game 7 Double Overtime win vs. Dallas this year!). But I suppose I would have also minimized some of the agony experienced from witnessing some really heartbreaking losses over the years (many of those to Detroit and Chicago).

In any case, I am eternally grateful to my Pop for the opportunity to see so many exhilarating games in this amazing sport and for the great times we had bantering on about our favorite team.

I also have to give a special shout-out to the late great Sid Salomon III. He had a dream to bring NHL hockey to St. Louis and he did it, running a first-class organization that players and fans adored. He didn't do it for the money but for the love of the game; and he took a genuine passionate interest in the sport and his players. Although he sadly had to relinquish ownership prematurely due to economic considerations and is often forgotten among the many heroes of this franchise, we diehard St. Louis Blues hockey fans would not have the Stanley Cup today were it not for him. Thanks Sid!

Acknowledgement

I want to thank my good friend and colleague Scott Hunt for encouraging me to take on this project and helping in its implementation. It's been a lot of work in a very short time, but I have truly enjoyed re-living the great moments in Blues' history and this magical year in exquisite detail. I also want to thank colleagues Jon Igoe and Julie Antoni for generously giving their valuable time to read drafts and lend editing guidance (I certainly needed the help, especially given the ridiculously difficult spelling of many hockey players' names). However, any remaining errors are entirely of my own.

I also want to thank the various unnamed former players and employees who agreed to be interviewed for this book and contribute their insights and experiences to bring color to this story.

Table of Contents

Introduction	1
The Beginning	8
The first game	15
The first year	21
Year 2	25
Year 3	31
The 1970's	35
The 1980's	58
The 1990's	83
The 2000's	117
The 2010's	131
The Cup-Starved Blues' Fans	150
The 2018-2019 Season	156
Regular Season Wrap-Up	181
The Winnipeg Series	185
The Dallas Series	204
The San Jose Series	227
The Stanley Cup Final vs. Boston	245

Postscripts

        The Stanley Cup............................ 286

        A Season to Remember in the Lou 291

        The Blues' historical connections to teams and places 296

        The Parade of all Parades 301

Conclusion 310

Introduction

News Flash June 12, 2019: **The St. Louis Blues have (finally) won the Stanley Cup – FIFTY-ONE SEASONS since they first laced them up in the Lou!** What a long strange trip it's been. And I'm so *grateful* that it happened before I'm *dead*.

Winning the Stanley Cup is a monumental achievement for *any* team; players endure an 82-game schedule in the most physically grueling of sports merely to (hopefully) make the playoffs and winnow the field to sixteen, and then must prevail in four best of seven-game series over the course of two additional *months* of playoff-style hockey. The sixteen wins it takes to carry home the sports world's most spectacular trophy demands extraordinary skill, determination, and the ability to absorb physical punishment every other night, including slashes to the body, pucks to the face (*See* Zdeno Chara and Vince Dunn for the gruesome details) and other undisclosed "upper and lower body injuries." The Stanley Cup is considered the toughest sports trophy to win for good reason.

But for THIS Blues' team to achieve this milestone in THIS year was astounding and defied all logic and probability. There were many twists and turns in the Blues' storied run to the Stanley Cup: the initial high expectations that accompanied the acquisitions of several new players; followed by the great disappointment of finding themselves dead last in the standings halfway through the season (a 300-1 proposition to win the Cup!); and then the magical metamorphosis and team-record 11-game winning streak behind a relatively untested head coach and a completely untested fourth-string rookie goaltender; the always taxing march to make the playoffs in a League where parity rules the day; and, finally, the conquest of four powerhouse teams from all corners of North America: the North (Winnipeg), the South (Dallas), the West (San Jose) and finally the East (Boston)

- each in a hotly contested, remarkably close and agonizingly compelling series.

There were many heroes that made it happen. There were the more apparent ones like Rookie Goalie Binnington, MVP O'Reilly, the Russian Tank, Hat Trick Schwartz, Captain Pietrangelo, the Shut-down Defensive Pairing of Parayko and Bouwmeester, Feisty Schenn, Sniper Perron, Boom-Boom (and sometimes Goalie) Gunnarsson, Hometown Hero Patty Maroon, and the "Chief," Coach Berube. But there were also less heralded but pivotal warriors like Sundqvist, Dunn, Edmundson, Sanford, Steen, and the killer B's: Bozak, Bortuzzo, Barbashev and Blais. And not to be overlooked General Manager Doug Armstrong who added significant pieces to the puzzle and had the conviction not to panic and sell off the team when others might have flinched, as well as a very committed ownership group who did everything they possibly could to finally bring the Cup to the St. Louis.

It took a village of dedicated players and coaches and owners, and, frankly, a lot of good karma and luck as well. There were great stories and characters along the way - from Bobby Plager's plea for a parade, to Jacks Bar and "Play Gloria" in Philly, to the emotional inspiration provided by little Laila to the Blues' biggest man, Colton Parayko. This book will get into all of that and much more.

But in order to fully appreciate the magic and magnitude of this miraculous season we need some context and to start at the very beginning - nearly 52 years ago. I use the pejorative "we" throughout this book since a great fan base always considers the team to be "ours." Even though we fans take no shots, make no saves and endure no checks (directly), we live vicariously through the players, and suffer and celebrate as if we were part of each and every play. Indeed, as a kid I would find myself bumping into the person next to me while watching the game at the old Arena or on TV, trying to elude a check or win the puck. Even when there was no game, I would often check my sisters, Plager-style, if they were foolish enough to come down our hallway with their head down.

My first introduction to the Blues and hockey was through Blues' former player (and very briefly Blues' coach) Bill McCreary. As a 7-year old in the early summer of 1967 attending a Cardinals game with my Dad, "Mr. McCreary" was seated next to me. We talked throughout the game with him, unaware of what he did or who he was. At one point he volunteered that he was a professional hockey player and would be playing for the new team that was coming to town. My dad, the consummate sports fan, asked all about the sport, and McCreary put on his best salesman hat for the new team, describing the tremendous skill and fast-paced action, and that hockey was the best sport on earth to see in person. (Also, unlike baseball and football where there is only about fifteen minutes of actual action, in hockey you get at least sixty minutes, and sometimes more, each game).

When my Dad asked what kind of season tickets he could get, McCreary advised that he could arrange to get him great seats. He had my dad, and I to the extent that mattered, sold on the proposition. The next thing you knew we were season ticket holders, paying about $6 per ticket to sit directly behind the penalty box. My life was never the same.

A new professional sports team is in many ways like a child. At the outset there is excitement and anticipation and the unpredictability about what she will be like or ultimately become. During the early years there are growing pains; the getting-acquainted process and lots of learning, challenges and disappointments. The Blues sure had more than their share, enduring many trying years and almost losing the franchise on multiple occasions. Early patience eventually yields to greater expectations and then, if not realized, mounting frustration. Success, measured most often by Championships, does not come easy. Thirty other teams currently (with another on the way) are vying for the same goal. Everyone knows that it takes talent, preparation, perseverance and good leadership to produce a winning team, successful playoff appearances and hopefully a championship. But there are no guarantees - sometimes the most skillful, hardest working and the best coached fall short of the goal and never make it to the Promised Land. That was certainly the Blues' story for much of the last five decades.

The reality is that there are numerous uncontrollable factors that can have a major impact on a team's success or lack thereof:

There are injuries (both on and off the ice as core Blues' fans know well) that cut a key player's season or perhaps an entire career short. And sometimes, unfortunately, there are even tragic deaths.

There are players with great promise who just don't seem to be able to achieve their potential - whether due to lack of determination, coachability or the willingness to sacrifice personal ambition for team goals.

There is the undeniable importance of a team's chemistry - that amorphous quality that allows highly competitive players with divergent talents and personalities to blend well together, put aside ego and make the whole better than the sum of the parts.

There is the important role of management; the difference between making good and bad trades, drafting wisely or unwisely, and having coaches who not only have a keen sense of talent and instincts for the game, but can also lead, is staggering. And there is always economics at play - not just the understandable desire to make money, but in today's world, the salary cap system which precludes a successful team as a practical matter from holding on to all of the players it desires.

There is the unpredictable role that officials can play in determining a team's fate. It's a game with many high-speed collisions and lots of "stick-work," where the difference between what constitutes a penalty from one night to the next can change radically and often depend on the score of the game and who had the last penalty. Similarly, there are actions by the NHL's well-meaning Department of Player Safety that decide who should (and should not) be suspended for a questionable infraction that can meaningfully impact a game, series and season. (Thankfully for our Blues, the suspensions of Oskar Sundqvist and Ivan Barbashev in the Stanley Cup Finals, whether justified or not, did not cost the Blues the Stanley Cup, but it *could* have contributed, as the Blues lost both games they didn't play).

And there are even legal actions that can dramatically affect a franchise's prospect of a winning team for years or even decades. The remarkable decision by NHL arbitrator Edward Houston to award Scott Stevens to the New Jersey Devils - the Blues' captain, best player, and future Hall of Famer - as compensation for signing Brendan Shanahan, a restricted free agent, set back the franchise for years. Stevens went on to lead the Devils to three Stanley Cups in a glorious 13-year career. During this same time frame the Blues had exactly zero Cups. Well, at least the Devils were responsible for starting the greatest trophy tradition in sports in 1995 by letting each player have his own day with the Cup.

And last, but certainly not least, there is the inescapable component of puck luck, karma, mojo or whatever you want to call it. Hockey is a game where the tiniest of fractions can separate winners from losers - a skate blade is offsides by a miniscule margin and costs a team a game-tying goal (*See Colorado vs San Jose*, Game 7 of their playoff this year) or a puck takes a crazy bounce and eludes a world-class goalie (*See* Boston's second goal in Game 6 of the Stanley Cup Final).

And it is often critical what opposition team you happen to draw in the playoffs and when you play them. In the Blues' best years, we seemed, more often than not, to run into a buzz-saw of a team that went on to win the Cup - whether it was Detroit, Dallas, Colorado, Los Angeles, Montreal or Boston.

Nowhere is luck more apparent than in the few times it seems every game that a shot beats the goalie cleanly but instead of reaching the twine, lighting the lamp and leading perhaps to victory, it strikes the cross bar instead and produces a non-event (not even a registered shot on goal). Having watched thousands of games, I have no doubt that every team that wins the Stanley Cup has to have at least some, and arguably a great deal of, lady luck along the way.

Some seek to control or influence luck with superstitions. Fans wear "lucky" shirts, hats and even underwear, and rotate seats on a couch or in the arena based on how the team is performing - anything that might enhance the fortunes of their beloved squad. Most know that this is logically absurd - that their silly superstition cannot change the bounce of a puck down on the ice or often thousands of miles away. But they do it nonetheless. The players themselves are not immune: you gotta love Blues' legend Bobby Plager using a different toothbrush on game days versus non-game days this year to help the Blues win the Stanley Cup! Whatever it takes!

But most of all you help make your own luck by having a strong team work ethic, by displaying character and, perhaps most importantly, by being resilient when things go badly or awry, as they inevitably will during the long journey of a season. If there is one word that describes the 2018-2019 Blues, and why they were successful, it is that they were resilient. Time after time they were able to overcome obstacles by accepting the reality of their situation, however difficult, self-imposed or unfair, and push forward even harder without looking back.

The truth is, as your mama probably used to say: Life ain't always fair. And that has certainly been the case for many sports franchises throughout history. In baseball, the Boston Red Sox and Chicago Cubs waited 86 and 108 years, respectively, between World Series Championships. In basketball, the Sacramento Kings have not won a championship since 1951, back when they were known as the Rochester Royals. In football, the Arizona Cardinals, formerly of St. Louis, have not tasted Championship champagne since 1947 when they were based in Chicago and when it was simply the "NFL Championship" (before the existence of the Super Bowl).

In hockey, the most compelling drought before this year clearly belonged to the St. Louis Blues - 51 years old and, unlike the Red Sox, Cubs, Kings/Royals, or football Cardinals, nary a single championship. To add insult to injury the Blues made the Stanley Cup Final in each of the first three years of existence but not only fell short each time, lost all 12 games! I suppose the closest thing in the history of sports to this is the Buffalo Bills having reached the Super Bowl four times in a row and losing each time.

So, when a team like the Blues finally breaks through and wins the ultimate prize after 51 seasons (over 52 years) and 42 playoff attempts, the dam of emotional baggage for those who have followed and worshipped this team for more than five decades unleashes in an unparalleled flow of euphoria that cannot be replicated by yet another Yankee, Patriot or Warrior Championship.

Absence does indeed make the heart grow fonder. I know this because I have personally experienced it. This is the story of the Blues, my favorite sports team.

The Beginning

In the beginning, there was almost no beginning at all. In a bold stroke of Louisiana Purchase-type expansion, the NHL decided in 1967 to double the size of the League from a mere six teams to twelve teams in a single year. The goal was to spread the great game of hockey from what had principally been a Canadian and Northern U.S. game (with teams in Montreal, Toronto, New York, Boston, Detroit and Chicago) to the hinterlands and even the west coast where there was no hockey, and in some cases no ice. The NHL had fallen severely behind the other major sports leagues in the number of teams and the breadth of their fan base, which would not serve them well with the bourgeoning importance of television ratings and revenue. New franchises were lined up in Philadelphia and Pittsburgh, Los Angeles and San Francisco, and Minneapolis and, it appeared, Baltimore. Or perhaps Buffalo or Vancouver would get the final spot. In other words, St. Louis was not scheduled to be part of the NHL's expansion in 1967.

Indeed, St. Louis' history and soon-to-be love affair with hockey and the opportunity to experience this incredible 2018-2019 season may have never happened if not for Arthur Wirtz and James Norris. That's right - the owners of the Chicago Blackhawks at the time!

Were they hoping to have a team with whom the Blackhawks could build a great rivalry, like the Cardinals and the Cubs? Or a shorter and less expensive travel schedule?

While both were no doubt true, it was mostly about self-interest. Norris and Wirtz owned a large arena on Oakland Avenue in St. Louis, the second largest indoor arena in America at the time it was built during the depression of 1929. The building had hosted hockey - the St. Louis Flyers and Eagles played professional hockey there in the 1930's, and even the Chicago Blackhawks had played several home games there in the 1950's. *(*Apparently there were large numbers of empty seats in Chicago Stadium at the time and the owners felt there was a more receptive crowd in St. Louis!*)* More recently, since

1963, it had been the home for the St. Louis Braves, a minor league team affiliated with these same Chicago Blackhawks.

But the Arena, affectionately known as the "Old Barn," was dilapidated and it had experienced more than its share of misfortune, including a tenacious tornado strike in 1959 which ripped off much of the roof. The building needed major repairs and was deeply in debt. Bottom line: Wirtz and Norris desperately wanted someone to take that building off their hands.

Sidney Salomon, Jr (commonly referred to as "the Boss" or "Mr. Salomon"), and his son, Sidney Salomon, III (commonly referred to as "Sid", or by the family as "Sonny") were affable owners of a successful independent insurance agency who loved sports - they had previously owned small portions of the St. Louis Cardinals and St. Louis Browns (now the Baltimore Orioles) in the past. Mr. Salomon was a well-connected man and big wig in Democratic politics - he served as Treasurer of the Democratic National Committee in the 1950's and as the Chairman for John F. Kennedy's Presidential Campaign in 1960.

Sid saw a hockey game a few years before and was transfixed. When he heard about the NHL expansion plans, he began working on his Dad to try and secure a franchise. Mr. Salomon was reportedly reticent to be a majority owner of the team. But when no one else stepped forward, he agreed to submit an application. Even so, St. Louis was not considered the front runner over the other cities vying to join the NHL.

The Chicago Blackhawk owners were intent on changing that. Wirtz apparently told the Salomons and their legal counsel, James Cullen, that if they bought the Arena from them he would make sure that they got an NHL team in St. Louis. When they asked how he, as just one owner, could be so sure, Wirtz reportedly explained that there were only six owners, two of which were he and his cousin who owned the Detroit team, so that he would only need to get two more votes and that, don't worry, he would get them - the owners of the small League were apparently pretty tight.

The Salomons decided to step to the plate or, perhaps more appropriately here, enter the goal crease. They were wealthy folks but not in the typical financial stratosphere of those who traditionally own professional sports teams. But with the help of investors they cobbled together the $4 Million asking price to buy the Arena, and the surprisingly small fee of $2 million to buy a professional hockey team at that time. The Salomons' investment group included the town's greatest sports hero, Stan Musial, and his sidekick restaurateur Julius "Biggie" Garagnani (who died only months before the first puck drop). And indeed, true to his word, Mr. Wirtz persuaded the NHL to award the sixth and final expansion franchise to St. Louis.

Who would have thought that St. Louis owes the very existence of the Blues to a rival Chicagoan? Perhaps we should cut Kane, Toewes, Keith and Seabrook some slack next time we see them? Nah!

Thus, the Salomons became the father of the franchise, and like their namesake biblical figure who built the first Temple in Israel, they built the Temple to NHL hockey in St. Louis.

As for the team name, the Salomons didn't have one when they learned that they had been awarded the last expansion franchise. They were in New York at the time and were being asked to say a few words to the press as part of the announcement. The marketing savvy "Boss" wanted to have a name for the team for the big announcement, since this would be the first and best chance for a swarm of media attention. So, the Salomons quickly huddled with their small team and racked their brains for names; most of the ideas centered around space - the Mercurys, the Apollos, etc. - since McDonnell Douglas (before it became Boeing) was the largest employer in the area at the time. But none of the names seemed to fit. Just moments before the announcement, Sid had an epiphany: What about the St. Louis **Blues**? It had an identity with the city and gave the team an instant theme song. It felt natural to Sid and his team, and that was it - no million-dollar marketing study or fan contest or concern about trademark issues.

The Salomons quickly grew to love the sport and this team like their own child. They treated the players like no owner in any professional sport previously had - they paid the players better than the other teams, often took them to fancy dinners on the road, and treated them and their wives to all expense vacations in Florida in the off-season (where a young John Kelly, the current team announcer and son of the late great Dan Kelly, would babysit the little kids). The Salomons even arranged for every Blues' player to have a Chrysler Barracuda car - naturally with a white body and a blue top and the name St. Louis Blues and the player's number written across the side. *So much for player obscurity in those days.*

However, the owners' generosity did not tend to ingratiate themselves to the other owners in the League. Toronto Maple Leaf's General Manager Punch Imlach *(What a first name for a hockey man!)* complained that the Salomons' actions put the other owners at a competitive disadvantage. It was a theme that would rear its head again a couple of decades later when free agency was finally introduced, and new Blues' owners sought to take advantage of that to improve the team.

The Salomons were also determined to make the old Arena a first-class place. It cost them an additional $2 Million (the same cost of the team itself) just to get the building in shape to play NHL hockey and to expand the capacity from approximately 9,000 to 14,000 fans. Sid was in charge of the project and he spared no expense in trying to build the best hockey venue in the country.

For the exterior of the building the Blues erected an impressive marquee neon sign lit up in blue and red with a Blues' hockey player shooting a puck toward a goal separated by the words "Home of the St. Louis Blues." Inside, the Salomons installed plush blue seats in the lowest "parquet" section and soft yellow seats in the middle section, a state-of-the-art scoreboard and some luxury boxes for the big corporate folks in town.

And then there was the swanky Arena club - dark and mysterious with low lighting, thick red carpeting, and a long stylish wooden bar with a large beautiful stained-glass mural hanging above it, depicting a hockey game between the Blues and the Detroit Red Wings (though I was surprised it wasn't against the rival Blackhawks). For a modest annual membership (a little over $100 as I recall) you could enjoy a dinner buffet before the game and sip cocktails during the intermission that could be ordered in advance and waiting for you when you arrived - it was all about customer service. (*I had my first sip of alcohol there - Kahlua and cream - as a 10-year-old. I know that's pretty young, but I was just trying to get my Canadian on!*)

For the players' comfort, the Salomons built a locker room that was the envy of the League at the time. It was carpeted with a large Blue Note in the center, with multiple whirlpools encased in fancy mosaic tiles, a huge sauna, a weight room, televisions, a billiards table down the hall and a separate medical room - perhaps routine today, but not back then. When Jacques Plante happened to mention to the Salomons that he liked to play ping pong to keep his reflexes sharp, the Salomons promptly arranged for a ping pong table to be delivered and installed. And for the players' wives and girlfriends the Salomons created a "better halves" room for them and their young children to congregate, socialize and have dinner before the game.

The Salomons were among the first owners in sport to truly care about the players as people and consider them their friends, not just hockey players. The Salomons lived, breathed and ate hockey and Sid even had a phone line by his bed dedicated to anything that would occur with his team at any hour of the day or night. His wife, Carol, was close with all of the players' wives and often had them over at her house when the players were travelling.

The Blues' employees were also treated like family; Sid knew the names and backgrounds of everyone from the Zamboni operator (Chester) to the person who cleaned the offices (Johnny), and would ask about them when he would see them. In Johnny's case, when Sid learned he couldn't read, he made sure that he signed up for reading classes and had a Blues' employee drive him there and then personally attended Johnny's graduation ceremony.

All of these efforts and passion were rewarded with players willing to accept deferred contracts and who wanted to give their all for the franchise, employees who loved the organization and always gave their best and fans who were heavily devoted to the team. The Salomons developed very early a foundation of trust and love among players, owners and fans.

The First Game

It all began on Wednesday October 11, 1967. St. Louis' iconic baseball team, the Cardinals, would defeat the Red Sox in Game 7 of the World Series the very next day in Boston, as Bob Gibson won his third game in the series.

The program for the first game, back when such things were popular, proudly proclaimed "The Birth of the Blues" and showed a picture of the game's greatest treasure - Lord Stanley's Cup - the Holy Grail of every NHL team and player. *Who would have known at the time that it would be **18,872 days** before the Blues and its soon to be passionate followers would finally get to raise that Cup in the Lou?*

The original roster would include only a handful of the names that even the most ardent Blues' fans from over fifty years ago would recognize. Yes, there was the aging 36-year-old Hall of Fame Goalie Glenn Hall, another gift from Chicago. Although he had just won the Vezina Trophy for the best goalie in the NHL the previous season, the Blackhawks left him unprotected in the draft based on Hall's announced plans to retire and their desire to protect their back-up goalie Dennis DeJordy. But the Blues boldly took him with their first pick in the goalie draft anyway and gambled that they could persuade him to continue to play. It was a great bet. Though near the end of his illustrious career, Hall still had a few years of magic left in him and became the Blues' salvation and first superstar.

And there was the beloved bespectacled defenseman and the team's first captain Al Arbour, who could block shots with the best of them. But his greatest hockey achievements would begin after he stopped playing the game and became one of the greatest coaches in NHL history. And of course, there was Bobby Plager, the hip-checking defenseman who is still, more than five decades later, the heart and soul of the organIZEation. After his glorious ten-year career with the Blues came to an end, he became the unofficial team mascot, cheerleader and history professor to the new Blues' arrivals. In the latter capacity, he made certain that they knew of the proud and dedicated men who wore the Note before them and reminded them what a honor and privilege it was to be a St. Louis Blue and to follow in the footsteps of his brother Barclay, Al Arbour, Glenn Hall and many others. He passed that on to younger leaders who continued the team's traditions and legacy - from Brian Sutter to Bernie Federko to Brett Hull to Chris Pronger to Al MacInnis to David Backes to Alex Pietrangelo. God help the player who let the Blue Note on the sweater touch the floor!

The most knowledgeable Blues' fans of yesteryear will recognize a few other names on that opening night roster. There was the highly versatile forward/defenseman Jimmy Roberts (the Blues' first non-goalie selection in the draft and one of my favorite players); the fighting French Canadian and later colorful announcer Noel Picard (once greeted by Pittsburgh Penguin fans with the memorable sign "Noel Picard is here courtesy of the St. Louis Zoo"); the diminutive redhead Terry Crisp (who later went on to coach the Calgary Flames to a Stanley Cup); the shaved-headed pair of Larry Keenan (who would become famous on opening night) and Ron Schock (who would have his own date with history later that year in the playoffs); and left winger and future Coach and General Manager, Bill McCreary (who turned me and my dad on to the awesome sport of hockey).

But I suspect very few will remember or have even heard of most of the others on that opening day roster: Goalie Seth Martin (who actually started the Blues' very first game when Glenn Hall had an allergic reaction to a tetanus shot - usually he just threw up before each game), Defenseman Fred Hucul and Gordon Kannegeisser, Centers Ron Attwell, Gerry Melnyk, and Don McKenney, and wingers Roger Picard (Noel's older brother), Wayne Rivers, and Norm Beaudin.

The entire Blues' roster - that's right 100% - were from Canada. *Bet you a loonie or a toonie, or even a mickey, that you didn't know that, eh?*

Most of these guys were not long for the Blues and it would not be until seven weeks into the season before the Blues acquired from the New York Rangers Gordon Arthur "Red"

Berenson, who became the team's first offensive star, and Barclay Plager, Bobby's older brother and the toughest 5 foot 10, 175-pound son of a gun I ever saw. And shortly before the playoffs they convinced Dickie Moore, named as one of the 100 greatest players to ever play in the NHL, to come out of retirement at age 37, *and after a three-year hiatus,* to join the squad and attempt to rekindle his scoring touch.

The coaching and the general manager duties were initially handled by Lynn Patrick, a highly honorable and likeable man who came from hockey royalty. Lynn's father and grandfather helped develop the rules of the game of hockey, and his father, uncle and son - the latter the assistant coach on the Miracle on Ice team that defeated the Russians in the 1980 Olympics - are all in the hockey Hall of Fame. Lynn himself was an all-star player and was later inducted into the Hall of Fame posthumously. Patrick's assistant coach was none other than Scotty Bowman.

It was not unusual back then to give the head coach the title of general manager as well, as having the hammer of deciding trades and contracts was thought could help to motivate the players' performance. And owners were also looking for any way to save some money by having folks wear multiple hats. Indeed, the Blues put the enthusiastic Gus Kyle, soon to be color man on broadcasts, also in charge of selling tickets.

The first game was sparsely attended - a little over 11,000 paid between $2.50 and $6 to be there. And I am proud to say that I was one of them now as an 8-year-old, sitting with my dad in a glorious seat to absorb the action - right behind the penalty box of the opposing team. Most of us in attendance had never seen a hockey game before, and barely understood the rules of the game beyond the simplest of objectives: to put more pucks into the opponent's net than they put in yours. We knew nothing about offsides, icing the puck or the forbidden two-line pass (now allowed). Fortunately, the program devoted two full pages to the rules, with humorous cartoon pictures of the various penalties that could be called.

The Blues' opponent in the first game was the Minnesota North Stars, who would later become the Dallas Stars in 1993 (naturally eliminating the "North"). The North Stars were led in goal by the "giant" Cesare Maniago. In an era where the likes of Zdeno Charra and Colton Paraykyo were nowhere to be found on a sheet of ice - indeed, many of the goalies from Gump Worsley to Rogie Vachon to Charlie Hodge were *under* 5-feet 7 inches - the 6-foot 3 Maniago was considered a gargantuan man for a hockey player. *Who could have imagined that Maniago would be small by comparison to the Stars' goalie fifty years later- the 6-foot 7 Ben Bishop?*

The Stars roster also contained a few other players of note: Jean-Guy Talbot, one of the many great French Canadian names in hockey who would wind up as an important Blues' player before the year was through; Billy Plager, the younger brother of Barclay and Bobby, who would also make it to the Blues the following year; and Bill Masterdon - the only player in NHL history to die as a direct result of injuries suffered during a game - only one year later.

There was much hoopla before the inaugural game - radio star Arthur Godfrey, Guy Lombardo and his Royal Canadians band, and Broadway singer Anna Maria Alberghetti were part of the pregame entertainment, with the late great Jack Buck, actually the Blues first announcer, serving as emcee. It wasn't until the next year that Jack was replaced with a young Irishman named Dan Kelly. Kelly's powerful voice, incisive knowledge of the game, and ability to bring excitement and passion through the airwaves, along with his trademark, "He shoots… he SCORRRES," had as much to do with the burgeoning popularity of the team as anyone.

I don't remember much about the initial game. I do recall that the game was played at a riveting pace and that I was hooked from the outset. And I was surprised that the players weren't very big - most players were less than six feet tall. But their toughness was unmistakable; crushing each other hard into the boards, slashing with their sticks and diving in front of slap shots - all without wearing helmets! And even the goalie had no mask to protect him from shots to the head! How no one died in this era, aside from Bill Masterton, is a miracle in itself.

For sports trivia buffs, this same Bill Masterton scored the first goal ever in Blues' history on a power play in the second period. The Blues' first goal was scored by Larry Keenan with an assist from Bobby Plager - who was not exactly known for his *offensive* prowess. (Bobby registered only four more assists and two goals the remainder of the season.) Far less surprisingly, Bobby took the first penalty as well - he was apparently trying to get himself into all of the record books. The Blues were trailing late in the third period 2-1 when with less than two minutes left, Wayne Rivers (#21) tied the game at two. When the buzzer sounded shortly thereafter, with no further goals, the game abruptly concluded. There was no Overtime back in the day, so there were a lot of games with endings that resembled "kissing your sister," as folks used to say.

The contest also featured an actual fight between grown men - or more accurately, a full-out brawl. Roger Picard got into "a scrap" with the North Stars' Ted Taylor. And then all of the players on both teams jumped over the boards and joined in the festivities - Hanson Brothers' style. That's just what the players often did back in the days; it was expected to support a teammate. As a young boy who was repeatedly told not to lose my considerable temper and get in a fight, it was all rather confusing and hypocritical, but nonetheless exciting.

After the game, Bobby Plager reportedly ran into the great comedian Bob Hope - of all places in the men's room. "I'm in the bathroom, and Bob Hope walks in and stands next to me to conduct his business," Plager told the St. Louis Post Dispatch. "Everything was blue that day to commemorate the team; we even had blue water in the bathrooms when you flushed the toilet." Standing at the urinal with Mr. Hope, Bobby recalls boasting: "Look at this. The water's blue here." Hope turned to him and said: "Oh, thank God you told me. I thought it was me."

The First Year

(The Blues' Plager Brothers: Bob, Barclay and Billy)

After the first game, the Blues fell on hard times. Indeed, seventeen games into the inaugural season, the team had managed to win only four of them. Nothing like getting off to a bad start as a new team in a new city! Less than 25% into the first season, Blues' coach Lynn Patrick voluntarily surrendered the job to his young assistant, 34-year old Scotty Bowman (Lynn apparently didn't like coaching). The team promptly proceeded to lose six of the next seven games under Bowman's leadership.

But then something suddenly clicked, and the Blues started turning things around. From late December 1967 through January 1968 the Blues lost only twice in sixteen games and started to play like a team with legitimate aspirations. The Blues rallied to a third-place finish in the division, making the playoffs. *A lot of parallels to the squad 51 seasons later!*

To be fair, the only reason the Blues made the post-season the first year was because the NHL showed the wisdom to put all of the expansion teams in their own separate division and let them compete among themselves in the playoffs first. It was designed to create interest and give new fans the splendid taste of playoff hockey. Not a single team in the expansion West division could hold a hockey stick to any of the Original Six East teams. Even the first place Philadelphia Flyers had a losing record. And that was with good reason. Unlike with the NHL's recent generous expansion rules for the Las Vegas Golden Knights that made them highly competitive from the outset, the NHL allowed the original teams to hold on to virtually all of their star players - only aged veterans who were planning to retire or younger players in the minor league ranks were generally available for drafting. Most of the players the Blues drafted never even made it on the opening roster.

Nevertheless, here were the Blues in our very first year competing for Lord Stanley's Cup. *How cool was that?* The Blues opened the playoffs against the expansion first place Philadelphia Flyers, due to an odd quirk in the format at the time that had the first-place team in each division play the third-place team and the second-place team play the fourth-place team.

It was not exactly a dream first-round match-up for the Blues, as the Flyers had been our nemesis all season long. Indeed, out of the ten games played against Philadelphia during the regular season (the large number of games against fellow expansion teams was another effort to give the new teams more chances at competitive games) the Blues won only one of those games. It was our worst record against any team in the League. And yet, the Blues managed to prevail in a tough seven game series, winning Game 7 in Philadelphia after dropping a potential series clincher at home in Game 6 in Double Overtime. *More parallels to the 2018-2019 squad!*

In the second round the Blues faced the Minnesota North Stars *(just as we faced their successor 51 seasons later)*. Like this year's battle against the Stars, that playoff series goes down as one of the most exciting in Blues' history.

Each team won three of the first six games and three of the games went to Overtime. In Game 7, held at the St. Louis Arena, goals were extremely hard to come by against the Blues' Mr. Hockey, Glenn Hall, and the Stars' Mountain of a Man, Maniago. *Does any of this sound familiar?* Indeed, the game stood scoreless for nearly 57 minutes. But then Stars' rookie Walt McKechnie scored what most assumed would be the game winner and send them to the Stanley Cup Final. Fortunately, Blues' veteran Dickie Moore ensured that would not happen, igniting the crowd with a goal of his own a mere 31 seconds later to even the score. It stayed that way to the end of regulation and throughout the first Overtime despite a plethora of shots by both teams, a total of 80 in all.

And then the Blues' number 10 - Ron Schock (who had been in Scotty Bowman's doghouse for a giveaway and subsequent goal in the previous series against Philadelphia and who had received limited ice time since) shocked the Stars and elated the capacity St. Louis crowd with a breakaway goal 2 minutes and 50 seconds into the Double Overtime. This scene would be eerily replicated 51 seasons later - in another Game 7 in the Lou against the same team (albeit now from a different city). Like in 1968, goals were extremely hard to come by on both sides with exceptional goaltending, and with the game tied after regulation and also after the first Overtime, the Blues finally and dramatically scored in Double Overtime to win the game and the series. *Is someone above directing this movie?*

The Blues' prize for their surprising and exhilarating playoff victories in their inaugural year? The opportunity to play the powerhouse Montreal Canadiens - the New York Yankees of hockey - for the Stanley Cup.

No one without a recent lobotomy gave the Blues a chance. The Canadiens' roster contained some of the greatest players of the era, not to mention some of the best French-Canadian names ever assembled. There was John Belliveau, Henri Richard, Jacques Lemaire, Yvan Cournoyer, Claude Larose, Jacques Lapppierre and Jean Claude Tremblay *(it's just fun saying these names)*. And there was tiny but feisty and effective goalie "Gump" Worsley. The Blues had not won a single game of the four games that we had played against the Canadiens during the regular season. It was the major leagues versus the minors. Had there been a line on the series, it undoubtedly would have been 20 to 1.

And yet, while the Blues did indeed drop all four games of the series, the games were surprisingly competitive; all four games were decided by a single goal and two of the games actually went to Overtime. That's not to say that the Blues were nearly equals to the Canadiens. The Blues just happened to have a man in goal named Glenn Hall who stood on his head throughout the series to keep the Blues in games. In Game 3, for example, the Blues were outshot by the absurd margin of 46 to 15 and yet Hall somehow managed to keep the game tied and get to Overtime. Hall's performance was so magnificent that he was awarded the Conn Smythe Trophy for the Most Valuable Player in the Stanley Cup Playoffs. I'm pretty sure that there has never been a player before who has *ever* won the MVP of a series *in any sport* when his team did not win a single game in the Final.

Year Two

Despite being swept in the Final the previous year, the team had gained tremendous credibility with the City and the fan base was ecstatic at the team's performance and how far the Blues had come in their first year.

The Salomons spent several million dollars to expand capacity from 14,000 to 18,000 under the theory if you build a great product they will come. And they did. The Blues went from an average attendance of under 10,000 per night in the first year to selling out the place every night.

The Old Barn vibrated with enthusiasm from the minute the team stepped on to the ice thanks in part to the silver-jacketed organist Norm Kramer. Norm would belt out W. C. Handy's catchy tune "St. Louis Blues" as the team marched on to the ice - a rhythmic beat that we youngsters would attempt to mimic as we began our own street or roller hockey games. And Norm also incorporated the famous "When the Blues [Saints] go Marching In" after goals.

Kramer was so effective at whipping up the crowd before and throughout the game that Blues' coach Scotty Bowman was quoted as saying that he was worth a half a goal a game. Unfortunately, Norm really took this compliment to heart and demanded a $10,000 salary, a huge increase over his previous fee of merely $35 per night. It was one of the few times that the Salomons refused to pay for an expense to enhance fan experience, and Norm took his organ elsewhere.

The players rewarded the fans' passion with inspired play and often lots of "fisticuffs" (Canadian lingo for fighting, which was far more common back in the day and a significant gate draw to some). And Blues' management was determined to make the team better and deeper.

For depth in goal, management dusted off their "You can't give up on hockey just yet!" speech that they had prepared for the 37-year-old Glenn Hall to coax him out of retirement and tried it on 40-year-old Hall of Famer Jacques Plante who hadn't played professionally in three years! The inducement? The Salomons would give him a three-year deal for $26,000 per year plus incentives (which would mushroom to $35,000) - more money than he had ever been paid in his illustrious career. Plante even typed up the contract himself since the agreement was reached on a weekend and there was no secretary around!

There were some concerns about how the gregarious Plante and reserved Hall would get along (they had been long-time rivals who hardly knew each other) and about how they would share the workload (both future Hall of Famers were used to being the top guy). But they set their egos aside; there would be no Number One goalie. They would simply alternate games.

And some worried how the team would respond to two completely different goalie styles: Hall was a stay in the net "butterfly" goalie and Plante the kind who would come way out of the net and cut down the angles. If there was a two-on-one Plante would play the shooter, Hall the pass. But the team adjusted well to both and sharing the goaltending duties helped minimize wear and tear on their aged bodies. The result was the greatest goalie tandem in the history of hockey. Hall registered eight shutouts, had a 2.17 goals against average and a .928 save percentage. Plante recorded five shutouts, a goals against average of 1.96 and a mind-boggling save percentage of .940.

The goalies were aided by a stellar defense, including Doug Harvey, one of the greatest defensemen to ever play the game that made Hall and Plante seem youthful at 44 years old! "Youngster" Al Arbour, at age 36, routinely threw himself in front of slap shots. And then there were the Plagers and Noel Picard. The threesome would protect the other players like a mama bear protects her cubs. They would skate around center ice during the warm-up and announce to the other team that if anyone messes with "the Redhead" (Blues' star Red Berenson) that they would have an "appointment" with one of them.

In addition, there was the reliable Jimmy Roberts who could play either defense or offense and Jean Guy Talbot who had won two Stanley Cups with Montreal. Occasionally the youngest Plager brother, Billy, now a Blue, suited up as well. Indeed, one night in Montreal when the game was being shown on Hockey Night in Canada (the longest running prime time show in our hockey-obsessed neighbor to the North), Scotty Bowman started all three Plager brothers as his *forward* line. The serious Bowman must have had a flair for entertainment as well.

Management also astutely sought to add some offense; the Blues had been third from last in goals scored the first year. To assist Berenson, speedy winger Gary Sabourin and steady center Frank St. Marseille, the Blues added lanky Ab McDonald and clever Camille "the Eel" Henry, likely the lightest man to ever play for the Blues. At 5 foot 7 and a mere 136 pounds the miniscule Henry looked like he belonged more on top of a horse than on the ice with brutes, but the man was slippery with the puck (thus "the eel "nickname) and could score. Indeed, Henry scored the first hat trick in Blues' history on November 3, 1968.

In short, the Blues were a veteran team that played immaculate defense and were very tough and intimidating. Armed now with a more complete team, the Blues literally blew away the rest of the expansion West division in year two, taking over first place in the first week and never relinquishing it. Indeed, the Blues won the division by a whopping 19 points over the second place Oakland Seals.

The Seals were the expansion team that many forget. They began as the California Seals but changed their name to the Oakland Seals in the middle of the first season. The name change did not change their futility on the ice, finishing dead last in the standings their first year with a mere 12 wins! Although their record improved in years two and three, and they made the playoffs (losing each year in the first round), it didn't last. In 1970 they were losing badly again and were back at the name game. They started the year as the Bay Area Seals, but after just two days changed to the California Golden Seals. Eventually they realized that their name wasn't the issue but rather their poor play - missing the playoffs in seven of nine years in the

NHL was not exactly a good recipe for a franchise's success. With declining attendance and financial losses mounting, the owners moved the team to Cleveland where they became the Barons. That experiment, however, only lasted two years, before they folded and merged their players into the Minnesota North Stars. They remain the only NHL team in the last half century to, in effect; go out of business (the Blues would come perilously close to becoming the second). And yet these same owners were rewarded in 1991 with the San Jose Shark's franchise that would have many significant battles with the Blues over the years.

So, just how good were the Blues in year two? At one point in the season the Blues went twelve straight games without a loss. How well did the team play *at home* in front of an adoring and vociferous crowd? The Blues lost only eight of their 38 games at the Barn on Oakland Avenue - pretty darn impressive for what was still essentially an expansion team. In fact, the Blues didn't lose two games in a row at home the entire season. Egged on by the crowd in close games, the Blues came from behind in the third period thirteen times to either tie or win in the final period, three times in the last five minutes.

One of the biggest moments of the year, and indeed franchise history, occurred that season on November 7, 1968 in Philadelphia, when Red Berenson scored six goals in a single game, most it seemed around Flyers' veteran defenseman Ed Van Imp. I can still hear Dan Kelly's great voice in my head over fifty years ago: "Berenson, around Ed Van Imp, he shoots, he SCORRRES!" Red's remarkable achievement tied a modern-day record for most goals scored in a game, a feat that still stands over five decades later. During the second intermission, with the Blues up 5-0, with all five goals by Berenson, Blues' veteran Doug Harvey, turned to him, and reportedly sternly joked: "If it wasn't for you, there would be a good game going on here!"

Among those celebrating the achievement was a large contingency of players' wives who had gathered at Sid's home with his wife Carol in St. Louis to watch the game on TV. When the Red Baron scored his six goals, the wives each put on two hats a piece for the *double* hat trick. Indeed, so overjoyed were the Salomons with Red's effort as true fans (much like current owner Tom Stillman and his fellow investors) that at the next home game, in front of a capacity crowd, they presented the outdoor enthusiast with a brand new 1969 Chevrolet Station Wagon with license plate RB 6666, a canoe on top and a 20-gauge shotgun inside.

Berenson, who had played previously in Montreal and New York, was stunned, noting that: "In New York or Montreal (where he'd played previously), all you'd get would be a handshake." Nevertheless, the Redhead may have committed a social grace blunder by selling the car only a few days later to of all people Blues' announcer Dan Kelly. That apparently didn't sit very well with some in the organization.

The Blues showed that their impressive regular season was no fluke when the playoffs rolled around, sweeping both the Philadelphia Flyers and Los Angeles Kings in four straight games each, and outscoring those teams by the prodigious margin of 33 to 8. In doing so, the Blues became only the second team in NHL history to accomplish that feat. And yet, despite the incredible season and much improved team, we once again drew those darn Canadiens in the Stanley Cup Final - a team that we *still* had never beaten in our history after fourteen tries (four in the inaugural season, four in the 1968 Stanley Cup Final and six in the 1968-1969 regular season).

The good news was that this Blues' team looked a lot stronger than the first year's squad and we were riding a ten-game winning streak (including the regular season) entering the series. This time things would surely be different - at least we weren't going to be swept in the Final this time.

And then reality set in. The Canadiens demolished the Blues in four straight games.

Year Three

Year Three of the Blues' franchise looked a lot like Year 2. The Blues once again ran away with the expansion West division, and by even a wider margin than the previous year, beating their next closest competitor, the Pittsburgh Penguins, by an impressive 22 points! As a team, we looked better than ever and seemed to be inching closer to the established teams. The Blues not only beat the Montreal Canadiens for the first time, we crushed them 5-0 on December 30, 1969 and did so at the Montreal Forum (the Canadiens' worst loss of the year). And to show it was no fluke, the Blues beat them again at the biggest hockey shrine in Canada a couple of months later.

By this time the Blues were not simply a hit in the Lou, but the most popular ticket in town. Hockey had become a happening in St. Louis. The Blues' *average* attendance exceeded capacity at 18,238 in 1970-71 and was the highest in the NHL. Indeed, so large was the love affair between the city and the Blues that we had the highest attendance in the League for five straight years! I recall one game against the New York Rangers on a Saturday night where the announced attendance eclipsed 20,000, undoubtedly a major fire code violation.

Saturday night at a Blues' game in 1970 was THE place to be in town. People actually dressed up for the occasion - women in sable and minks, men often in stylish suits or sports jackets - as if they were going to a party at the Ritz (or in those days, the St. Louis Playboy Club). And the place was raucous - the loudest building in the League. The crowd was so loud in those days that Pittsburgh Penguins' Coach Red Kelly actually had his players wear ear muffs in one game in January 1970 to try and drown out the noise. Aside from making the Penguins' players look ridiculous, it didn't help their performance as the Blues scored 29 seconds into the game and easily won 6-0!

Some Blues' fans took things to an extreme. The gentleman who had the season tickets next to ours, a man I will just call by his first name, Joe, would harass any opposition player from the time they entered the penalty box until the time they left. He would often bring a pretty woman to the game with him and show off his bravado with the opposing players (I wasn't sure as a young boy if his frequent changes in game partners was due to *his* choice or *theirs*.) Joe's other constant companion was a rubber chicken that he liked to dangle over the glass separating his seat from the penalty box into an opposing player's face. During one particular contentious regular season game with the Boston Bruins, there were several fights and multiple Boston players in the penalty box at the same time. Joe was in rare form, giving them the business, when Derek Sanderson, one of the Boston cellmates at the time, decided he had enough of Joe's antics and started to climb to the top of the glass separating the box from the fans. He was soon joined by other Bruins in the box. When their teammates on the ice saw what was going on, they actually stopped play in the middle of the game and rushed to the penalty box to join in the scrum - if there is one thing hockey players are taught at an early age is to stand up for your teammates.

Although Joe was supposedly a pretty tough guy, he was no match for the swarm of Bruins. As a feisty young lad, I wanted to participate in the festivities but was quickly pulled away by my Dad. At one point, as I recall, Sanderson had Joe by his necktie (*I told you folks dressed up for the games*) with his fist cocked and had him pleading for reconciliation. Sanderson turned to Joe's date for the night and said, "He's not such a tough guy now, is he?"

The altercation eventually subsided with the help of the police and the game continued. It was quite exciting for a 10-year-old. Not so much for good old Joe. Far worse than the embarrassment was that the Blues took away his season tickets behind the penalty box as a result of the incident and relegated him to seats higher up in the stands.

For the third consecutive year, the Blues made it through the expansion team West playoffs unscathed, although this time it required two six-game series wins over the Minnesota North Stars and Pittsburgh Penguins; all of the expansion teams were gradually improving.

There was good news and bad news for the Blues: The good news? We finally had an opponent in the Stanley Cup Final not named the Montreal Canadiens. The bad news? The new opposition was every bit as daunting. The Boston Bruins had become the most talented team in the NHL with high scoring big center Phil Esposito, small but speedy winger Johnny McKenzie, talented and tough wingers Johnny Buyck, Ron Hodge and Wayne Cashman, playboy skillful center Derek Sanderson and most notably, the irrepressible Bobby Orr, the most exciting defenseman to ever wear a pair of skates. Orr was the only player I ever saw who could routinely start with the puck behind his own net, and with his speed and puck handling acumen, take it all the way down the 200-foot slab himself, maneuvering around the opposition's entire team all by himself.

The Bruins and Orr didn't disappoint *(unless, like me, you were a Blues' fan)* and obliterated the Blues once again in four straight games. Only the last game was close as the game stood tied 3-3 after regulation play. But it didn't last long for Orr to work his magic: Merely forty seconds into the extra session, Orr raced to the front of the goal from his defensive position, received a pass from behind the net and scored. Just as Orr had unleashed his shot, he was tripped by Noel Picard causing him to literally fly through the air, parallel to the ice, arms outstretched in celebration for what seemed to be long enough to defy the laws of gravity. Glenn Hall would later comment that "by the time (Orr) landed, I had already had a shower and a cold one."

The photo of Orr post-mortem has become one of the most iconic photos in NHL history. To Bruins' fans it commemorates the greatest defenseman (and they likely say the greatest player period) to ever play the game and one of the most memorable moments in Stanley Cup history. To Blues' fans, it represented *(at least until this year)* the culmination of their 0-12 record in Stanley Cup Finals as well as the very last time the Blues stepped on the ice in a Stanley Cup Final.

The 1970's

(Blues' Traveling Secretary Tim Madden with Barclay Plager, Floyd Thompson and Bob Gassoff)

The Blues had made it to the Stanley Cup Final each of the first three years - aided by an NHL expansion system that doubled the number of teams and mercifully allowed the new teams to play each other first before getting whooped by the big boys. While the Blues lost all twelve Stanley Cup Final games, it was nevertheless a significant accomplishment that the team and the City of St. Louis could take pride in. I am not aware of any expansion team in any sport making it to the Finals in their first three years of existence, and I suspect it will never happen again. Still, the goal here was not to be the bridesmaid but the bride.

Unfortunately, things were about to change for the Blues. The NHL decided that it was time to break up the expansion party so that the Stanley Cup Final would represent a contest between the two best teams in the League. So, they arranged for the winners of the first round to cross over and play teams from the other division after that. That meant that the Blues would have to beat an "Original Six" team in the second-round before making it to the Final. The change was designed to put a quick end to any West team making the Final for a while and diminishing the value of the Stanley Cup Final.

Not surprisingly, a West team would not make the Finals for the next three years. But then the Philadelphia Flyers broke through the glass ceiling and not only made the Final but beat the Bobby-Orr led Boston Bruins for the first Cup win by an expansion team. The Flyers even repeated the same feat the following year.

That Philly team, popularly known as the "Broad Street Bullies," had some talent led by the smallish, toothless diabetic Bobby Clarke at center - one of the best players I ever saw play - and Bernie Parent in goal. But what mostly distinguished the Flyers from other teams was their brawn; they hit everything that moved and fought anyone who complained about it or retaliated. They were big, tough, and intimidating. And they showed that you could win championships with "old-style hockey" (something that the 2018-2019 version of the Blues have been accused of or worshipped for, depending on your point of view).

Before the 1970-1971 season, the NHL also moved an Original Six team, the Chicago Blackhawks, to the West division to balance the scales a bit and arguably help create a bigger rivalry with the Blues. In order to accommodate the switch, and with no other West teams interested in heading east to get routinely demolished, the NHL decided to make the new expansion team Vancouver Canucks - the most Western team geographically - play in the East conference. *Say what? I wonder how many total miles the Canucks were forced to log that year?*

In the first year under the new format, the Blues, as expected, finished second in the West division behind the Chicago Blackhawks. But before making it to the second round against the East, the Blues uncharacteristically lost in the first round to the North Stars in six games. It was the earliest ending and the longest off-season in Blues' history to that point.

It wasn't just the change in playoff format and the Blackhawks move that changed the Blues' fortunes. The foundation of the Blues was veteran leadership. Indeed, the team's run of success was aided greatly by selecting, signing and trading for aging superstars at the twilight of their careers - several of the greatest players to ever play the game from that era (Hall, Plante, Harvey, and Moore) donned the Blue Note. But with that strategy also came a judgment day, and a need to replace the talent when even the great ones succumb to the ravages and reality of age. As the Blues grew older and as other expansion teams got better, the Blues no longer were dominant.

Moreover, a great deal of the Blues' success was due to the team's young coach Scotty Bowman. He was a master tactician, keen evaluator of talent, creative thinker and stickler for details. Before he signed 40-year old Jacques Plante, who had undergone knee surgery over the summer, Scotty invited him to a Cardinal game on a 100-degree day, just so he could observe firsthand how he walked up and down the steps and handled the sweltering heat to make sure he was up to the task. When the Blues struggled on the West coast he put the team on a routine for meals and bedtime that matched the Midwest time zone.

Bowman was also a bit of a control freak. Knowing the propensities of young Canadian hockey players, he wanted to make the sure they were not out too late or getting themselves into trouble. One successful tactic Scotty employed with respect to players whom he felt he needed to keep a close eye on involved asking them for a cigarette light (lighters were not common in those days and players, many of whom smoked in the day, would grab free packs of matches at the bars they went to). Scotty didn't smoke but he would use the ploy to see the name of the bar on the matches when they gave him a light. He would then go into his office and call the owner of the establishment and interrogate him about what his player was doing at his bar last night and how late he stayed. The players never seemed to figure out how Scotty knew where they had been - hockey players are not always the most educated lot.

When the team was at home he could also keep tabs on the players by the cars they were given by management. That didn't pan out too well for Floyd Thompson who managed to smash his car up so badly along highway 40 near the Arena after a night out on the town that all that could be seen were the words "St. Louis Blues" on the abandoned vehicle. It didn't take long for Don Miller, the long-time noted KMOX chopper guy to make note of that fact on the air in his early morning report - and for the public relations-conscious Blues' management to scramble to get that car out of there.

On the road Scotty would resort to other clever maneuvers to ensure his curfew was met. He would make sure that all players had hotel rooms on his floor and he would verify that each player was in his room before the deadline. At times he would wait in the hall for a while, like a high school hall monitor, trying to ensure that no one would slip out. At other times he would even hire kids to stand in the hallway to ask for the autograph of any player who left his room. Scotty would then have a nice list of the players who had snuck out.

But that didn't always prevent the boys from being boys - after all they were Canadians who liked to carouse. One time in Philly, Noel Picard was assigned to break out of the Bowman penitentiary and go get the beer. The big man was able to sneak out somehow and took a cab across the river to New Jersey where he loaded the trunk and entire back seat with beer - Canadian hockey players just love the stuff. He managed to make his way back to the hotel and sneak the contraband into the room as Bowman left for his traditional late-night dinner with announcer Dan Kelly - the ultimate foodie who had a go-to spot in every city.

As Bowman and Kelly got into a cab to begin their journey the driver asked what they were doing in town. When they told him that they were the coach and announcer for the St. Louis Blues, respectively, the driver mentioned that he had just dropped off one of their guys at the hotel. Bowman's interest peaked and asked the cabbie to describe the fellow and was told that it was a big man with a French-Canadian accent. Bowman had the driver swing back to the hotel where he made a beeline to Noel Picard's room and found a large party assembled - and a massive quantity of beer. Scotty's apparent comment to the group in breaking up their fun, and likely handing down some fines, was simply: "That's what you get for putting the dumbest French-Canadian in charge."

It was often said that the players hated Bowman until they got their first playoff check - a concession that despite his onerous ways, he was a great coach who got results. But Bowman's success with the expansion Blues naturally attracted attention. None other than the Montreal Canadiens began recruiting him - the Canadiens had been disappointed that their plethora of talent hadn't produced the Championship results routinely expected in the City of Saints.

At the conclusion of the 1970-1971 season, Bowman shockingly decided to leave St. Louis for Montreal despite having three years still left on his contract. Some say it was the lure of coaching the greatest franchise in hockey, but others blame his growing frustration with Sid who began to increasingly meddle in hockey operations.

As it turns out, Bowman's departure propelled his career to the Mount Everest of coaching royalty. Bowman went on to win an arsenal of Stanley Cups with the Canadiens, a full handful of five, before moving on to Pittsburgh where he won another, and then on to Detroit where he won three more! In the process he became the winningest coach in NHL history. If it wasn't for his first opportunity with the expansion Blues would any of that have happened? And Blues' fans hesitate to think how many championships might have come our way under his leadership had he remained. At least we can take comfort in knowing that our organization helped contributed to the success and euphoria of *other* teams and their fan bases. *Not!*

In mid-season before his departure Bowman traded the Blues' biggest star, Red Berenson. It was part of a four-player swap, with the biggest prize in return a young promising center named Garry Unger. The trade was immensely unpopular in St. Louis at the time as Red was the seventh leading scorer in the NHL the prior season, was thought to be in his prime at 31, and was the most popular player among the fans. Few in St. Louis knew much about the 23-year-old Unger although he had already scored over 90 goals in his first three seasons.

Some suggested at the time that Berenson was traded for serving as President of the Player's Association; others because he "double-crossed" Salomon in breaching an alleged deal he was trying to work out with the Players Association on licensing rights; and others because Red was not well liked by some in the organization. The sale of the car the owners gave him to another Blues' employee didn't likely help his cause much either.

The trade proved to be one of the best deals the Blues ever made. Unger was a tremendous hockey player and became one of the greatest Blues ever. During his eight plus seasons with the Blues, he scored 292 goals and had 575 points. Berenson's production during this same time dropped considerably, averaging less than 20 goals over nearly four seasons with Detroit, before eventually rejoining the Blues for his last three and a half years.

Like Berenson, Unger was a center. Like Berenson, he would wear Number 7. And like Berenson, Unger had very colorful hair - except that Unger had a lot more of it and wore it real long, unlike the crew-cut Berenson.

Indeed, Detroit was apparently anxious to trade its young star because of his hair! Unger was very serious about it. He would shower right before every game and then apply a can of hairspray to his long locks to ensure that his glowing hair was never disrupted regardless of the intensity of the action. But Detroit's owner did not like long hair. In fact, he had a crew cut rule and Unger refused to cut his hair.

It's amazing how ownership egos can impact a team's fortunes for decades. Around this time, the St. Louis Cardinals traded 20-game winner and budding superstar pitcher Steve Carlton to Philadelphia because he had the audacity to ask for a paltry five thousand dollars more money than owner Auggie Busch was offering and had spoken to the media about it. Carlton apparently realized that he had upset the Beer Baron and called the General Manager to accept Mr. Busch's original offer but was told that it was too late; he had already been traded. Carlton merely went on to win the Cy Young award the next year and three more years in a long Hall of Fame career as one of the greatest left-handed pitchers of all time.

Some fans on opposing teams took Unger's big beautiful hair to be a sign that he was "weak" and would serenade him with whistles when he stepped on the ice. In fact, nothing could have been further from the truth. Although "Ungie" was not a big man - he has been described by one former player as "170 pounds soaking wet" - he was extremely tough. Though he rarely got in a fight, he reportedly had the best boxing skills on the team - which is saying a lot for a team with the Plagers, Picard and a new young stud, Bob Gassoff.

Moreover, Unger played in a remarkable 914 consecutive games, setting the all-time record at the time in a sport where injuries are as commonplace as football, but where players can play four times a week instead of just one. In the course of his eight plus seasons with the Blues, there were undoubtedly times that Unger was pretty banged up and even fairly seriously injured, but he suited up nonetheless and played through it, earning him the well-deserved moniker "Iron Man." Unger's explanation for his refusal to surrender to fatigue or pain: he had a sister who was confined to a wheelchair. He reportedly told himself that he could not consider complaining about his injuries when she couldn't even walk.

On defense in the 1970's, the Plager brothers still ruled the back end for a good portion of the decade with toughness, smarts and the instinctive reactions that only brothers could have with each other. Barclay was the undisputed team leader and team captain for over five years - the second longest stint in Blues' history. No one took liberties against the Blues' players when Barc was on the ice. He was afraid of no one, including guys twice his size. He had 13 broken noses to prove it!

Pittsburghers had a special thing for the elder Plager and would sing his name derisively with the chant "Bar- Clay, Bar- Clay, Bar- Clay" over and over every time he would step on the ice. But it only made him play better, as he seemed to have some of his best games against the Penguins.

As for the middle Plager brother, God help the poor player who was skating with the puck through center ice (or anywhere) with his head down when Bobby was in the vicinity. Needless to say, it would not be a beautiful day in the neighborhood for them; Bobby would routinely deliver a brutal hip check that would make the surprised opponent fly over his back through the air and land hard, often face first, on the ice.

It was also in the early 1970's that the Salomons gave an ambitious young man whom they had known for many years as their caddy at Westwood Country Club, and whose father had suddenly passed away, an opportunity to work for the team. He was attending college at Notre Dame at the time, but Sid told him if he would transfer to Saint Louis University, he could finish his studies and still work for the team as assistant publicity director. Tim Madden grabbed the opportunity and, upon graduation, became the team's travelling secretary at a mere 20 years old. The Salomons placed great trust and faith in Tim and put him in charge of all sorts of projects; besides flight, hotel and bus arrangements and making sure the players and all equipment and bags got where they needed to be, distributing meal money, handling ticket requests, paying for team dinners and all tips, he was also entrusted with dealing with all kinds of personnel issues and other problems that arose (and to no surprise, hockey players have a propensity to find "trouble" now and then).

One of his more challenging assignments (before the advent of the cell phone and google apps) was finding a certain unnamed player who had a bit too much to drink and who called him from a pay phone desperately needing a ride home. He could only describe his location as the intersection of "Walk" and "Don't Walk."

Remarkably, and unbeknownst to most folks, the Salomons built Tim his own pseudo-apartment inside the Arena across from the visiting locker room where he lived throughout the year, even during the long hot St. Louis summers. For five years he was the lone resident of the place (if you exclude the mice and the various cats that roamed the premises to take care of the mice and other creatures that might surface in the ancient building). As a young man, Tim had the undoubted distinction of living in the largest "home" in the St. Louis area. He also had the master key to the Arena Club and perhaps most importantly, for a young man, to the beer kegs located there (all with Sid's blessing, by the way, as long as he and his friends made sure to keep the place spotless). Between his home, his private club on non-game days, and his own ice rink, Tim had to be one of the most popular guys in town.

One of the more memorable games in Blues' history took place that season on January 6, 1972 in Philadelphia. With the Flyers leading 2-0 at the close of the second period, Coach Al Arbour sought to complain to Referee John Ashley about a Flyers' goal (aided by a premature puck drop when the Blues' players were not ready). Arbour followed after the referee onto the ice. The Philadelphia faithful showed their displeasure with Arbour - or perhaps they were just being Philly fans - by pelting him with trash and dousing him with beer. Others apparently grabbed at him and ripped his shirt and coat from the body of the normally mild-mannered man. *Philly could have used back then the "rage room" the team set up just this year to allow their fans to "break stuff" as a way to get out their anger and frustrations.*

Bobby Plager, who had followed Arbour onto the ice to protect him, was incensed at the Philly fans and did not take kindly to their transgressions against his friend and the beloved coach. He led a difficult charge over the glass into the crowd with his skates still on, followed by brother Barclay and brother Billy - determined to show the Philly fans the *real* meaning of brotherly love! Soon much of the team was in the stands fighting with unruly fans when 200 of Philly's finest arrived on a special call and started using billy clubs on the Blues.

When asked by a St. Louis Post Dispatch reporter what was happening, one officer purportedly said, "Right now, it's the Philadelphia Police against the St. Louis Blues, and we're winning." Indeed, several Blues' players received serious gashes to their head, requiring stiches, including Al Arbour and player John Arbour (no relation) who needed forty stitches for his wound. The Salomons who were in Philly at the time were outraged at the police behavior calling it some of the worst police brutality they had ever seen (perhaps not all that familiar with Philadelphia standards for police brutality).

Inspired by the attack on their coach and the police behavior the Blues rallied in the third period to score three goals and win the game. After the game, the police waited outside the Blues' locker room to arrest several Blues for "assault." Floyd

Thompson, Phil Roberto, John Arbor, and Al Arbour were all handcuffed, fingerprinted and spent the night in jail. However, the leader of the charge, Bobby Plager, cleverly hid in the locker room and had trainer Tommy Woodcock lock the door. He waited to leave until after the police were gone and was never charged. *Who says leaders can't be self-preservationists as well?*

The incident got widespread media attention - even the New York Times wrote about it - and inflamed a rivalry that had begun from the Blues' first year upset of the Flyers in the playoffs. From that point forward whenever the Blues came to town, the Spectrum was packed, and the Flyers were at their best. Indeed, the Blues did not win another game in Philadelphia in the next 32 tries, spanning an incredible 16 years!

As a kid I was struck by the disparity in justice between the Blues entering the stands in response to fans physically harming their coach and the Boston Bruins climbing up over the glass in St. Louis because a fan's abusive language and rubber chicken, only a year earlier. In the former, the Blues were beaten by police and then arrested and charged with crimes themselves and there were no apparent repercussions to the offending fans. In the latter, the fan permanently lost his season ticket privileges near the penalty box and the Bruins' players who infiltrated the stands incurred no adverse consequences. Apparently, disparate treatment by officials is not limited to on-ice activities. It was also a good lesson about how the justice system can be very different depending on where you are.

On the ice, the 1971-1972 playoffs presented two very familiar foes and two remarkably similar outcomes. In the first round the Blues once again drew the Minnesota North Stars. By now the North Stars were considered the better team, with the better record and home ice advantage. Indeed, home ice dictated the outcome of every game of the series until Game 7.

With the series tied 3-3 in games, the deciding game was, as in 1968, a very low scoring affair - tied at 1-1 through regulation. Once again, the Blues prevailed in Overtime in glorious fashion. Little used right winger Kevin O'Shea took a pass from his brother Danny (part of the Blues' special history with siblings along with the Plagers, the Cavallinis and the Sutters) and fired a slap shot that hit the goal post, bounced out and ricocheted off the back of the large goaltender Cesare Maniago, and then trickled into the net.

The 2-1 final Overtime score against the Stars was identical to the Blues' Game 7 Overtime win in this year's 2019 Stanley Cup Playoffs! And the game-winning goal was scored in an astoundingly similar manner. The only difference between the two really was that the hockey gods had the foresight this year to make sure the puck didn't slip in behind goalie Ben Bishop, after it hit the goal post and struck his back, so that the local kid, Patty Maroon, could tap it in and be the hero. *You just can't make this stuff up!*

In the second round, the Blues came up again against the Boston Bruins. It wasn't the Stanley Cup Final this time around, but the result was similarly disappointing for Blues' fans as the Bruins once again swept the series, outscoring the Blues by the lopsided margin of 28-8!

In the following 1972-1973 season, the Blues lost more games than we won but made the playoffs due to the generous playoff format at the time. However, the Blues were easily dispensed with by the Chicago Blackhawks in five games, our first playoff encounter of many with our rival to the North Side - *few of which have turned out well for the good guys.*

In 1973-1974, the Note missed the playoffs for the first time in the team's seven-year existence and managed a mere 64 points. Late in the season veteran winger Lou Angotti was made player-coach, a move that was not especially popular with some of the players.

Angotti continued as the head coach the next season, though no longer as a player. But just ten games in to the 1974-1975 campaign, the Blues had only two wins and Blues' management had seen enough. Angotti had only coached 36 games thus far but the Blues had only won six of them, by far the worst record of any coach in Blues' history.

Unfortunately, the Blues were in a pickle; having signed Angotti to a long-term deal. But fortunately, Angotti helped bring about his own demise. When pressed by management about his performance as a coach, and apparently oblivious to his own unpopularity on the team, Angotti offered in response to put the matter to a vote of the players whether he should stay or go. A secret ballot was held with answers put in separate sealed envelopes. Angotti was present as the envelopes were opened. After ten ballots were counted Angotti had received zero votes from the players for him to remain as coach! He reluctantly conceded that he should resign. But someone in the room with a special disdain for Angotti, suggested that they should open *all* of the ballots - after all, they had only opened half of them. It was agreed, and the remaining ballots were opened revealing that it was a unanimous 20-0 that Angotti should go. *Ouch!*

With Angotti gone as coach, the team improved considerably under new coach Garry Young and finished the season with more wins than losses and the Blues once again made the playoffs. It didn't last long, though, as we lost both games in the new two out of three "preliminary round" format to the Pittsburgh Penguins and were once again done early for the summer.

The mid 1970's teams had several players of note beyond Unger, Berenson and the Plagers. There was Larry Patey who established (and still holds) the record for most shorthanded goals in Blues' history (22). More importantly, as far as I was concerned, when Patey was controversially acquired for goal scorer Wayne Merrick (who had scored 144 goals over four seasons) the Blues now had three redheaded centers on the same team. (*I'm counting Unger as part of the tribe as he clearly had some red in there.*) I doubt that the NHL keeps statistics on such things - only a young redhead like me would probably have noticed - but that has to be a record, given that only about 1% of the population are redheads.

Other folks who stood out to me were Pierre Plante (the handsome French-Canadian who winked at my young step-mom every time he skated onto the ice to start the game; he apparently really liked the ladies and also really liked to score goals and reportedly sulked when he didn't get either); Bob Hess (a 20-year old defenseman who was the fastest and most skilled Blues' defenseman I ever saw but was perhaps cursed by comparisons to a young Bobby Orr); and Bruce Affleck (who had a few good years with the Note before an abysmal minus 56 rating one year encouraged him to try a different vocation; he has since held numerous jobs with the Blues from sales to broadcasting to currently an Executive Vice-President). *But I can't help but think he may have missed a golden opportunity to be spokesman for a certain insurance giant.*

One of the most colorful players to ever wear the Note joined the Blues in October of 1975: ex- Boston Bruin Derek Sanderson - yep, the same guy who climbed into the stands of the Arena just a few years ago. "Turk", as he was known, was among the flashiest guys in the League, with his big burly mustache and good looks. He was often accompanied by beautiful women on his arm or, lying on top of his famously photographed round bed, and reportedly had a "lady friend" in nearly every city on the road. Sanderson was hockey's version of Joe Namath, and even opened a bar with Broadway Joe. To add to his image, he owned a stretch Rolls- Royce limo which he reportedly purchased for $40,000, a lot of change back in mid-1970. He was known to drive it down Madison Avenue in New York with a chauffeur hat on to boot.

Putting aside the flair, Turk was a great hockey player; an outstanding passer and penalty killer and one of the best faceoff men to ever play the game. He was an integral member of the Boston Bruins Stanley Cup team that defeated the Blues in 1971 Stanley Cup Final and that won another Cup in 1972.

After the 1972 season, however, Sanderson was enticed to leave the NHL to join the Philadelphia Blazers of the upstart World Hockey Association. The inducement? $2.6 million! It made him the highest-paid athlete in *any sport in the world* at that time. But due to injuries, and perhaps other shenanigans, he appeared in only eight games for the Blazers, and they paid him a startling sum of $1 million just to leave and immediately return to the Bruins. After a couple less than stellar years with his old team, he was traded to the New York Rangers, where he appeared to regain his form, scoring 25 goals with 25 assists in the 1974-75 season. His flashy ways, though, may have rubbed the conservative coach Emile ("the Cat") Francis the wrong way. The next year Turk found his role diminished and was traded early in the season to the Blues for a first-round draft pick.

With the Blues, Sanderson reminded everyone the kind of player he still was. In the team's final 65 games of 1975-1976 season, he registered 67 points, more than a point a game. Moreover, with Sanderson as his playmaking center, Chuck Lefley emerged as a superstar, scoring 43 goals in one season, incredibly eight of those shorthanded - a Blues' record equaled five years later by Larry Patey. One of Sanderson's signature plays was to tell the Blues' speedster with the big shot to just take off right after the faceoff; he would win the draw and hit him with a long stretch pass, often for a breakaway.

But Sanderson's time with the Blues was short-lived. Ironically, the Rangers coach who traded Sanderson away to the Blues, would soon wear out his own welcome in New York (the *coup de gras* when he released popular goalie Eddie Giacomin). And then the Cat came to St. Louis to coach the Blues in January 1976. Not surprisingly, Sanderson was once again soon "traded" by Francis - this time simply exchanged for cash. Lefley's goal production dropped to 11 goals and was never again a big scorer.

Although Sanderson made a lot of money, he spent it just as fast, and not just on himself. He was reportedly one of the nicest and most generous guys around. If someone asked for money or a loan, he would give it to them - no questions, no documentation, and no efforts to keep tabs on whether he got repaid. While with the Blues, he would often give an employee a 10% cut just to cash his checks for him and bring him the money. And of course, he also did some pretty stupid stuff, like purportedly lighting a $100 bill and then using it to light his cigar. It is both sad and shocking that, despite all of the money he made and the kindness of his heart, that he apparently spent some time later in life living on the street in a cardboard box.

My beloved Blues were also on the verge of financial collapse. In 1976 the Salomons announced that they were in a very difficult financial predicament and would have to sell the team without some assistance from the City. They would even have to consider moving the team from St. Louis, if a suitable local buyer could not be found.

There was a litany of reasons. Chief among them was the Arena, which was a financial nightmare. The Salomons had spent four times the cost of the franchise and twice the cost of the building making it a great venue to see a game (some might say they spent way too much to do so). The Old Barn cost a fortune to maintain (purportedly another $11 Million over the years), but the Salomons had never spared a dime ensuring that the place was kept spic and span.

And a major economic problem with the Arena was that it had no air conditioning, rendering it unable to be rented out for concerts and other events five months of the year. Moreover, the Salomons had to compete for events with Kiel Auditorium owned by the City which offered its space for rent at a discounted rate. Blues' counsel James Cullen pointed out that that the team itself was doing just fine; it was the Arena that was bleeding them dry.

And then there was the City of St. Louis and its politicians. Unlike in today's world where cities fall all over themselves to offer tax breaks, incentives and handouts to professional sports teams, St. Louis offered no help to the Salomons. Indeed, while the average NHL team was paying

4.5% in city and state taxes, the Blues were paying 9.5%, and the City refused to give the Blues any tax break. It also refused to buy the Arena at a fair market value and lease it back to the Blues. Further when the Blues sought to build a parking garage in Forrest Park across from Highway 40 with an underground tunnel, seeking use of seven acres of the more than 1400, and promised to allow the City to use as it pleases when there was no game, they were blocked.

But there were also some extravagances that the generous owners bestowed on not just players but their employees, always paying them well and keeping probably more folks around than needed to run a tight ship. Indeed, the Salomons were the consummate employer-friendly organization, throwing a Christmas steak and champagne lunch for all employees and their families, and helping out any employee in need. When a young Blues' stick boy was diagnosed with cancer, Sid personally went to the hospital and gave the billing coordinator his information and directed that all bills be sent to him for payment.

The financial problems of the team were no doubt also compounded by the Salomons' own personal financial decline. The primary source of revenue for father and son was their insurance agency, which experienced a significant financial setback when their biggest client terminated their relationship after 47 years. The company? The Crown Life Insurance Company of Saskatchewan - a province in Canada that would rear its head again big-time in Blues' ownership lore before too long. Nor did it help when the Salomons lost their wrongful termination suit against Crown in the U.S. Court of Appeals in 1976.

And there was the team's declining performance. The team had become mediocre which naturally lowered fan interest, attendance and revenues - and at the worst possible time. Sid clearly bore some of the blame as he got more involved in hockey operations, had no background to do so, and adopted an almost schizophrenic approach, going through six different general managers and eleven coaching changes in only six years.

If that weren't enough heartache, Mr. Salomon suffered two actual heart attacks in January 1977, the last leaving him in a temporary coma. And then Sid's long-standing battle with cancer and Hodgkin's disease reared its head. No doubt the stress of these financial doldrums and the potential loss of their beloved team were taking a toll and contributing to their poor health.

On "Black Monday" January 31, 1977, numerous Blues' employees were fired so that the team could meet its February 1 payroll. Among those let go was long-time Senior Vice-President Lynn Patrick, the Salomons' loyal lieutenant and the first employee ever hired by the Blues in 1966. A gracious Patrick told the St. Louis Post-Dispatch that he understood the necessity of it: "I could see this coming. The team was short of money and something had to be done. I know the situation and I know it isn't good."

With all of these clouds hanging over the Blues, hockey continued on the ice in 1976-77. Just two games into the season, a hard decision was made that time had caught up with the team's long-time captain and leader Barclay Plager. It was determined that he should become the player-coach of the Kansas City farm team to help him launch a new career as a coach and groom future Blues for the NHL, including promising young players Bernie Federko and Brian Sutter. Barclay, as always, took his assignment seriously, and led his team into the finals. He was even named the League's Most Valuable Player.

Midway through the season, the Blues called up Sutter from Kansas City (Federko was furious that he was left behind at the time, but he would get his own call-up just a few games later). Sutter was the ultimate lunch-pail hard-hat guy. When he began with the Blues, he was not much of a skater or a shooter - indeed his skills were arguably not even at a professional level. But don't tell that to Brian Sutter. No one worked harder on the ice and had more heart than he. And Sutter, probably more than any Blues' player in history, made himself into an exceptional player by sheer willpower. He went from scoring four goals and then nine goals in his first two seasons to forty-one the next.

It naturally didn't hurt that he played alongside the far more talented Bernie Federko throughout virtually his entire career. Bernie could do much of the skating and puck handling and feed him the puck. But Sutter had to do the dirty work in the corners and along the boards and had to fight hard for position in front of the goal - the man had nearly 1800 penalty minutes, a Blues' team record to this day, much of that dropping the gloves to protect Bernie and other teammates. Ultimately, Sudsy had to put himself in a position to put the biscuit in the basket - something he did over 300 times for the Blues.

Sutter was a natural leader and, in many ways, the embodiment of the Blues' first legendary leader, Barclay Plager. Like Barc, he was not an especially big man (both men were 5 foot 11 and only weighed about 170 pounds), but he had a very loud bark and was not afraid to get into a scrap with anyone to protect a teammate. Like Barc, he was the oldest of multiple brothers who played in the NHL. Like Barc, he played for only one NHL team, the Blues, his entire career. Like Barc, he was a team captain - indeed, they are the two longest serving captains in Blues' history. Like Barc, he went on to coach the Blues, and in his case several other teams as well. And like Barc, Sutter's Number 11 hangs in the rafters, fittingly, right next to Barc's Number 8, as one of the team's seven cherished retired numbers.

Despite having a losing record in 1976-1977, the Blues actually finished first in the extraordinarily weak "Smythe" division (the NHL has repeatedly changed the names and configurations of its divisions). Our first-round opponent under the new playoff format was the Montreal Canadiens. It was a completely different team than the one that had dismantled the Blues in the 1968 and 1969 Finals, but they were no less effective or powerful. Indeed, as had become a custom with all thing Canadiens, the Blues lost in four straight games to the now Scotty Bowman-coached squad. The goal differential was a rather embarrassing and less than competitive 19-4. The only conceivable comfort in being mauled by the Canadiens yet again was that the Habs went on to win the Stanley Cup that year.

If the potential loss of the ten-year-old franchise and being swept by the Canadiens in the first round of the playoffs was not enough to put the team and its loyal fans into a somber mood, then the shocking death of young 24-year-old defenseman Bob Gassoff from a motorcycle accident about a month later on May 27, 1977, really did the trick. Gassoff was attending a post-season Sunday barbeque with his nearly eight-month pregnant wife at Garry Unger's 200-acre farm in Gray Summit, Missouri.

Gassoff was not a great player initially but was steadily improving and starting to come into his own as a defenseman, with a promising career ahead of him. He was also one of toughest guys on earth - he had over 500 penalty minutes in the previous two seasons. We had now moved our seats behind the Blues' penalty box, and Bob was a frequent guest to our neck of the woods. I would recall him coming in to the box after a particularly tough fight with his hands all cut up and bleeding, and he would just stick his hand into the bucket of ice that held the spare frozen pucks for minutes on end. *If you don't think that hurts like hell, just try it sometime and see how long you last.*

As a young man a car reportedly fell off of a jack right on top of Bob and he managed to survive. So, it seemed inconceivable that he of all people could be killed by anything. But I learned that no one is invincible. Bob jumped on one of the motorcycle dirt bikes on the property to take it for a spin before dinner joined by Blues' fellow defenseman Bruce Affleck and Bobby Plager and a 12-year-old boy who was related to one of the players. A 19-year old working for Unger parking cars had been dispatched to get some more ice for the party and was returning fast on the dirt road and coming over a hill. The bike riders didn't see the car because of the approaching hill. The driver apparently swerved missing Affleck in front, and the young boy, but struck Gassoff, apparently shearing off his leg and he bled to death.

Bob left behind a pregnant wife and a son he never got a chance to see. Like his Dad, Bobby Jr. was one tough dude and, indeed, went on to become a Navy Seal. Bob would have been very proud. It was a tragedy beyond contemplation - one of the darkest days in Blues' history - and for a long time it felt as if there was a large black cloud hanging over the team.

And if things couldn't get any worse, stricken by financial and health woes and with no solution in sight, the Salomons announced that they would not be operating the team for the 1977-1978 season, which had to have been devastating for them. Thus, in order for the franchise to survive in St. Louis, a new ownership group would need to step up and buy the team.

Some good news finally arrived in late July 1977 when Emile Francis helped convince R. Hal Dean, the Chairman of Ralston Purina, to have his St. Louis-based pet food company buy the Blues and the Arena and assume its substantial debts as a civic gesture. Ralston Purina stepped in at the last minute when no one else would with the apparent goal to get the team's finances in order until another suitor could be found. Dean's actions would be one of the greatest saves in Blues' history, one that even the great Hall and Plante wouldn't have been able to make. The Arena was also renamed "the Checkerdome" to promote the company's checkerboard logo.

Despite the new temporary stability of the franchise, the wheels really came off on the ice in the 1977-1978 season. With Francis stepping aside as coach, the Blues started the year about as dismally as possible, winning just 11 of their first 54 games. Following back to back home-away massacres at the hands of the Canadiens, the Blues fired coach Leo Boivin and replaced him with legendary leader Barclay Plager in hopes that he could turn things around.

The Blues did play better but still missed the playoffs. And then we really hit rock bottom. In the 1978-1979 season, the Blues managed only 18 wins for the entire year for a mere 48 points - a franchise low to this day. To put the team's futility into perspective, over a two-year period, the team won a meagre 38 times in 160 games played. It was the first time in Blues' history that we had missed the playoffs in consecutive seasons and that the team was not even remotely competitive.

As the team continued to struggle in the 1979-1980 season, the Blues relieved Plager of his coaching duties after only twenty-four games, deciding to try another former Blues' legend, Red Berenson, at the helm. The team promptly responded by losing the next four games (which seems to be a trend with even the best Blues' coaches). But then, the team began to jell and got on somewhat a roll, finishing the season in a flurry and even surprisingly making the playoffs. Unfortunately, the season and decade ended with a first-round playoff loss once again to their rivals from Chicago, with the Blues losing all three games in the best of five series.

The last season of the decade also came with a significant rule change - NHL players were now *required* to wear helmets for the first time. This was a huge safety breakthrough and benefit to players in reducing the number and severity of head injuries. But it did take away some of the fan experience and identification with the players - no more so than those with flamboyant hair. Ungie was no doubt relieved that current players were grandfathered in and he could choose to opt out (which he naturally did). The last NHL player to go helmetless? The Blues' Craig MacTavish who retired in 1997, eighteen years after the rule was implemented.

Recap of the 1970's

The 1970's was a very challenging decade for the Blues on several levels, after such a promising start for the team in its first three seasons. Off the ice, the Blues lost their first-class owners, and also a young and promising player to tragedy.

On the ice, the Blues had some good and colorful players but had a losing record most years and made no serious challenge for the Stanley Cup. Indeed, although the Blues made the playoffs in six of the ten years, we only won *one* playoff series the entire decade!

Much of our troubles could be laid at the goalpost of the goalies, a theme that would haunt the Blues for much of the next four decades. Once Plante and Hall put away their goalie pads for the last time in 1970 and 1971, respectively, the Blues couldn't seem to find anyone who could consistently fit the bill. Indeed, the Blues switched starting goaltenders almost every year - from Jacques Caron *(who could not hold Plante's Jacques-strap)* to Ed Staniowski to Wayne Stephenson to John Davidson to Ed Johnston to Phil Myre.

As the decade drew to a close, it was unclear where this team was headed. The silver lining was that the team's new ownership had financial means, the Blues still had a strong niche following and there was a plethora of young players in their early 20's that were hoped to be rising stars in Bernie Federko, Brian Sutter, Mike Zuke, Wayne Babych, Perry Turnbull, Blake Dunlop, Larry Patey, Rick La Pointe and Joe Micheletti. The 1980's couldn't come soon enough.

On a personal level, my dad had moved to Florida and was no longer a season ticket holder and I had headed off to college in Austin, Texas, hardly a hotbed for ice hockey. But I continued to try to follow my Blues as much as I could before the advent of the internet, ESPN, and Fox Sports network. Thank God for KMOX radio and its 50,000-watt signal that can transmit broadcasts at night in most states, across Canada and as far as the Netherlands, if the conditions are right. I would take my beat-up station wagon to the highest elevation I could find in Austin's hill country - often Mount Bonnell overlooking Lake Austin. Between gaps of static, I could listen to the wonderful and powerful voice of Dan Kelly that made you feel like you were right at the Old Barn.

The 1980's

And just when we thought we would be singing the blues for a long time, something magical happened. The first Blues' team of the 1980's started the season on a winning note and just kept winning. Halfway through the season the Blues were a phenomenal 29-6-6. Indeed, we already had almost as many wins as the last two full seasons combined! We finished strongly as well, securing not only first place in the Smythe Division, but also second overall in the NHL with 107 points, our highest total ever.

It was a remarkable turnaround season and Coach Red Berenson was rewarded with the Jack Adams Trophy for Coach of the Year in a unanimous vote, the first time that had ever happened. The Blues went from the bottom one-third of the League in scoring to second in the entire NHL. And it wasn't just one or two players. Yes, young guns Wayne Babych and Bernie Federko had the finest years of their careers with Babych scoring 54 goals and Federko dishing out over 70 assists and tallying over 100 points. But the Blues had exceptional offensive balance with five thirty goal scorers (in addition to Babych and Federko, there was Jorgen Pettersson, Brian Sutter, and Perry Turnbull), and five additional players with at least 20 goals (Mike Zuke, Tony Currie, Larry Patey, Blake Dunlop, and Blair Chapman). Indeed, the Blues scored more goals that season on a per game average than any in team history.

But the biggest story was goaltender Mike Liut. Although his numbers on paper (such as save percentage and goals against) were not overly impressive, his play for this offensive-minded team certainly was, as he was often left alone on breakaways and odd-man rushes to fend for himself. In fact, so impressive was Liut's play that he was runner-up for the Hart Memorial Trophy for Most Valuable Player, losing to Wayne Gretzky, the man widely considered the greatest to ever play the game, by less than one percent of the vote. And Liut actually won the NHL *players'* vote that year for Most Outstanding Player. In terms of League-wide recognition, Liut's season was the second best ever for a Blues' player, eclipsed only by Brett

Hull's wining the Hart trophy following an 86-goal performance one decade later.

The Blues started what many hoped would be a glorious run to the Finals against the Pittsburgh Penguins, a team with a losing record and only 73 points. The Blues did manage to get through the first round by winning the best of five series, but it took a much tougher than expected five games. Indeed, Game 5 of that series was one of the Blues' classics of all time. The teams traded lots of punches - literally (there were several fights, extremely rare for a playoff game these days) and even more shots (each goalie faced more than 50 shots!). The game went to Double Overtime - a pattern it seemed for Blues' deciding playoff games - with the unlikeliest of candidates, defensive-minded Mike Crombeen, who had hardly played in the game due to a bad cold, scoring the game winning goal. It was the Blues' first playoff series win in nearly ten years!

But the closeness of the Pittsburgh series did not bode well for a team with much higher aspirations. After all, the Blues were the second-best team in the NHL during the regular season and this was our first serious chance to win a Stanley Cup in history (you can't really say that we had much of a chance in the first three years). Fortunately, the next opponent, the New York Rangers, was another mediocre team that year with a losing record and a team that the Blues had handled well all year; in fact, the Blues had beaten the Rangers all four games that we played against them during the regular season - most recently by a lopsided 7-2 margin.

Unfortunately, as Blues' fans have come to learn all too well over the last five decades, the playoffs are not the same thing as the regular season. Perhaps the Blues were not as good as their record indicated, or the Rangers had figured out how to play them, but the Rangers shockingly dispatched the Blues in six games, winning four of the last five games. It was a heartbreaking playoff loss and something that would be a common theme over the next several decades for the Note.

Although the personnel did not change materially the next year (1981-1982) the Blues suddenly somehow were no longer a dominant team. Indeed, we had a losing record and, with just twelve games left in the season, GM Emile Francis let Berenson go as coach and installed himself at the helm. (Berenson would become Head Coach of his *alma mater* Michigan and lead the Wolverines to two NCAA titles in a distinguished 33-year career). Despite the poor record, the Blues still made the playoffs in the newly named "Norris" division, and even won in the first round versus Winnipeg. But we never led in the next series versus our rivals from Chicago. Trailing three games to one, Bernie Federko scored an Overtime goal in Game 5 to extend the series, but we were shut out in Game 6.

The following year (1982-1983) the Blues had even fewer points (a mere 65) but again managed to make the playoffs thanks to a very weak division. Again, though, we were sent home for the summer by the Blackhawks - this time in the first round. The Blues impressively erased a two-goal deficit with four third period goals to win Game 1 in Chicago, only to lose the next three games of a best of five series.

But there were bigger problems brewing in the beer city than the team's performance on the ice. R. Hal Dean, the Ralston Purina's Chairman who saved the Blues from demise, retired and his replacement cared little about hockey. Ralston's Board decided that a pet food company, however much they liked their hometown city, did not want to be in the hockey business, especially when the team was costing it millions every year - allegedly over $10 Million during its brief ownership.

Ralston Purina would soon go from hometown hero to disloyal deadbeat in many folks' eyes. Unable to find someone locally interested in buying the team, the pet food giant announced in January 1983 that it had sold the team to Billy Hunter, the swashbuckling salesman from Edmonton who once owned the Edmonton Oilers when it was part of the rival World Hockey Association. Most shocking, it was Hunter's plan to move the team to Saskatoon, Saskatchewan, a city 1,221 miles from St. Louis in remote farmland 250 miles north of Montana with a population of only about 150,000 folks at the time (today it is a more bustling metropolis with a population of nearly 300,000, so perhaps Hunter may have seen the future).

Hunter and his fellow investors agreed to pay Ralston $11.5 Million for the team and were planning to build a $43 Million 18,000-seat Arena (which represented, if full, about 12% of every man, woman and child in Saskatoon on game days, though they were presumably planning to draw rabid hockey fans from all over the province).

In light of these developments, Emile Francis (who was himself born in Saskatchewan - *a pure coincidence?*) sought release from his contract with the Blues and immigrated to Hartford (where the NHL Whalers resided and subsequently moved, with no League objection, to become today's Carolina Hurricanes). Barclay Plager took his place as coach. Ralston then proceeded to fire 60% of the Blues' employees. The only folks left were Plager, the scouting department and accounting folks.

The one obstacle to the sale of the Blues was that the NHL Bylaws required that all sales of franchises had to be approved by at least 75% of the owners - i.e. 14 of the 18 owners at that time. This provision was designed to ensure that an owner would not sell or move a team against the best interests of the League as a whole. In addition, the NHL could, at least in theory, give cities and fan bases that spend so much money supporting the team some comfort that an NHL team would not leave absent poor support or some other compelling reason.

While this provision exists in a similar form in all professional sports league Bylaws, the leagues have, in practice, generally been loath to bar fellow owners from moving their teams even when they lack good cause (*as fans of the St. Louis Rams know all too well*). Perhaps it falls under the "there but the grace of God goes I" mentality of fellow owners, or a desire to avoid expensive and burdensome litigation. Indeed, on the extremely rare occasions where leagues have actually tried to block teams from moving it has not always gone so well. *See* Al Davis antitrust lawsuit against the NFL for blocking his move from Oakland to Los Angeles in 1980. Davis ultimately won his right to move as well as money damages - and his team won the Super Bowl that year just to throw some more salt in the wound.

But in this case, the other NHL owners almost universally opposed the Blues' move to Saskatoon. They did not consider it good economics for the NHL to move a franchise from one of the twenty largest markets in the U.S. to a town a fraction of the size in a remote part of Canada - not good for revenue, television market size or the NHL's reputation. And then I suspect, some were not wild about having to travel to Saskatoon to play hockey as opposed to the far more centrally located and more easily accessible St. Louis.

I would like to think that the other owners also felt that it was the wrong thing to do to folks in St. Louis who had supported the team so well over the years - leading the NHL in attendance many of those years. Then again, had the move been to a larger U.S. city, I'm not so sure the other owners would have cared much about St. Louis or its fans.

When the vote was held for approving the sale and move, Ralston managed to get only 3 of the 14 votes it needed, with one of those being its own. Ralston did not take kindly to this development and intrusion on what it saw was an invasion of its free market right to sell its own property. Like most people and entities do in this country when they feel aggrieved, they sued.

And in the sports world, the favorite choice of a lawsuit is an antitrust claim, since none of the sports leagues other than baseball have an antitrust exemption. Further, if the actions are deemed to be a restraint of trade, the penalty is three times the actual damages plus attorney fees. Leagues are also often concerned about the precedential impact of any adverse antitrust ruling against them since they all conspire in one form or the other by their very nature. In short, an antitrust lawsuit often serves as great leverage in getting a matter resolved to the plaintiff's satisfaction. To make sure that they sufficiently got the NHL's attention, Ralston filed a $60 Million-dollar antitrust lawsuit against the League and all of its owners individually.

Ralston did not stop there in its effort to flex its legal muscles. It locked the doors to the Checkerdome and threatened to sell off all the players and assets. Moreover, it announced that it would not take part in the League's draft that was scheduled to occur in Montreal only a few days later.

Four loyal Blues' scouts who had been working their butts off on the draft went to Montreal on their own dime hoping to get approval to at least make selections in the draft until things got worked out. After all, how could it be beneficial to Ralston, even if it was trying to sell or dispose of the team, to diminish the value of the franchise by failing to add top young talent to the franchise? But Ralston refused to allow any draft of players, marking the first time in NHL history then or since (and in any sports league I suspect) that a team has simply just skipped the entire draft altogether.

After that development and following the typical blueprint of most sophisticated folks who get sued in this country and are well-represented, the NHL and its owners countersued Ralston for even more money - $78 million. The Counterclaim accused Ralston of bad faith in failing to attend the NHL draft and seeking to damage the League by "willfully, wantonly and maliciously collapsing its St. Louis Blues' hockey operation." Moreover, Ralston, it urged, had violated the NHL's constitution that required "an owner to give two years notice before suspending the operations of a hockey franchise." The NHL sought $3 million in actual damages, plus punitive damages of $75 million or an amount equal to five percent of Ralston's assets ($105 million).

So there - Game On! *Perhaps they should have settled it by having the toughest and most fearless Blue, Captain Brian*

Sutter, take on a Ralston Purina pit bull. For the record I would have bet on Sutter surviving.

One Blues player that had to have been very conflicted about this development was the team's biggest star at the time, Bernie Federko. Federko was born and grew up in Saskatchewan and had lots of family there, had even played for the Saskatoon Blades of the WHL and no doubt thought it would be very cool for them to have an NHL team and for him to play in his hometown. At the same time, he loved St. Louis, his immediate family was settled here, and knew how devastating the loss of the Blues would be to many St. Louisans. The future Fox sports talk man knew that sometimes it was best to remain quiet.

In light of Ralston's actions, the NHL temporarily took over running the Blues and announced that it was searching for a new owner. The League advised that it preferred to keep the team in St. Louis, if a suitable person/ group could be found. But if that did not occur by August 6, 1983 (a very short deadline), the NHL would likely disband the team. The NHL Players Association then joined the fray and threatened a legal battle if the team was disbanded and players were consolidated into other teams, thereby reducing the number of jobs for its constituency.

Enter Harry Ornest to the rescue. Harry was a Beverly Hills, California businessman who had made a lot of money in the vending machine business and later in real estate. He had also grown up in Edmonton, been a minor league hockey referee in the 1940's, and had invested in several minor-league sports clubs and parks as his fortune grew. He was now living a comfortable Southern California lifestyle and presumably didn't need the headache of trying to revive a franchise thousands of miles away.

But Harry had always relished the opportunity to own a professional sports team. He had owned some minor league teams, but previous efforts with other investors to buy the Seattle Mariners baseball team and other clubs had fallen through. "We grew up listening to dad on the phone trying to convince his wealthier friends to buy various teams over the years and it didn't happen," Laura Ornest told the Los Angeles Times. In addition, from all indications, Harry also really liked the green stuff. Here was a golden opportunity to perhaps do own a team and make money since the cost of the flailing Blues' franchise was pretty darn cheap for a professional sports franchise.

By late June 1983 Ornest had emerged as the main investor in a consortium of local companies and individuals looking to buy the Blues. To meet his $12 Million purchase offer, Ornest put up the proceeds from his sale of the Triple-A baseball Vancouver Canadians, paying $3 million in cash and providing $9 million in unsecured notes. He simultaneously offered to purchase the Checkerdome from Ralston for $5 million. To meet operating expenses for the club, Ornest raised $3 million by selling debt securities to civic-minded local companies like Anheuser-Busch, Emerson Electric, Maritz, Mercantile Bank and Stifel, Nicolaus and other individuals.

As it turned out, Ornest's bid was the only formal one that was submitted, so it was likely that the St. Louis Blues would have disappeared after 16 seasons had he not been able to close the deal. Fortunately, only ten days before the deadline, Harry's offer was accepted by the NHL, and the Blues would stay in the Lou by the skin of our teeth.

While certainly a great development for the City under the circumstances, Ornest was notoriously tight with the buck. He hired his family to take on much of the management of the team: His son, Mike, was appointed president of the Arena (restoring the old name) and Vice-President of the hockey team, and his daughter, Cindy, was made Vice-President of the Arena company. A third child, Maury, also joined the family business. Only his eldest daughter Laura, already in broadcasting in Vancouver, was not on the payroll. "He wanted to save money and people talked about it being - what's a nice way of putting it besides bare bones? - economical and efficient," Laura said of her father.

Indeed, the team operated on a shoe-string budget; the Blues had only 23 players under contract, whereas other teams had twice that number. Players were given below market salaries and limited perks, but most players were willing to oblige since they liked St. Louis and wanted to stay and make it work.

Ornest was initially given a free pass by the media and many fans because he had been the team's savior. However, the honeymoon began to crumble when he traded away star players in moves that looked like they were made solely for financial reasons. Chief among these was trading young star Joey Mullen for basically Eddy Beers and Gino Cavallini. Beers would only play 24 games with the Blues, injure his back in training camp the next year and never play again in the NHL. The older Cavallini brother played several years with the Blues and was a hard-worker who once scored 20 goals in a season - 91 for his entire career with the Note. Mullen, on the other hand, had scored 151 goals in his first four plus seasons with the Blues and would go on to become the first American-born hockey player to score both 500 goals and 1000 points and be selected for the Hall of Fame.

It was clearly one of the worst trades the Blues ever made. Harry was lambasted: "He rode in on a white horse and was God for a while. Then he started doing all of those things and ticked everybody off," Bob Plager told the excellent hockey journalist Jeremy Rutherford in the book "100 Things Blues Fans Should Know and Do Before They Die."

With the new season and ownership, the coaching reins were turned over to Jacques Demers, who had previously coached the Quebec Nordiques (which eventually became the Colorado Avalanche). Demers had not been a head coach in three years and, as it was later learned, was unable to read or write (apparently due to abuse as a child). Ornest likely made him coach because he could be had very cheaply. But as it turned out, Demers was an excellent coach. He was actually a very smart man who was bi-lingual, related well to his players and got the most out of them and was a likeable and colorful personality.

More importantly, he was able to keep the Blues competitive despite having a lot less money and players to work with.

In his first season with the Blues (1983-1984) the team had a losing record but was able to finish second in the still weak Norris Division. One unlikely emerging star was center man Doug Gilmour. Drafted only in the seventh round in the prior year due to his small stature, the Blues relegated him to junior hockey where he led the entire League in scoring. Demers saw something in him, primarily as a defensive forward specialist and played him against the other team's best players. It turned out that Gilmour could not only shut down the opposition but also score himself, tallying 25 goals in his first season at the very young age of 20. He was also a feisty and aggressive player and bore a physical resemblance, in Captain Sutter's eyes, to Charles Manson, leading to his nickname "Killer." Gilmour would go on to have a Hall of Fame 20-year career, though the vast majority of it after he left the Blues.

In the playoffs, the Blues made a bit of a splash. In the first round against Detroit, the Blues won the three out of five series with back to back Overtime wins in Games 3 and 4, the first one in Double Overtime and the second on a hat trick from our lone resident Swede, Jorgen Pettersson. The Red Wings weren't exactly a great team that year, finishing even behind the Blues, but Blues' fans did not take any playoff wins, especially against the team from "Hockeytown," for granted. In the next round, against a much better first place Minnesota squad, the Blues pushed the North Stars to seven games, and even took the lead in that game with less than six minutes remaining, but quickly surrendered it, forcing yet another Game 7 Overtime versus the Stars. This one, however, went to the Minnesotans.

The following 1984-1985 season would be impacted by injury. When you play a sport with large men crashing into one another at high speeds in a limited enclosed space there is always a decent chance that players will get hurt - sometimes severely and in a career-altering way. It's a risk that every player assumes when he steps on to the ice and every franchise takes when it signs a player for millions of dollars to a long-term deal. The risk is naturally magnified when it is a young star player whom you are betting a lot of the future on. So, it is an especially difficult thing to accept when such a player is injured *off* the ice and *outside the bounds of hockey* and when the injury stems from stupidity and could have been easily prevented.

March 13, 1985 was an off day for the boys in blue, but that didn't stop them from acting like frat boys; it was time for an annual Blues' prank to haze rookies referred to as the "snipe hunt." In the course of the festivities a highly talented young Blues' player jumped onto the back of a pick-up truck. His name: Doug Wickenheiser - the number one pick in the entire NHL draft in 1980 by the Montreal Canadiens after scoring 89 goals and being Player of the Year in the Canadian Junior Hockey Leagues. Doug had been acquired the previous season for Perry Turnbull, the Blues' number one pick, second overall, in 1979 and a three-time 30-goal scorer. Before Wickenheiser was settled the truck sped off and he fell off the truck onto the street. If that wasn't enough, he then got hit by a car.

Somehow fortunately, unlike Bob Gassoff, he was not killed. But he was seriously injured, tearing both his ACL and MCL in his left knee and requiring reconstructive surgery. He was out nearly a year. While Wickenheiser was able to return to be part of a very dramatic moment in Blues' history late in the following season, his high promise was never realized, and he was claimed off of waivers a few years later and ended his career as a shell of himself as a part-time player.

More tragedy followed him several years later when he developed cancer and ultimately succumbed to the disease at the very early age of 37. His memory lives on through the "14 Fund," a Blues' charity that raises funds for cancer and is dedicated to him.

Despite the loss of Wickenheiser in 1984-1985, Demers was able to transform the Blues into an improved and winning team, finishing first in the division. But once again we lost to the

North Stars in the playoffs - this time in the first round and by a sweep.

And then came the 1985-1986 season. The Blues had a typical regular season for the times: 37 wins, 34 losses and 9 ties - pretty much the definition of mediocrity. While we made the playoffs, there was no particular reason to feel optimistic about our chances. To the extent that momentum is important, the Blues won only one of the last five games. And our first-round opponent was naturally, once again, the North Stars, the team that had eliminated us in the playoffs the previous two years.

The Blues had Sutter and future Hall of Famers Federko and Gilmour, as well as steady defensive leader Rob Ramage. But we had foolishly traded one of our best players, Joey Mullen, to Calgary for very little in return. And the Blues didn't even have a number one goalie that year, with Rick Wamsley and Greg Millen splitting the duties almost evenly and each performing at an equal level of below average.

Nevertheless, we managed to squeak by the North Stars this time around in five games (in a three out of five format), losing the potential clincher in Game 4 on home ice but winning the deciding Game 5 in the City of Lakes. Then, against the Toronto Maple Leafs, the Blues did something not achieved in 16 years: we won a second-round playoff series. It was another close one that went the distance with the Blues winning in seven games; relatively unheralded Kevin LaVallee scored the game winner in the third period for the 2-1 victory in St. Louis.

We were heading to the Conference Final - only one step away from the Stanley Cup Final! The last image Blues' faithful had had of that was Bobby Orr's arms outstretched.

The Blues' opponent would ironically be the Calgary Flames - the team to whom we had essentially gifted Joey Mullen. The Flames were also led by a young hard-shooting defenseman named Al MacInnis. The Blues pulled off an upset in Game 1 in Calgary, but then lost three of the next four games, setting up a highly memorable Game 6 in St. Louis where the Blues had to win or be eliminated.

The game started off more like a war than a hockey game. In the first period the referees called an astounding 21 penalties, mostly offsetting and seven of them as the buzzer sounded as a melee broke out. But neither team had broken through for a goal. It appeared like it would be a close checking defensive affair. That would soon change dramatically.

Just twenty seconds into the second period, Dan Quinn (who would himself later become a Blue briefly) scored the game's first goal for Calgary. And then he did it again about a minute and a half later, giving the Flames a big two goal lead. The Blues' Cliff Ronning countered with a goal soon thereafter, but that was wiped out a few minutes later by yet another Calgary score. And then the Flames put the icing on the cake with their fourth goal of the period.

The 4-1 lead at the end of two periods, especially in a playoff game, seemed insurmountable. But Blues' intense Captain Brian Sutter was having none of it. He reportedly got in the faces of his teammates during the intermission and sought to rally them, proclaiming, in effect, that "We are NOT losing this game!" The Blues came out strong in the third period and Doug Wickenheiser narrowed the deficit to 4-2 with a goal at the six-minute mark - still a long way to go. But then Joey Mullen got revenge on his former team by scoring a back-breaking fifth goal for Calgary only one minute later (5-2). Now Sutter's prophecy looked like mere bravado to all who heard it.

Sutter, however, remained undeterred; he promptly responded with a goal of his own at the eight-minute mark - the third goal in three minutes (5-3). Still, there were only twelve minutes left to get two more goals, while preventing any further scoring by the Flames.

Calgary employed a defensive approach and the clock began to tick down quickly, as it always appears to do when your team is trailing. And then, with a little more than four minutes left in the game, the Blues' Greg Paslawski scored a goal, assisted by Sutter naturally, to cut the lead to just one (5-4).

The Blues put on a full court press trying to tie things up and prevent going home for an 18th straight season without a Cup. Time was winding down with just over one-minute left in the game and the Blues' season. Flames' defenseman Jamie Macoun had clean possession of the puck behind his net, waiting and just taking up time. With the hometown crowd in a loud frenzy, Paslawski snuck behind a surprised Macoun and stole the puck, and then in one quick motion directed it behind the befuddled Calgary goaltender Mike Vernon to tie the game! It was an incredible one-man effort and goal and a phenomenal comeback.

Although it tied the game, there was still Overtime to play. No problem! Buoyed by the amazing turnaround and the energy of the crowd, the Blues were not to be denied; we scored seven and one-half minutes into the Overtime to win 6-5. It was Wickenheiser who scored his second goal of the game to pull off what has generally been considered (until at least this year) the greatest win in team history (it was certainly Doug's greatest game in the NHL).

Sutter had willed the team to victory - which I suppose was why he was the longest serving Blues' captain. His ability to lead men would also propel him to the job of head coach just two years later - a position he held with the Blues from 1988-1992, the longest tenure for a Blues' coach at that time.

It was a rare playoff game that I did not attend in those years, but I was not there to watch the incredible comeback in Game 6. My soon-to-be wife and I had just moved into our first home that day (a home we still live in today) and were marveling that we had a place of our own and didn't want to leave. We had no bed or couch or TV or other furniture. But we sat on the carpet in the living room with an old transistor radio listening to the game that became known as the "Monday Night Miracle."

To call it a miracle, however, stretches how desperate Blues' fans had become. It certainly doesn't live up to the most famous miracle on ice, when a bunch of college kids who got their asses kicked by the Russians at Madison Square Garden only weeks before (by the embarrassing score of 10-2) somehow managed to defeat the greatest hockey team in the world in the 1980 Olympics. To this day that's still the most unlikely outcome and greatest sports moment in American history in my and most sports folks' opinion.

Moreover, despite the Blues' dramatic win, the outcome merely served to extend the series to a Game 7. The Blues would still have to make the 1,800-mile trek back to a red-hot inspired Calgary. And, of course, the Blues lost that game and, thus, failed to advance to the Stanley Cup Final yet again. Game 7 wasn't as close as the score sounded at 2-1. (*Why does every Blues' Game 7 end 2-1?*) After the Flames seized an early first period goal by Al MacInnis, the Blues had very few meaningful opportunities, with only 18 shots on goal for the entire game. We didn't score our goal until we were trailing 2-0 and with less than two minutes remaining in the game.

When the best game and moment of your team's history until this year occurs in a losing playoff series, it tells you a lot about the psyche of Blues' fans.

Shortly following the season, Blues' fans were shocked to learn that popular coach Jacques Demers was leaving the Blues and had signed a contract with rival Detroit. Blues' owner Harry Ornest was irate and claimed Demers was under contract for three more years. He even took the highly unusual step of suing the coach to force him to remain and/or bar him from coaching for any other team until his contract ran out.

For his part, Demers was perplexed and agitated - he had never been sued before and took pride in his integrity. He had been greatly underpaid relative to other coaches in the NHL, consistent with Ornest's bare-bones financial philosophy

(Demers was making $75,000 when the average coach's salary at the time was nearly double that). Demers agreed that Ornest had *promised* that he would provide a three-year contract for considerably more money but asserted that he had never delivered on the promise or provided a written agreement to that effect. Had he done so, Demers insisted, he would have stayed with the Blues.

Ultimately, Demers was allowed to leave. And he made Blues' fans regret Harry's frugality, turning Detroit from a last place team to a first-place team in two years, winning back-to-back coach of the year awards (the only coach to ever do so) and later winning a Stanley Cup coaching Montreal. He was just one of the many great coaches the Blues let slip away. Interestingly, Demers is now a Senator in the Canadian Parliament - an incredible journey for a man who couldn't read or write.

The heroic but cheap Ornest didn't stick around much longer himself. In October 1986, he sold the Blues to a local group headed by Michael F. Shanahan, CEO of Engineered Support Systems, Inc. (a company that produced ground support equipment for the military based at the time in my neighborhood of Olivette, Missouri). The purchase price for the team was $19 million, which included $10 million in cash and the assumption of $9 million in notes. Ornest also sold the Arena to the City of St. Louis' Land Clearance Redevelopment Authority for $15 million - $5.5 million in cash, a $2.7 million note due in 1993 that paid 9% in yearly interest and the assumption of his $6.8 million mortgage on the Arena. *I'm sure Sid and his dad was wondering where that kind of help was from the City when they owned the team.*

All told, Ornest returned to California with a $3.4 million profit on the Blues and an $8.2 million profit on the Arena - a total haul of more than $11 million. Not a bad three-year investment! *Who said saviors couldn't profit from their salvation?*

Mike Shanahan's group represented a fresh start for ownership and a return in some ways to the Blues' beginning - with local ownership by people who genuinely loved St. Louis and the Blues. Shanahan, the youngest of eight children of Irish immigrants, was an avid sports fan with a gregarious personality and a local sports hero of sorts, having played soccer on St. Louis University's National Championship teams of 1959 and 1960. It was hoped that he and his fellow new owners would restore stability to the franchise.

With new ownership came yet another coach, and another Jacques: Jacques Martin. *The Blues have had a love affair with that name since nearly the beginning.* Unfortunately, Jacques Martin was not quite the coach of his predecessor. In his first-year stint at the helm, the Blues lost one more game than we won and were in the bottom one-third in offense. Fortunately, 23-year old Doug Gilmour had a break-out year, scoring 42 goals along with 63 assists, finishing fifth in voting for the Hart Most Valuable Player. Although Gilmour was able to carry the team on his back to the playoffs, even managing to finish first in the weak Norris division, the Blues quickly proved that we were not a legitimate first-place team by losing in the first round to fourth place Toronto in six games.

1988 was also a sad year for the Blues' family as we lost two St. Louis Blues' icons. On February 6, 1988 the great Barclay Plager succumbed to brain cancer at the age of 46 years old, only three days before the NHL All-Star game was held in St. Louis. And on December 18, 1988, Sidney Salomon III, the man most responsible for St. Louis having a hockey team in the first place, being the NHL's exemplar expansion franchise, and creating and energizing a passionate fan base, also passed away from cancer at the age of 51. He was survived by three children and thousands of grateful hockey fans and players.

As for the 1987-1988 hockey season, it looked a lot like the previous one - a slight losing record with a weak offense. One very short highlight was Doug Gilmour's record setting goal against Boston, when he scored an astonishing two seconds after a Boston goal - the fastest goal following another goal in NHL history (though remarkably since been tied by two teams). A much bigger highlight occurred on March 7, 1988, when the Blues made a trade with lasting implications for the franchise, acquiring a young man from Calgary named Brett Hull.

Hull came from impeccable pedigree - his Dad, Bobby a/k/a the Golden Jet, was not only a Hall of Famer, but has been listed among the ten best players to ever play the game. Like his dad, Brett appeared to be a special goal scorer with an amazing shot (though his was more of the wrist shot variety that he could unleash with uncanny quickness and accuracy rather than the explosive slap shot of his father). Moreover, Hull was only 23 and was just beginning his career. He had already scored 26 goals in 52 games in his first full season and his trajectory was expected to only go up.

Nevertheless, the trade for Hull was not universally endorsed at the time - the Blues had to part ways with steady and popular defenseman Rob Ramage along with Rick Wamsley, a reasonably reliable goaltender who shared the starting job. While Hull was considered to have the *potential* to be an offensive superstar in the League, he was considered a liability on defense and not an especially hard worker, and Ramage and Wamsley, in some minds, had *proven* value.

Once again, Blues' management hit the jackpot. Although Ramage was a decent player who would contribute to helping Calgary win the Stanley Cup in 1989, he played only two seasons for the Flames and moved to multiple teams as his skills declined (sadly, after he retired, he was involved in a drunk driving accident in which former Chicago Blackhawk Keith Magnusson was killed and Ramage was sentenced to prison). Wamsley would be essentially a back-up goalie for the rest of his career who only played sporadically in the playoffs. By contrast, Hull would become the superstar that the Blues had hoped – launching a Hall of Fame career over 16 seasons, more than a decade of that with St. Louis. In most hockey minds, he is the greatest player in Blues' history.

And in the post-season, the Blues finally beat Chicago in a playoff series when Doug Gilmour tallied the game-winning goal in the deciding Game 5. For his part, Hull scored six goals in the five-game series, Blackhawks' fans who worshipped Bobby Hull must have been at least a little bit conflicted.

But the exuberance of that win and having the next great Hull in our midst was short-lived as the Blues dropped four out of five games in the second round to Jacques Demers' Detroit Red Wings.

The Blues switched jockeys again for the 1988-1989 season, naming long-time Blues' Captain Brian Sutter to be coach. It only seemed natural that his leadership skills as captain would translate well to earning the respect of players as coach.

But before the first puck was dropped on the season there was a killer development for the Blues (back when "killer" was not considered a good development). The Blues' team's best player at the time, Doug Gilmour, was accused of having sexually assaulted a 14-year-old girl. A million-dollar civil lawsuit was filed by her parents, naming Gilmour as well as the Blues, asserting that the team knew or should have known about the assault.

Only one week later, and just before the season started, the Blues traded Gilmour, along with the team's second-best goal scorer over the course of the last couple of seasons, Mark Hunter, to Calgary for Mike Bullard and Craig Coxe.

Clearly, the Blues wanted to disassociate from Gilmour as quickly as possible and gave him away at a bargain basement price. It was highway robbery even before management added Mark Hunter, who averaged more than 33 goals in his four seasons with the Blues (in fact he is still the Blues' all-time leader in shooting percentage, having scored on over 20% of shots he took while with the Blues). Like Hunter, Mike Bullard was a high former first-round draft pick who could score goals (he had even scored 51 one year with Pittsburgh), but he managed to score only four goals with the Blues in twenty games during the season before he was traded away. As for left winger Craig Coxe, he scored ZERO goals for the Blues in his brief forty-one game history before he was shipped to Chicago as compensation for a free agent signing and then waived by the Blackhawks.

It was the second time the Blues had just handed Calgary a Hall of Fame player for very little in return. Then again, Calgary had done the same with respect to Brett Hull so perhaps it was a *quid pro quo*. (*We'll have to ask the President!*) For the record, Gilmour denied the assault and a grand jury chose NOT to indict him. The civil lawsuit was also dropped shortly after that (though who knows what, if anything, Gilmour and the Blues paid to make it go away). Gilmour then went on to play 15 more years in the NHL. One can only imagine how good the Blues might have been had we had Mullen and Gilmour for the next decade to go along with Hull.

With Gilmour and Hunter gone, and more in line with his general proclivities, Coach Sutter implemented a more disciplined defensive approach. But the team's regular season performance did not materially change, finishing two games under .500. And the playoff results were also similar, with the Blues winning the first round versus the North Stars and then losing to the Blackhawks in the second round in five games.

As for Brett Hull, in his first full season with the Blues he scored an impressive 41 goals with 43 assists. But he also carried a minus 17 rating when he was on the ice at even strength, reflecting his defensive shortcomings. The goal for Sutter was to make Hull realize how to become a better overall player and to emphasize the importance of getting into better shape.

The end of the 1989 season also marked the end of another era - the playing career with the Blues of one of its greatest players, Bernie Federko. Federko may have been one of the most underappreciated players of all time, perhaps in part because he played during the Gretzky era and in part because he played in the Midwest for a team that rarely advanced beyond the first or second round of the playoffs. But Federko's stats are right up there with some of the best players to ever wear a pair of skates for a living. In exactly 1000 NHL regular season games (927 with St. Louis), Federko had more than 1000 points, and in 91 playoff games he had over 100 points, averaging more than a point a game for his entire career.

Though he could put the puck in the net, once registering over 40 goals in a season, his calling card was his ability to help others score, as he was a masterful passer and playmaker. He was the first player in NHL history to have more than 50 assists in ten consecutive seasons (a record only matched by Gretzky) He ranks 11th all-time in assists per game. Those few ahead of him include the likes of Gretzky, Lemieux, Orr, Crosby and the young man he was traded for - Adam Oates.

And Federko was a Blue true and true - the rare breed who played virtually his entire career for the same organization. After 13 years wearing the Blue Note, it must have felt extremely awkward to be wearing the red of the rival Red Wings. Indeed, after only one season, Bernie retired and returned to St. Louis to live and work and has forever since remained active in the St. Louis hockey scene. One of his jobs included coaching and managing the St. Louis Vipers, a professional *roller* hockey team. The Vipers were actually the last team to play a sporting contest at the historic old Arena and it seemed only appropriate that the person who had played the most games for the Blues, and the most games in that building, should be there that night. For decades now, Federko has worked for Fox Sports as a hockey announcer and analyst.

For the final season of the 1980's, the Blues' record regressed in the regular season. However, the good news was that Brett Hull was emerging as a superstar. The now 25-year-old scored a Blues' record 72 goals and 113 points. But Hullie would have never reached that plateau had it not been for his new linemate and center Adam Oates, whom the Blues had acquired in 1989 as part of a four-player trade involving Bernie Federko. (The two others exchanged as part of the deal, Paul MacLean to the Blues and Tony McKegney to Detroit, were also solid players who had each scored 40 goals in a season, but both were toward the end of their careers, and never came close to that level of production again). Hull and Oates would prove to be a dynamic pairing - one of the greatest of all-time.

It was the second time in Blues' history (after the Berenson trade) that the team traded its biggest star late in his career for a rising star. And boy did it work out well. Federko had his worst performance in more than a decade in his only season with the Red Wings. Oates, on the other hand, was a star right off the bat with over 100 points in his first season.

Individually Oates, like Hull, was a great player who could excel on his own, and each is in the Hall of Fame. But together, working collaboratively, they were like their band's namesake big song, "Maneater," and boy could they chew you up.

Oates had a magical ability to not only pass the puck with perfection - right on target and in a smooth manner so the puck didn't bounce - but to do so at the ideal time. Everyone knew Hull would be shooting and pulling the trigger every chance he got and other teams guarded him like he was the President. But Hull would circle about searching for an opening or space, however small or brief, and Oates had the uncanny ability to get the puck to him in that fraction of a moment.

Despite another sub-par regular season, the Blues were hoping to have a better playoff run. For the third straight year, the Blues won the first round - this time versus Toronto. For, the second straight year we faced a strong Chicago Blackhawks team led by Jeremy Roenick and Dennis Savard with Eddie "Bel-Four" in goal. The Blues made the series interesting and competitive. After six games, the series was tied at three games apiece. But in Game 7 at the old Chicago Stadium - one of the loudest stadiums in the NHL and ironically built in the same year as the Arena - the Blues were literally blown out of their building by a score of 8-2. It was the team's worst performance in a Game 7 in the team's history - the St. Louis Post declared it the "Monday Night Massacre." *Needless to say, not a great evening in the Sophir household.*

But my day was a lot better than one that Blues' defenseman Paul Cavallini had earlier in the year. As hockey players tend to do with little regard for their safety, Cavallini stationed himself directly in front of a wicked slap shot by the Blackhawks' Doug Wilson. The puck hit him solidly on his left hand. Although he was wearing a hockey glove, the sheer force of the blast somehow managed to amputate the top of his index finger. Cavallini located the severed tip inside his glove. Doctors later tried to reattach it but were unsuccessful. Naturally, Cavallini only missed 13 games and scored a goal in his first game back. *He's a hockey player!*

Also, during the season - nearly a year to the date of Barclay Plager's passing - the long-time voice and soul of the St. Louis Blues was silenced when Dan Kelly passed away. Cancer had taken yet another of the early St. Louis greats. Following his death, the NHL Hockey Hall of Fame awarded Dan the Lester Hewitt Memorial Award given to announcers who make an outstanding contribution to the game of hockey. His most lasting legacy is that two of his children have broadcasted Blues' hockey, including the current TV announcer, John Kelly.

And before the new season unfolded, the Blues had another change in ownership. Mike Shanahan, the Chairman of the Blues who had helped steer the team back into popularity with the City with an obvious affection for the team, sold his 10% minority stake to his other business leader partners comprising Kiel Center Partners. Shanahan would stay on as team Chairman for several more years to add some continuity before being replaced by former Cardinals' executive Jerry Ritter.

Recap of the 1980's

For the decade the Blues lost three more games than we won and had exactly one great season with nine mediocre ones at best, including several where we had a losing record. And yet the Blues somehow made the playoffs every single year of the decade, which would start a rather impressive run of making the playoffs 25 years in a row - the third longest such streak of all-time. While granted it is a lot easier to make the playoffs in hockey than other sports, and the Blues benefitted during this era by playing in a very weak division, it was nevertheless a remarkable record of longevity of at least *very modest* success.

More importantly, St. Louis still had the Blues after an extremely close call with losing the team forever. Once again, the future appeared bright. The ownership group seemed more stable, we had our own legitimate budding superstar in Brett Hull, and it looked like the Blues would be upgrading the talent in the near future. But few could have foreseen just how big that upgrade would be.

The 1990's

The first team of the new decade started with a bang, led by the hottest rock and roll tandem in hockey: Hull and Oates.

In the 1990-1991 season, Hull scored more than one goal per game on average, a ridiculous 86 in total, which was the third highest number of goals in a season in NHL history. Only a man by the name of Gretzky had ever scored more goals in a season. And his sidekick, Oates, concluded the campaign with 90 assists - the most ever by a Blues player – with more than half of those to Hull.

The team also had a very solid second line led by Rod Brind'Amour, the current successful coach of the Carolina Hurricanes, and Geoff Courtnall, an outstanding and underrated player. Sometimes Paul MacLean, a mustachioed former sharpshooter who also tried his hand at coaching for a while, played on that line, but the more effective linemate was the diminutive Cliff Ronning, who was becoming a consistent 20-goal scorer.

The defense included stellar offensive-minded Jeff Brown and intimidating defensive-minded Scott Stevens. Stevens was one of the best defensemen to ever don the Blues' jersey, though he barely had time to wash it before he was gone.

The Blues' acquisition of Stevens was highly controversial around the League. Contrary to the wishes of the NHL owners who had somehow gotten away with not signing a single free agent in five years, despite a Collective Bargaining Agreement ("CBA") that allowed for restricted free agency, the Blues went ahead and signed Stevens to an offer sheet what was considered exorbitant by some. (The contract was large only by the standards of the day - four years for a little over $5 Million total, which put him at the top of the pay scale for defenseman before he was considered one of the top few elite defensemen in the NHL.). This made his former team, the Washington Capitals and the rest of the teams very unhappy with the Blues for disrupting the NHL's effort "to control exorbitant spending" or, alternatively, "to conspire to hinder players' true market value" -

depending on which side of the labor negotiating table you were sitting on.

Under the CBA, the Capitals had the right to match the Blues' offer or receive compensation. They chose the latter and were awarded the Blues' next FIVE first round draft picks! This was unprecedented "compensation" clearly designed to punish the Blues for signing a free agent, and something that I cannot imagine would pass antitrust muster if challenged. The Blues risked the ire of their fellow owners because, to their credit, management was all in to win the Stanley Cup, and thought Stevens could be the critical missing piece.

And the Blues were potentially on pace to do just that. It was probably the most balanced team the Blues had to date - we had the fourth best offense and the third best defense statistically in the NHL. In early March of 1991, we were riding high in first place in the entire NHL standings - at one point the Blues had a stretch where we only lost once in 14 games.

And then well-meaning management blew it. They decided to make a major trade late in the season, sending goal scorers Geoff Courtnall and Cliff Ronning, tough winger Sergio Momesso (*who was living in the house I grew up in as a kid - yet another reason not to trade him*) and Robert Dirk to Vancouver for defenseman Garth Butcher and center Dan Quinn.

The trade made no sense. The Blues did not appear to be getting equal value on paper. Moreover, the team was playing great and on a roll. Why mess with team chemistry? But Blues' brass apparently relished Butcher's toughness and leadership ability that they thought would serve the Blues well in the playoffs, discounting his lack of speed, his lack of offensive skills (he scored 11 goals for the Blues in 200 games spread across four years) and his propensity to spend far too much time in the penalty box (289 to be precise in 1990-1991). They also greatly miscalculated Quinn's value - he was a former first-round draft pick from years ago with skill but who never quite materialized as a top player. He seemed more interested in golf than hockey. (Indeed, he would win the annual celebrity classic among entertainers and top athletes from other sports five times). Quinn was gone from the Blues at the end of the year, all of 14 regular season games - and two years later was released from the North Stars after rape allegations surfaced (though charges were never brought).

It's always easy to second-guess in retrospect, but most Blues' fans saw this as a terrible trade at the time. To their credit, Blues' management had in the past shown that it often knew more than the fans when it came to horse trading (putting head before heart) - including the great trades of getting Unger for Berenson, Hull for Ramage and Oates for Federko (at least when there weren't *non-hockey* factors that forced their hand, like the trades of Mullen and Gilmour). But clearly not this time.

Following the trade, the Blues won only one of their next seven games, though we did reel off wins in the final seven. In the playoffs, the Blues mounted our most impressive comeback in a playoff series, beating Detroit after falling behind 3-1 in the series. But the up and down end of the season finished down as we fell to Minnesota in the second round in six games.

The news however would get much worse; the Blues were about to lose Scott Stevens, the captain and leader on defense after just one year and having just spent much of the team's foreseeable future talent on him. In an effort to further buttress the team the following year, the Blues once again thumbed their nose at owner-wide efforts to prevent a meaningful free agency system and signed another young promising player to a free agent offer sheet - this time a strong and tough right winger who could score named Brendan Shanahan. On first blush this was great news. But what would be the *compensation* this time around? The Blues had no first-round picks left for the next half-decade thanks to the Stevens' signing.

The Blues tried to negotiate fair compensation with the New Jersey Devils (Shanahan's team) to no avail. The Blues offered a substantial package that included young and highly-regarded goalie Curtis Joseph, second-line center Rod Brind'Amour and two conditional draft picks. But New Jersey's General Manager Lou Lamoriello had other ideas. Sensing that he had the Blues over a barrel and the NHL and its arbitrators on his side, he rejected all overtures and absurdly demanded that the Devils receive Scott Stevens instead - the Blues' most valuable player whom we had just given up five first round draft picks for. And on September 3, 1991 the arbitrator, Ed Houston, gave Lamoriello exactly what he asked for - undoubtedly as punishment for the Blues' "renegade" approach in actually adhering to the spirit of free agency that the owners had agreed to. It was perhaps the most outrageous decision by a sports arbitrator in history, and would set the Blues back for years, and arguably more than a decade.

Stevens initially refused to go to New Jersey - not only because he and his family liked St. Louis and planned to make this their permanent home (*and, after all, he was being sent to New Jersey!*), but also, because he couldn't understand how the Blues' signing of Shanahan had anything whatsoever to do with *him*. Eventually, however, he felt forced to capitulate if he wanted to play hockey in the NHL - the only professional ice hockey league in the western hemisphere. *Where was Curt Flood when we needed him?*

And then to really pour some salt in the wound, Stevens promptly led the Devils to not one, not two, but THREE Stanley Cups, became the best and most intimidating defensemen in the League (as the Blues correctly assessed that he would be), and entered the Hockey Hall of Fame in his very first year of eligibility after a long and distinguished 22-year career. *Ouch!*

Stung by Stevens' departure, the Blues fell back considerably in the standings the next year (1991-1992) falling dramatically from 105 to 83 points. The Blues started the year with some serious fire power at the top of the line-up with the future Hall of Fame trio of Hull, Oates and Shanahan, along with promising youngster Nelson Emerson. Oates, in particular, was having a monster year - in fact such a big year that he was unhappy with how much he was being paid.

Oates had just signed a four-year, $3 million contract extension with the Blues prior to the season. But when he found out how much the Blues were paying Shanahan, Butcher and Ron Sutter (Brian's brother and one of an incredible five brothers to play in the NHL), Oates felt he was greatly underpaid - which he was. He threatened to leave the team following his participation in the All-Star game if the Blues did not renegotiate his contract. That did not sit well with the fan base at the time, many who felt that you should stick by the contract you signed and quit complaining when you are making nearly $1 million a year to play a sport for a living. *When the fans booed him loudly at the next home game I cringed and was sick to my stomach. I sensed that the Blues would panic and feel the need to trade the best playmaker in hockey, which is exactly what happened. I also knew enough about negotiation that it was never a good idea to make a trade when you were desperate to unload someone. Hadn't the Blues learned this basic lesson with Gilmour?*

Just a couple weeks later on February 7, 1992, with Gilmour-like speed, the Blues traded Oates to Boston for Craig Janney and Stephane Quintal. It was a horrible trade, and everyone knew it. With no disrespect to Janney, who was a solid playmaking center, one year even accumulating an extremely impressive 86 assists, he was no Oates. In fact, Oates finished tied for second for the Blues in scoring that year despite missing 26 games. And he merely went on to record 1,420 points over a 19-year career, had the seventh most assists in NHL history, and was named one of the 100 greatest hockey players to ever play the game. *For the next decade hard core Blues' fans could be found contemplating what his and Hull's numbers might have been like had they played with each other their entire careers.*

On the plus side, the Blues handed the goaltending reins to 24-year old Curtis Joseph, who looked like the first Blues' goaltender since the early days that might be a star. In the 1992 playoffs, the Blues gave fans some reason to believe in the future potential of this team, taking a two games to one lead against the mighty Blackhawks in the first round. But then the boys in Blue dropped three straight games to bring us back to reality - another playoff loss to our neighbors to the north.

After the season, the Blues unwisely canned Coach Brian Sutter somehow blaming him for the significant drop in performance when the team lost two Hall of Fame quality players in Stevens and Oates. Sutter followed Oates to Boston the next year and led them to 109 points and a first-place finish in their division. The Blues replaced Sutter with another Blues' legend, Bobby Plager. Bobby's debut as a head coach of the Blues was inauspicious and especially short-lived; he quit after only 11 games, with 4 wins, 6 losses and 1 tie - though at least he was able to win the last game he coached against his former coach Scotty Bowman. Apparently, Bobby did not enjoy the difficult emotional parts of coaching - like replacing a friend in Brian Sutter and sitting out players who he liked.

In Jacques Demers- Jacques Martin tradition, Bob Plager was replaced by another Bob - longtime Coach Bob Berry, who led the team to a record of 33-30-10 the rest of the way. It was barely enough to get the Blues into the playoffs. The Blues were expected to make another early exit against the Chicago Blackhawks but shocked the hockey world by not only beating the first place and reigning Stanley Cup Finalists but sweeping them in four games! The star of the show was clearly the new young goaltender. "Cujo" shut out the powerful Blackhawks in Games 2 and 3, stopping a combined 81 shots without yielding a goal. Perhaps the Blues finally had a goaltender like Hall and Plante, who would lead us to the summit.

The second round that year was against a talented Toronto Maple Leafs team led now by ex-Blue Doug Gilmour - the Blues' propensity to run into great ex-players in the playoffs with a chip on their shoulder to punish their old squad was becoming routine. The Blues lost the first game in Toronto in Double Overtime, with Doug Gilmour naturally scoring the game-winning goal. The Blues returned the favor in Game 2 winning in another Double Overtime game and then won Game 3 in regulation, taking a surprising series lead of two games to one. After losing the next two games, the Blues were able to win Game 6 at home and force a Game 7 in Toronto. But like Game 7 in Chicago in 1990, the last game of the season would prove to be a disaster, with the Blues getting crushed 6-0. Doug Gilmour scored the last goal to put the cherry on top.

On the strength of a decent playoff performance, Bob Berry would be given another chance to lead the Blues in 1993-1994. The results in the regular season would prove better, though not exceptional, with 91 points. But the playoffs would not - the Blues were swept in the first round by the Stars, who were making their home for the first time in Texas.

As the 1993-1994 season drew to the close it was the end of an era for the Blues' home. April 14, 1994 marked the last Blues' regular season played at the Old Barn. The last goal in the regular season was scored by the Winnipeg Jets' Keith Tkachuk, who would make a big contribution with the Blues in a few years. The last game at the old Arena was on April 24, 1994 against the same team that had played the very first game there against the Blues, nearly 27 years ago. And the last goal ever scored in the building on Oakland Avenue was by the Stars' Mike Modano. Thus, both the first and last goals ever scored at the beloved Barn were scored by the Stars.

Come Independence Day of 1994, Blues' fans had a couple additional reasons to celebrate. First, the Blues acquired Al MacInnis from Calgary for Phil Housley. Housley was a great skater and good offensive defenseman, who actually had quite a 21-year career, but he did little with the Blues, was weak defensively, and never really seemed to fit in. In MacInnis, the Blues were getting a defenseman with the best slap shot in the game and a great leader who had won the Stanley Cup before.

"Chopper" would go on to play ten seasons in St. Louis, score 127 goals and record 325 assists, wear the "A" and the "C" on his jersey, and go down as one of the greatest Blues ever -

with his number 2 retired and a statute sitting outside the building alongside Hull and Federko. He also chose to raise his family in St. Louis and helped build an outstanding youth hockey program here (in the 2016 draft, four of the first six U.S. born players and four of the top fifteen kids overall played their youth hockey in St. Louis, more than any city *in the World*). Al would remain with the Blues after his playing career ended and served as a critical advisor to the 2018-2019 Blues' team.

Perhaps Calgary felt bad about stealing Mullen and Gilmour but score a big victory for Blues' management on that exchange! It's hard to believe when you look back that four of the most lopsided trades in NHL history occurred between the same two teams, with each side fleecing the other twice (unless it was all part of some orchestrated long-term equalization pact). But, at the end of the day, I would take Hull and MacInnis for Mullen and Gilmour.

A second reason to shoot off some additional fireworks: the team signed Scott Stevens once again to an offer sheet to return to the Blues. Although New Jersey could match the offer since he was a *restricted* free agent, they would have to pay $17 Million over four years to do so - a very hearty sum at the time. The conventional wisdom at the time was that they wouldn't at that price. The Blues would then be subject to losing significant unknown compensation with other players or draft picks. But the Blues' love affair for Stevens knew no bounds, and the dream pairing of the best defensive defenseman in the NHL with the most dangerous offensive defenseman in the League had Blues' fans salivating like a St. Bernard on a hot July 4th!

Naturally, New Jersey decided to match the offer. Not only that, General Manager Lamoriello was not through with messing with our franchise. He claimed that the Blues had contacted Stevens earlier than was allowed under NHL rules, before the deadline began for free agency, and that the Blues, therefore, should be punished.

Once again, the NHL agreed. This time the Blues were fined $1.5 million dollars AND New Jersey was awarded a Blues' first round draft pick as well as the opportunity to swap draft positions with the Blues during a four-year window. All in all, the signing of Stevens and Shanahan cost the Blues six first round draft picks and dropped us in the drafting order for a seventh first-round pick. And for all of that, we got the use of Stevens' services for one stinking year (and Shanahan for a few years) - clearly a big mistake by the Blues in retrospect and the biggest screw job in NHL history. Although he has some competition, Judge Houston should probably go down as the most hated man in Blues' history.

Less than two weeks after the MacInnis/Stevens announcement, the Blues had another startling surprise: the team had hired Mike Keenan as coach and general manager, fresh off his Stanley Cup win with the New York Rangers. One problem with that was that Keenan was still under contract to the Rangers. He maintained, however, that the Rangers had breached his contract and that he, therefore, was free to go elsewhere. Of course, he did. The Blues were determined to win the Stanley Cup no matter what it took and whom they pissed off in the process. After some legal wrangling, the NHL allowed Keenan to go to the Blues, but he was suspended for 60 days, the Blues were fined, and also naturally we had to part with players as compensation. The Blues were making no friends in the NHL in the insatiable quest for the Cup.

To add to the excitement and a new era, the City's leaders, "Civic Progress," built a brand-new 18,400-seat hockey stadium in downtown St. Louis. The new Kiel Center, which would later be called the Savvis Center, then the Scottrade Center and now the Enterprise Center, was scheduled to open on October 11, 1994. It had much better amenities - more room, better concessions, and restrooms, and many more boxes and suites for the elites - but it lacked some of the charm, the cats and the noise that the Old Barn generated.

And then, after all of those efforts by Blues' management to rock the boat and try to bring a Championship hockey team to the City, the season never began. That's right - due to a nasty dispute with the NHL Players over the Collective Bargaining Agreement (undoubtedly influenced by the way the owners were handling free agency signings and compensation with the Blues), the season was delayed for months.

Finally, on January 26, 1995, play resumed for hockey-starved Blues' fans. Over 20,000 people crammed into the brand-new Kiel Center to witness the first game there, which the Blues won 3-1 against the Los Angeles Kings. The first goal at the new building was scored by Blues' rookie Craig Johnson, and the first and lone opposition goal by none other than Wayne Gretzky. In the strange and eerie category: the two would be traded for each other the following year. Appropriately, the star of the first game was the team's biggest star, Brett Hull, who scored two third period goals to break the tie.

The Keenan era would prove to be highly tumultuous. Some considered him to be a brilliant coach (Blues' President Jack Quinn proclaimed him to be "the best in the game"), and others considered him a hot-headed power freak and egomaniac. He came to town with a reputation of being contentious and difficult to get along with. But what the Blues cared most about at this point were results and winning a Stanley Cup. There is a sense in sports that if a coach has won a championship before or advances a team beyond expectations in a single season (no more so than the coach of a small school who wins a few games in the NCAA basketball tournament) that he is somehow the next Vince Lombardi, Mike Krzyzewski and Bill Belichick wrapped into one and will propel your team to greatness. Perhaps he is truly a great coach, or perhaps he just had great players, got lucky or the Championship year was an aberration.

In any case, Keenan was the hottest coaching commodity in the NHL because he had just won the Stanley Cup. In eight previous seasons coaching with Philadelphia and

Chicago, his teams had generally done well but had never won the grand prize.

The first season under Keenan - actually half-season - looked promising. The Blues added some aging stars to go along with Hull, Shanahan, and MacInnis in Steve Duchesne, Esa Tikkanen, and Glenn Anderson. And with Curtis Joseph playing well in goal, the Blues had a very solid regular season, finishing thirteen games over .500 in a shortened season, which was good for second in the NHL.

But then the Blues lost in the first-round of the playoffs in seven games to Vancouver. It was a series that we could and should have won. With the series tied 2-2, the Blues outplayed the Canucks but lost Game 5 in Overtime on a goal naturally by ex-Blue Cliff Ronning. The team responded well in Game 6 and destroyed the Canucks 8-2, but then lost Game 7 despite outshooting Vancouver 44-21. For all the hoopla surrounding the great Mike Keenan, he had delivered essentially the same script as many prior coaches - a very solid regular season followed by a highly disappointing playoff performance.

It was back to the drawing board. In the off-season, Keenan completely rearranged the team. He traded Curtis Joseph and brought in former Edmonton star and four-time Stanley Cup Champion Grant Fuhr to play goal. Joseph would go on to have a long career with a plethora of different teams - Edmonton, Toronto, Detroit, Phoenix and Calgary. Until recently he held a record that seems particularly appropriate for someone affiliated with the Blues: having the most wins in NHL history by a goaltender *without* winning the Stanley Cup.

Keenan also got rid of Duchesne and Tikkanen and replaced them with several other players also closer to the back side of their careers: 37-year old Craig MacTavish, 33-year-old Geoff Courtnall (back for a second stint), 32 -year old Dale Hawerchuk and 29-year-old Shayne Corson (a veritable child by comparison). Keenan sure liked veteran players - until he didn't.

And then Keenan really showed his commanding, some would say erratic, style by trading the highly productive and insanely popular Brendan Shanahan to Hartford for a twenty-year-old gawky looking defenseman named Chris Pronger. Shanahan had been outstanding for the Blues, scoring over 50 goals in back-to back seasons of 1992-1993 and 1993-1994, and adding a lot of grit, experience and team leadership. He had it all. *Who was this Pronger fellow?*

The fans were flabbergasted; it seemed to many an outrageously one-sided deal and designed mostly for Iron Mike to flex his muscles and let the players know that if Shanahan could be traded that none of them was safe. Others suggested the trade may have had something to do with a tryst that the handsome Shanahan was alleged to have had with the wife of fellow Blues' player Craig Janney - not exactly good for maintaining a cohesive locker room.

Shanahan would soon move on to the Detroit Red Wings and become an integral part of a team that won two Stanley Cups. But to give Keenan his due (*not easy for me to do*) he must have seen something special in the young Pronger who struggled mightily out of the gate with the Blues. Whether he was a great assessor of future talent, was just lucky, made the deal to avoid bad team chemistry because of the Janney thing, or just to stroke his own ego can be debated. But regardless, Pronger would turn out to be a superstar in his own right and, surprisingly, a lot more valuable than Shanahan.

It certainly didn't start out that way; in his first year with the Blues the 21-year old Pronger had the worst plus/minus rating on the team at minus18. But it wasn't long before "Prongs" became the best defenseman in the entire NHL. He was hard-hitting and intimidating and perhaps the meanest man on skates, whacking anyone within distance of his long reach who dared to stand near HIS goalie's crease. He was also one heck of a player whose long stick and anticipation could single handedly kill penalties. And he had some significant offensive skills as well; he was a great passer especially on the outlet and long stretch passes, was a strong skater and had a decent shot.

But in the first full season under Mike Keenan (1995-1996) the Blues were not exactly setting the world on fire. We were essentially a mediocre team and all the buzz and excitement from the previous summer's activities had waned, replaced by a giant dose of reality.

And then Keenan helped pull off the unthinkable: On February 27, 1996, as a late birthday present for my wife (*ok, that would be for me*), Keenan was able to orchestrate a trade to bring Wayne Gretzky - yes, THE Wayne Gretzky - to our humble town. We had to give up a lot - a promising young player in Craig Johnson (the fellow who scored the first Blues' goal at the new Kiel center against Gretzky's Kings), along with Roman Vopat, Patrice Tardif, the 5th round pick in the 1996 draft and the 1st round pick in the 1997 draft as part of the deal. But please, we were getting Wayne bleepin' Gretzky!

Gretzky was only the leading scorer in NHL history. He had more goals and more assists than any other player who had ever played the game; indeed, more assists alone than any other player had *total points*. Gretzky tallied over 100 points in a ridiculous 16 seasons, and is the only NHL player to garner over 200 points in a single season - a feat he accomplished four times. By the time he ended his career Gretzky had captured nine Hart Trophies as the League's Most Valuable Player, ten Art Ross Trophies for most points in a season, two Conn Smythe Trophies as playoff MVP and five Lester B. Pearson Awards (now called the Ted Lindsay Award) for most outstanding player as judged by his peers. He also won the Lady Byng Memorial Trophy for sportsmanship and performance five times. Gretzky holds 61 NHL records: 40 regular season records, 15 playoff records, and six All-Star records. The NHL eventually retired his number 99 League-wide, Jackie Robinson style, making him the NHL's only player to receive such an honor.

The greatest hockey player to ever play on the planet was coming to play in the Lou - it was like Babe Ruth deciding to leave New York and play for the Cardinals! Many wondered why the Great One would come to middle America when he had been playing in the big lights of Los Angeles, and was coveted no doubt by New York, Boston, Toronto and every other major market team. He could go anywhere and be welcomed as a hero. And yet he chose St. Louis!

Some of his decision had to do with the fact that his wife was from St. Louis and that they could raise their family here with relatives. And for all his fame, Gretzky is at heart, like many Canadian players, a humble farm boy. Although he grew up in the small city of Brantford, Ontario, he regularly spent time on his grandparent's farm and St. Louis and the Midwest is generally a down-to-earth humble kind of place.

But most of all he liked the nucleus of this team and its chances to do well, and that he would be rejoined with many former Edmonton Oiler buddies: Grant Fuhr (who he once called the greatest goalie ever), Glenn Andersen, Charlie Huddy, and Craig MacTavish. And he could play with his friend and fellow scoring machine Brett Hull. The thought of Gretzky, the greatest passer and assist man of all time, playing with the Golden Brett, arguably the greatest goal scorer at that time was downright orgasmic. *If Hull scored 86 goals with Oates, Blues' fans wondered what he could do with Gretzky.*

And St. Louis wasn't just getting the biggest star in the game to follow on a nightly basis; we were greatly enhancing our chances to win a Stanley Cup. Winning followed Gretzky wherever he went. With the dynasty Edmonton Oilers he won four Stanley Cups. After he was traded to Los Angeles he promptly made the Kings relevant and hockey popular in the sunbaked beach metropolis and even carried them on his back to the Stanley Cup Finals in 1983. Captain Shayne Corson gladly relinquished his "C" to Gretzky with the hope that the Great One could lead the Blues to hockey's highest mountain peak.

No Blues' fan wanted to get ahead of themselves, but the thought had to cross the minds of many in the land of Blue, as it did mine, that this could actually be the year. The team had extraordinary talent and potential. Between Gretzky, Hull, MacInnis, Pronger, Anderson, Fuhr and Dale Hawerchuk, the Blues had seven eventual Hall of Famers on the roster at the same time!

And if Gretzky was able to help produce the franchise's first Stanley Cup, he would be a hero in his wife's hometown forever!

The City was all abuzz about our newest real life superhero. He was instantly embraced with deity status like no athlete in this town since Stan the Man. In his very first game with the Blues, on leap year February 29, 1996, Gretzky scored a goal in a 2-2 tie in Vancouver. When the Blues returned home for Gretzky's first game in the Lou (on March 5, 1996 against the Florida Panthers) I was fortunate to be in the house. The building was as electric. Gretzky got ovation after ovation. Although he didn't score in the game, the Blues won, and he made several great passing plays giving the fan base a glimpse of what may be about to come.

And yet, following the trade, the Blues did not overwhelm teams over the remainder of the season and did not look much like a Stanley Cup contender. Indeed, after acquiring Gretzky the Blues lost more games than we won and finished the season on a huge downer, winning just once in the last 12 games! It wasn't Gretzky's fault; he played well and scored 21 points in the 18 regular season games with the Blues that year. But the huge lift the Blues and fans were expecting was not forthcoming - at least not yet. Perhaps it just took an adjustment period and the Blues would rise to the occasion in the playoffs when it really mattered.

The Blues opened the 1996 playoffs against the Toronto Maple Leafs, a team that had the same number of points (also with a losing record) but who gained home ice advantage by virtue of more wins. And, encouragingly, the Blues beat the Leafs in six games with Gretzky getting at least one assist in every game of the series except Game 6, with three assists each in games 1 and 4. The win over Toronto and Gretzky's prominent role in it were reasons to be optimistic. But a devastating season-ending injury to goalie Grant Fuhr when the Leafs' Nick Kypreos crashed into him early in Game 2 was a crippling blow to the team's chances. Fuhr, with his arsenal of Stanley Cups, was thought to be critical to the Blues' prospects for the Cup.

Further, the reality was that Toronto was an average team and next up were the Detroit Red Wings, the best team in hockey that year. Coached by former Blues' Coach Scotty Bowman, the Wings won a record setting 62 games and accumulated 131 points, the most in the NHL and the second most of all-time. They had two winning streaks of nine games and an unbeaten streak of thirteen throughout the year. The Red Wings were also the only team to have never been shut out the entire regular season.

Bowman had assembled an international arsenal of talent the likes of which had never seen before; from Canadian Captain Steve Yzerman to young highly talented Swedish defenseman Nick Lidstrom to the amazing Russian Five of Federov, Larionov, Fetisov, Konstantinov and Kozlov. It would take a minor miracle for any team, much less this Blues' team with a losing regular season record, to beat the Detroit juggernaut.

And, indeed, things pretty much went expected through the first two games in Detroit. The Blues put up a good fight in Game 1 but lost 3-2, and then got smoked in Game 2 by a score of 8-3. Gretzky had an assist in both games, but it was a case of far too little against this squad. The likelihood of the Blues winning the series at this point was virtually nil as we would have to win four of the next five games against a team that hadn't lost two games in a row the entire season!

But back on home ice, the Blues managed to eke out a 5-4 win in Game 3. After blowing a two-goal lead to fall behind 4-3 in the third period, Tony Twist - the Blues' resident enforcer with limited skating or scoring ability - scored a goal to tie the game and send it to Overtime. To say that was a surprise was a major understatement - it turned out to be the only playoff goal of Twister's entire career! And then, just a few minutes into the Overtime, the Blues won the game on a goal by our lone Russian, Igor Kravchuk. *At least we wouldn't be swept.*

And then in Game 4 Gretzky scored his first goal in the playoffs and Jon Casey, in for the injured Grant Fuhr, stopped all 29 Red Wing shots, even getting a rare assist on Gretzky's goal, for the shocking 1-0 victory. The Blues had miraculously beaten the Red Wings two games in a row, albeit barely, and had even shut them out - both firsts against Detroit for the season.

Nevertheless, the reality was that it was back to Detroit for Game 5 and a very different atmosphere at Joe Louis Arena. Perhaps buoyed with confidence by the success in Games 3 and 4, the Blues took the lead early in Game 5 - Hull from Gretzky - just as we all envisioned it! After Detroit tied the game in the second period, the two Blues' superstars switched roles - this time Gretzky scored his second goal in the playoffs on a pass from Hull with only about a minute left in the period. The teams traded goals in the third and the Blues hung on to win Game 5 by a score of 3-2 despite being outshot 39-21.

The Blues were now only one game away from upsetting the best team in hockey and arguably one of the best teams ever assembled. The Blues had won three games in a row and Gretzky was on a roll having scored in two straight games and now having had points in ten of the eleven playoff games played with the Blues. The Note headed home to a passionate crowd hoping to make a difference in propelling the team into the Conference Final, a place we had rarely seen.

The crowd was pumped up and feeling strangely confident. But as had become a pattern over the years for Blues' fans, optimism was followed by failure and discontent. And it didn't take long for Detroit to shower disappointment and frustration all over the team and Blues' fans. The Red Wings took an early lead which they quickly turned into a 2-0 lead in the first period. Halfway through the third period Detroit scored again for the presumably insurmountable 3-0 lead. With less than five minutes remaining in the game the Blues finally got on the board on a goal by Stephen Leach with assists from MacInnis and Hull. And then again one minute later on a goal by Hull from Gretzky and Leach. *Was there another Monday Night Miracle in store, except on a Wednesday night?* Unfortunately, Nick Lindstrom put an end to those hopes with an empty netter.

So, it was back to Detroit for Game 7. The Blues had made this a surprisingly competitive series, but could we somehow pull out one more game and in Detroit's building no less? The Red Wings had only lost THREE games at home during the entire regular season, but the Blues had beaten them in the most recent game there. Could that be a source of confidence against the considerable odds?

It didn't help when the Red Wings were given three power plays in the first period. But the Blues managed to weather the storm and maintain a scoreless tie after one period, which felt like a big victory. From that point on the teams played fairly cautiously, and the referees kept their whistles in their pocket, aside from one unsuccessful power play by the Blues. The game entered the third period scoreless. The longer the game remained tied, the greater the Blues' chances became.

As the clock ticked down in the third period, it was pretty clear that one goal, the next goal, would decide the series and the season. The goal could be due to a bad turnover, a great shot, or pure luck. It could be scored by one of the many superstars in the game on both sides or perhaps by someone who rarely if ever scores. In any case the winning goal in a seven game playoff series, especially one in Overtime, would be memorialized throughout time and the shooter or goat would be forever remembered in that capacity.

Regulation ended like a soccer game, with the extremely rare score of 0-0. The Blues had now, in effect, blanked the explosive Red Wings twice in three games, something that no other team had accomplished even once the entire season. But the Blues hadn't won or accomplished anything yet.

In a highly stressful Overtime with both sides having some chances and on the brink of their season ending, neither side was able to break through. The game remained tied after the first extra period. At this point Chris Osgood had stopped all 29 shots from the Blues and Jon Casey had stopped all 39 shots from the Red Wings.

It was on to the second Overtime. But it didn't last long. As all serious Blues and Red Wing fans from that era well remember, Gretzky turned over a puck in the neutral zone to the great Steve Yzerman who gathered it quickly, skated toward the Blues' blue line and, just as he crossed it, unleased a long slap shot that somehow baffled back-up goalie Casey and found the twine. Some folks blamed Gretzky, but the turnover was not in the defensive zone and should not have led to a great chance, as there were still two defenders back and this was a LONG shot. The fault, if there is any to go around, belonged primarily to Casey. Blues' fans liked to claim that if Fuhr hadn't been injured that he would never have given up a goal on such a shot. That may be true, but would he have shutout the Red Wings in Game 4? Or stopped the 39 shots that Casey did in Game 5? Or held the powerful Russians, Yzerman & Co scoreless through more than four periods in game 7, including a great point-blank shot by Federov in Overtime?

It was simultaneously *almost* the biggest series win and upset in Blues' history and also an abrupt and disappointing ending to the season.

To make matters worse, the seemingly always irritable Coach Keenan publicly criticized Gretzky for his play. Indeed, he ticked Gretzky off sufficiently enough that instead of staying on with the Blues and finishing his career in St. Louis (the Blues had generously offered him $15 Million over three years) he signed instead with the New York Rangers on July 21, 1986 (a lousy birthday gift for me) for a mere $8 Million (plus incentives) over two years. Gretzky later recalled: "If I had my druthers, I would have finished my career here (in St. Louis)." How well would an aging Gretzky have fared with the Blues with a full year or several to work with? I suspect VERY well. But it wasn't to be thanks to Mike Keenan. Move over Ed Houston!

Indeed, Keenan managed to alienate nearly everyone in his path. His mean-spiritedness knew no bounds at times. As one prime example, the Blues were playing the Sabres in Buffalo and Dale Hawerchuk's dying grandmother, who lived in nearby Fort Erie, Ontario came to see him play one last time while she was alive. Upset with Hawerchuk's play, Keenan benched him for the game. An unhappy Captain Brett Hull rallied to his teammate's defense and screamed at the surly coach. Keenan responded by stripping Hull of his captaincy.

But it was Iron Mike who would not last much longer. Just 33 games into the next 1996-1997 season, with a losing record and lots of bad blood created, Keenan was fired, much to the delight of this Blues' fan. Fittingly, Brett Hull - a frequent target of Keenan's wrath - scored his 500th goal of his career just three days after Keenan was fired.

Keenan had a special knack for making enemies wherever he went and yet somehow continually enticing new teams to hire him as if he was Magic Mike because of his one Stanley Cup. In the eight seasons he coached in the NHL after he left the Blues - with Vancouver, Boston, Florida and Calgary - his teams collectively lost more games than they won, only two of those teams even made the playoffs, and he never won a single playoff series. *"Best coach in the game?" Really?*

In October 1996, the Blues pulled off another blockbuster trade, though few realized its great importance at the time. The Blues acquired Pierre Turgeon and Craig Conroy (along with Rory Fitzpatrick) from Montreal for Murray Baron, Shane Corson and a 5th round draft pick.

Turgeon was a tremendous player for the Blues, a great two-way center who was consistent, steady and reliable, and perhaps the most underrated Blue in team history. In five seasons with the Blues spanning 327 games he registered 355 points, easily more than one per game. In 50 playoff games he recorded 45 points. In every season with the Blues he had a positive plus/minus rating, uncommon among many scoring forwards.

For his career, spanning 19 years, Turgeon scored more than 500 goals, the most ever by a player who is not in the Hall of Fame - a reflection of how much he fell under the radar not just in St. Louis but throughout the NHL. Perhaps he is still being penalized in some Canadian voters' minds because as a young man playing in the World Junior Hockey Championships for Canada against the hated Russians, the mild-mannered Turgeon was the only player on either side who remained on the bench when a bench-clearing brawl ensued, refusing to join in the madness.

As for Conroy, he was similarly underappreciated. Relegated to the third or fourth line for much of his time with the Blues, and never seeing any power play time, Conroy was never a big goal scorer for the Blues - 14 goals was the most he scored in a season. But man could he play defense and kill penalties, and often drew the assignment of guarding the top player on the opposing team. He was twice in his career a finalist for the Selke Award for the NHL's best defensive forward. I always thought that Conroy had the skills to be a solid offensive player as well if he was afforded the opportunity. It wasn't until he was later traded (to Calgary naturally) that he got that chance and showed his offensive side, scoring 27 goals and recording 48 helpers in his very first year there.

The latter half of the 1990's saw the incubation of another great Blues' head coach and the Joel Quenneville era - a stint that would eventually span six full seasons and two partial ones. By the end, Coach Q would become the winningest coach in Blues' history. Quenneville took over at the halfway point of 1996-1997 season from interim Coach Jimmy Roberts (who owns the record for the least number of games coached for the Blues at nine - *Sorry Bobby Plager, you don't get that record too*), after Keenan had been fired.

Like many of his great coaching predecessors, the Q lost his first game at the helm. But the Blues then reeled off wins in five of the next six games and seven of the next nine games. The team cooled off toward the end of the year but still made the playoffs. It was one of the more talented teams to date. Hull, Turgeon, Courtnall, Jim Campbell and Joe Murphy (the first pick in the entire draft by Detroit in 1986 who petered out quickly) led the offense, and three Hall of Famers led the defense - defensemen Pronger and McInnis and goalie Fuhr. Adding to the mix was a talented youngster who joined the Blues late in the season, Pavol Demitra, and excellent defensive forwards and penalty killers Craig Conroy and Scott Pellerin. And now we had a great young coach that wasn't a first-rate A-hole. This was a playoff team to be reckoned with. Indeed, the Blues looked, at least to me, like one of the best teams in the League.

Unfortunately, the opponent in the first round was, once again, the ridiculously talented Detroit Red Wings and their Russian Army led by Scotty Bowman. The Russian Five played a brand of hockey not seen in the NHL. They were such good skaters and puck handlers and instinctively knew where each other was at all times. Bowman would smartly play them all together, and it seemed that they would control the puck their entire shift. They would circle around, often going backwards and leaving the offensive zone to regroup - they were all about having the puck and never letting you play with it. They were amazing to watch as a hockey fan but frustrating if you were trying to beat them. It almost didn't seem fair that one team would have so much skill. I also found it highly ironic that the country's most "America First" city due to its dependence on the auto industry and their demagogical insistence that folks buy

American cars, would be the ones to import five star Russian players for their beloved hockey team.

It was a powerhouse match-up, arguably the best first-round match-up in Blues' history. The Blues actually took the first game in Detroit. And were leading Game 2 by a lone goal in the third period when we gave up the dreaded shorthanded goal to penalty killing specialist Kris Draper, which tied the game, and completely changed the momentum. Detroit scored again only a couple of minutes later to take the lead and win 2-1.

The Red Wings then won a critical Game 3 back in St. Louis, with Steve Yzerman scoring a late second period power play goal to break a 2-2 tie, which held up for the 3-2 victory. The Blues stormed back in Game 4, winning convincingly 4-0 with Geoff Courtnall scoring twice, Demitra and Pronger once each and Grant Fuhr pitching the shutout. But the Blues dropped the next two games and the series leaving Blues' fans with that familiar pain in the gut. The pain was exacerbated by the performance of ex-Blue Brendan Shanahan who proved to be a particular handful in the last two deciding games scoring two goals and registering two assists.

The Red Wings went on to crush Anaheim in the next round, sweeping them in four games, then beat an excellent Colorado team led by Joe Sakic, Peter Forsberg and Patrick Roy in six games, and then swept Philadelphia in the Final for the Stanley Cup. In some ways it was vindication for the Blues; although the Blues lost in the first round, we had lost to the Stanley Cup Champions and played them the toughest of any team. One might legitimately argue that the Blues were the *second-best* team in hockey that year (*as if there was a consolation prize to be awarded*). But the sting of what could have been and another early playoff exit, especially to those darn Russians from Detroit, was excruciating.

That said, many of us who bleed blue were really looking forward to the 1997-1998 campaign; we had many great players returning with extra motivation, would have rising star

Demitra for the entire season and welcomed back a veteran puck-handling defenseman in Steve Duchesne. And as great as Detroit was, most teams have a bit of a hangover the following season after winning the Cup and rarely repeat. (*It must be all that alcohol the hockey players drink from the 34 ½ pound silver chalice celebrating their achievement for months.*)

Adding to the excitement in Blues' nation, we got off to a tremendous start the next season. After dropping the first game, the Blues reeled off seven straight wins to start the season. It was an entire season of winning streaks; the Blues had additional separate winning streaks of six games and five games and three other four game winning streaks during the year. The team finished first in the entire NHL in goals scored - a shocker for a team known throughout its history for its defense and the only time that has ever happened in 51 seasons! And Chris Pronger had a monster year on the back-end with his plus 47 rating at even strength to lead the NHL. The Blues somehow only finished with 98 points but seemed primed for a big run.

In the first round, we annihilated the Los Angeles Kings, sweeping them four games to none. But once again the vaunted Detroit Red Wings stood in our way of achieving hockey immortality. Despite being reigning Stanley Cup Champions, they did not appear to have lost a step or any of their determination. (*Please take Note 2019-2020 Blues!*).

Just as in the 1997 playoffs, the Blues stole Game 1 on the road at Detroit. But once again, we lost game 2 (actually crushed 6-1). And the teams headed back to St. Louis. Could the Blues win Game 3 at home this year and seize the momentum and put Detroit perhaps back on their heels? *I didn't have tickets to the game. I also had an early morning deposition and it was a late starting time. I spoke to a doctor buddy who is as passionate about hockey as me and was told he had an even earlier morning surgical procedure the next day. But this was the playoffs and critical Game 3 against the reigning Stanley Cup Champions after all, and we decided that we had to be there.* It would turn out to be one of the classic games of all time.

The Red Wings scored first, but Al MacInnis answered back with a power play to even the score after one period. Just a little over one minute into the second period, the Red Wings took the lead again 2-1, a back-breaker of a goal in a very tight checking and defensive struggle. From that point on, the Red Wings put on a clinic on team defense and puck possession. The Blues fought hard but could never seem to get many quality chances - on those rare occasions where we even had the puck. Detroit had shot after shot, and at one point in the second period had outshot the Blues 17-5. But Hall of Famer Grant Fuhr kept the Blues in the game, and the score remained 2-1 after two periods.

In the third period, the Blues stepped up the pressure and had a couple glorious chances from close in by Hull and Demitra, but Detroit's goalie Chris Osgood was better than good.

And then he wasn't. As time was winding down, with less than a minute left in the game, Al MacInnis unleashed a LONG slap shot just as he crossed center ice. His objective presumably was simply to get the puck down at the Wings' end and hope somehow to force a face-off in their end or have the boys gain possession before Detroit was able to exit the zone and play their special game of keep away. But somehow, incredibly, the puck eluded Osgood and went into the net!

It was the longest goal (other than an empty netter) that I had ever seen. To do it in a playoff game where goals were at a premium and in the last minute of the game, no less, to force Overtime was like winning the lottery. The Arena erupted in a cacophony of joy (at least the folks who had not driven down from Detroit for the game with their pet octopus). We knew we had caught a monumental break. Moreover, when something like that happens you feel like the hockey gods are on your side - that they had finally realized what we Blues' fans had been through over the past 30 years and how deserving we were. This was certainly going to be *our* game and, more importantly, it was going to be *our* year!

It was getting very late, and I was dreading the few hours of sleep I would get before I had to be mentally sharp. My equally passionate hockey friend/doctor had a patient who was counting on him not to fall asleep during his medical procedure. But we couldn't exactly leave at this point. Hopefully the Blues could seize the momentum and win this thing soon.

But the Red Wings were far less cooperative with our plan. They weren't throwing in the towel or acting as if this game belonged to the Blues. When the hockey gods called they must not have been listening - Russians tend to be agnostic. Indeed, Detroit continued to bottle up the Blues squelching the very few opportunities we had. Good scoring chances were hard to come by on both sides, and neither team could break through during the 20-minute Overtime period. *Urgh!* I really had to leave, but it didn't compare to my friend's predicament. If I screwed up the next day, I took a lousy deposition; if my buddy screwed up, there was a life potentially on the line. We stayed.

The Blues seemed to come out stronger in the second Overtime and for a while seemed like the better team finally. But we still couldn't manage a score, and at 11:12 of the second Overtime - after over four and a half periods - ex-Blue Brendan Shanahan broke the exhausted blue hearts of the capacity crowd. I said it was a classic; not that it was a *good* classic.

As in the previous year, the loss of this critical game propelled the Red Wings past the Blues. Detroit took Game 4 as well in St. Louis. The Blues rallied to win Game 5 in Detroit to cut the series lead to 3-2, but the Red Wings won the series back in St. Louis in six games. So, in three playoff games at home against Detroit - and lots of time, money and energy spent by the loyal fan base - we had exactly zero wins to show for our efforts. *This year's squad was not the first Blues' team to struggle at home during the playoffs.*

One of the scariest moments in Blues' history occurred during this playoff series when Blues' Captain Chris Pronger sought to block a hard shot from Red Wings' defenseman Dmitri Mironov. The puck hit Pronger squarely in the chest, just to the left of his heart. He fell down, covered up the puck, and began to get up when his eyes rolled back into his head and he collapsed. His heart had stopped, and he was unconscious for twenty seconds. Fortunately, somehow, it started up again on its own. After a precautionary night stay in a Detroit hospital Pronger, unlike his heart, didn't skip a beat and was back on the ice. *Hockey players are the toughest professional athletes.*

After bidding farewell to the Blues, Detroit went on to defeat Dallas in six games and then sweep the Washington Capitals in the Final to capture back-to back titles. *So much for that Stanley Cup hangover.* Once again, the Blues played the Stanley Cup Champion as tough as anyone.

The following season (1998-1999) the Blues were not nearly as good a team as our long-time reliable scoring machine, Brett Hull, left town to sign a free agent deal with the rival Dallas Stars. It just didn't seem right. Hull should have finished his career in St. Louis like Stan Musial or Albert Pujols (*oh yeah, he didn't either*). But economics, his advancing age (now almost 34), a career-low 27 goals the previous season, along with a perception that Hull was slower and less committed to defense, and perhaps some remnants from his squabbles with Coach Keenan and the perception that he was a "problem" dictated the outcome.

Despite dropping to 87 points, it was still good enough for the Blues to make the playoffs. On the positive front, we won an exciting first-round match-up (barely) against the Phoenix Coyotes. The Blues rallied from being down three games to one in the series and won Game 7 by a score of 1-0 in Overtime, with Pierre Turgeon beating the big Russian goalie with the great name, Nikolai Khabibulin, to advance. And there was more good news: we didn't have to play the Detroit Red Wings for a change.

But the next opponent, the Dallas Stars were no push over. They had a star center and the greatest active American-born player in Mike Modano along with newly acquired Brett Hull, as well as Joey Nieuwendyk, Jere Lehtinen, Jamie Langenbrunner, Sergei Zubov, and Darryl Sydor. And they had former Blackhawk and Blues' nemesis Eddie Belfour in goal. The series went more like one you might expect where home ice actually made a meaningful difference. The Stars won games 1 and 2 in Dallas, the Blues won games 3 and 4 in St. Louis and the Stars returned to Dallas to win Game 5. But the pattern unfortunately ended in Game 6 when Dallas beat the Blues 2-1 in Overtime in St. Louis - with Modano scoring, naturally on an assist from Hull, to win the series. Last year ex-Blue Shanahan ended the Blues' season in Overtime and now Hull assisted on the series' winning Overtime goal - both in front of the Blues' faithful. *Just how much do they think we Blues' fans can take?*

Once again, the Blues appeared to inspire our playoff opponent to greatness (or catch a bad break playing the Stars early) since for the third straight year the team we lost to in the playoffs went on to win the Stanley Cup. And to add insult to injury, who scored the Cup-clinching controversial goal in TRIPLE Overtime of Game 7 against Buffalo and all-world goalie Dominik Hasek? *Our* Brett Hull. The man plays over ten seasons with the Blues as our best player and never advances past the second round of the playoffs, and then joins Dallas and wins the Stanley Cup in his very first year - and he's the hero.

Losing Hull was a tough pill to swallow, but it became that much tougher - like swallowing a hockey puck - when Hull won the Stanley Cup with Dallas (and later again with Detroit). *Is there no end to the punishment?*

Off the ice, the Blues were once again hemorrhaging financially. The team was drawing reasonably well but was saddled with debt - $96 Million of it, mostly associated with the new Kiel Center. The consortium of 19 well-meaning business leaders that owned the Blues had enough of their civic-inspired investment, feeling the pain of Ralston Purina, and they began looking for a buyer. Up to the plate stepped an unlikely source - Nancy and Bill Laurie.

Nancy was the daughter and thus the heir of Sam Walton of Walmart fame and among the wealthiest people in the world. Bill started out as a teacher and basketball coach at CBC High School in St. Louis after having played college ball. Perhaps his biggest claim to fame as a basketball player was that he was a starter on the Memphis State basketball team that lost to UCLA in the NCAA Final at the Old Barn in 1973 when Bill Walton (no relation to the Arkansas clan!) had likely the greatest game of his illustrious career, shooting 21-22 from the field. (Bill Laurie, by contrast, didn't score a single point in the final game.)

Perhaps inspired by his fellow Bill's performance, Mr. Laurie decided to marry himself a Walton. He became manager of an extensive real estate portfolio but always maintained a strong interest in basketball and made no secret about wanting to own an NBA team. He had tried to buy the NBA's Denver Nuggets along with the NHL's Colorado Avalanche and the Pepsi Center where both play earlier in the year for $400 Million but was thwarted. Ironically, his brother-in-law Stan Kroenke of St. Louis Rams infamy, bought these same assets instead just a year later for $450 Million. *Just a good investment or to spite his brother-in-law? Stan reportedly helped seal the bid by promising that he was committed to the City of Denver and would not move the team for at least 25 years. Hmmm!*

So, as the 1999 season began, the Lauries decided to become the seventh owner of the Blues, paying $100 Million (essentially leaving the sellers with virtually nothing after assuming the debt). It was an odd purchase for a man who didn't know a thing about hockey and, allegedly, had never even skated. Perhaps he was hoping that his acquisition might give him some pro sports world credibility and help him land an NBA team. And the cost was paltry for a professional sports team and chump change to the Columbia, Missouri natives.

For the last year of the decade, the Blues tried a new approach. The team decided to become younger and more international in flavor like Detroit. *If you can't beat them, join them.* Instead of Russia, though, the Blues went with a Slovak/Czech invasion adding young Michal Handzus (22), Lubos Bartecko (23) and Ladislav Nagy (20) and big goalie Roman Turek (a back-up with Dallas whom the Blues thought could be a quality starter). And we added a promising 22-year old German Jochen Hecht as well to the established core of Pronger, MacInnis, Turgeon, Demitra, and Scott Young.

While the Central Europeans were hardly the equivalent of Detroit's all-star Russians, they added skill, speed, depth and variety to the soup. And the recipe really seemed to work. But a large part of the team's success was due to one man - Chris Pronger. In 1999-2000, when Prongs was on the ice the Blues always seemed to be the better team, no matter how good the team we were playing. Indeed, Pronger was so good that year that he led the entire NHL with a plus 52 rating and was voted not only the best defenseman in the League (James Norris Memorial Trophy), but also the Most Valuable Player (Art Ross Trophy). Only one other player in NHL history had ever accomplished that - yep, that Bobby Orr guy. And no one has done it since.

After losing the first two games of the season, the Blues were a veritable wrecking crew. At one point the team won 12 of 13 games. By the end of the year, the Blues had finished first in the entire League at 114 points. It was the best Blues' regular season in history and the first (and only) time that the Blues have won the President's Cup. Surely this season would produce a magical ride deep into the playoffs and possibly our very first Stanley Cup!

As the first-place team, the Blues opened against the eighth place San Jose Sharks. The Sharks had some talent - a tough scoring winger in Owen Nolan, a top defenseman in Gary Suter, a veteran center in Vincent Damphousse, a promising 20-year-old Patrick Marleau and a few other pieces. But they were not the great team that the Sharks would later become. The Blues had played the Sharks five times during the regular season and had *never* lost to them, although there was one tie mixed in there.

But this was the playoffs - everyone starts with a clean slate and the style of hockey is different. The Blues, as expected, won Game 1. But then inexplicably we dropped the next three games in a row. Games 3 and 4 were particularly hard to digest as the Blues outplayed the Sharks but lost both games by a single goal. In each case a third period goal broke up a tie game for the loss. Down 3-1 in the series and facing elimination the Blues did what the team has rarely done when down big in a series - we rallied big time. The Blues won Game 5 at home and then crushed San Jose 6-2 in San Jose to win Game 6.

The Blues were now heading home for Game 7, a game that we were heavily favored to win. If the Blues could pull this series off, we would have momentum, and this just might be the springboard we needed for a Stanley Cup. Indeed, most teams that come from the depth of despair to find a way to survive an early challenge are able to use that to their advantage (See e.g. the Red Sox defeating the Yankees in the ALCS in 2004 after being down three games to none and trailing in the 9th inning of Game 4 with the greatest relief pitcher in history, Mariano Rivera, on the mound for the Yankees. After their improbable comeback in Game 4 and subsequent wins in Games 5, 6 and 7, they swept the Cardinals for their first World Series in 86 years).

I was in the Kiel Center for Game 7 against San Jose. I was nervous but reasonably confident about this team's chances *(and confidence and I are rarely partners)*. We were the better team, at home, had the momentum and these Sharks were not exactly the Red Wings of 1998 or even the Stars of 1999.

Hadn't history taught me anything? Despite having the best record in the NHL and rallying from a 3-1 series deficit to force a Game 7 at home, the Blues could not finish off the Sharks. We fell behind 2-0 in the first period and then 3-0 and never really mounted a serious threat, losing 3-1 with only 22 shots for the entire game. It was arguably the biggest loss in Blues' history at the time given the expectations for this team and the team we lost to. At least it would be the first time in four years that the team that defeated the Blues in the playoffs did not win the Stanley Cup! In fact, the Sharks would get crushed in their next series against Dallas, winning only one game in the series - adding to the shock that we had lost to that team.

The end of the 1990's was also the official end of the old Arena. Pressured by City Progress that built the new facility and did not want another building competing for events, and over the objections and protests of many, the City tore down the place that had served as the host for so much excitement and angst - my favorite home away from home as a boy.

The Old Barn had quite a lengthy and impressive sports history. In addition to hosting three Stanley Cup Finals, it was the venue for lots of great basketball - occasional games of the NBA's St. Louis Hawks, the full-time home for the short-lived but entertaining ABA's St. Louis Spirits (with Movin' Marvin Barnes, Moses Malone, Freddie Lewis, Don Chaney, Maurice Lucas and a very young Bob Costas as the announcer), the scene where UCLA won its 7th straight NCAA Championship in 1973 and where the University of Kentucky beat Duke for the 1978 NCAA Championship, and the regular location for the annual Mizzou vs Illinois "Braggin' Rights" basketball games. The Arena also served as a home for indoor soccer: the St. Louis Stars, Steamers and Ambush played their games there. In addition, the longest tennis match in Davis Cup history took place there as John McEnroe defeated Mats Wilander of Sweden in five sets - 79 games which took over 6 hours. And it also hosted numerous memorable concerts from the Rolling Stones to the Who to Michael Jackson.

Yet, in the dynamite blast of 15 seconds, the large structure and its 70 years of memories vanished into rubble.

Recap of the 1990's

It was a wild decade for Blues' fans. Without question the 1990's brought St. Louis the most talented hockey players of any decade in our history. With Hull, Oates, Shanahan, MacInnis, Pronger, Stevens, Joseph, Fuhr, Turgeon, Demitra, Courtnall, Janney, Anderson, Hawerchuck, Duschene, Tikkanen and, ever so briefly the Great One, St. Louis arguably saw the best and widest assembly of hockey talent of any NHL team in the decade.

Nevertheless, the team was not able to fully capitalize on that talent. The Blues once again made the playoffs every season in the decade but could never quite pull it all together in the critical juncture between mid-April to mid-June; all that talent and all those great teams did not translate into a Stanley Cup. And we didn't really ever get close. In fairness, we had the great misfortune to run into the eventual Stanley Cup Champion in several of those years. It seemed as though the Blues may have been the second-best team in the NHL on more than one occasion but never got a chance to prove it or to gain the experience of having gone deep in the playoffs.

The Blues also shot themselves in the foot with bad trades, hired a coach who helped run Gretzky and Hull out of town and lost a franchise player and five draft picks to a terrible legal ruling. More than ever the Blues felt like a cursed franchise.

But there was always next year and a new decade of hockey and hopes. We had our customary change of ownership - two in fact - and a spanking new home for hockey, though I and many old-timers preferred and missed the old one. And with the best backline in the business in Pronger and MacInnis, each playing roughly half the game, there were reasons to be optimistic - *if* you were so inclined.

The 2000's

The Blues began the new decade with a new name for the place where the team played hockey - the Savvis Center - but were essentially the same team. *Why mess with success?* The only significant addition was a feisty forward with a name more suited for the entertainment or even the porn industry - Dallas Drake.

Although not quite as strong a team as the previous season, the 2000-2001 version of the Blues was still clearly one of the top teams in the League. The Blues also pulled off arguably the two most miraculous comebacks in the team's five decades of hockey (sorry Monday Night Miracle fans). On October 11th, 2000, the Blues trailed the Los Angeles Kings by the score of 4-0 entering the third period (the Kings having scored all four of their goals on the power play). But the guys in Blue did not quit and rallied in the third period with a goal by Demitra, two goals by Scott Young, and a fourth goal by Hecht with less than a minute remaining to tie the game. Turgeon assisted on the last three of those goals. Although the game ended in a tie after Overtime (no shoot-outs back then), it sure felt like a win under the circumstances.

And the Blues topped that incredible achievement a month or so later in the hockey hotbed of Toronto. This time the Blues fell behind by five goals (5-0) early in the third period to a strong Maple Leafs' team. Starting goalie Roman Turek was pulled and replaced by Brent Johnson to change the momentum. Pronger finally got the Blues on the board to prevent what appeared might be a shutout. Alexander Khavanov and MacInnis followed soon thereafter with goals to make it 5-3 and at least prevent a blowout loss. But when Michal Handzus scored with about five and a half minutes left in the game to cut the margin to just one goal, it was suddenly quite an exciting game. Could the Blues actually rally back from a five-goal deficit in the third? No team had ever done that before on the road. (The Los Angeles Kings had accomplished a virtually identical feat at home in 1982, winning 6-5 in Overtime.)

And sure enough, with just 25 seconds left in the game, Khavanov had himself a game, collecting a loose puck and sticking it in for the tying goal. And for icing on the cake, the Blues scored a mere 18 seconds into the Overtime - once again it was the German born Hecht scoring on a pass from Demitra for the most improbable win in Blues' history. Brent Johnson got the win in goal facing merely two shots on goal in his nearly 17 minutes of action – it was undoubtedly the lowest save total ever recorded by a Blues' goaltender in a game that we won. And who was the Toronto goalie who gave up all six goals in less than twenty minutes? Surprisingly, former Blue Curtis Joseph.

While we were unable to match the record-setting season of the season before, the Blues still finished the 2000-2001 season with an impressive 103 points, and were often dominant, with separate seven game and eight game winning streaks during the year. And the Blues - players and management - were determined this year to make a better showing in the playoffs.

To enhance the team's chances, management went out and acquired Keith Tkachuk with only twelve games left in the season. "Big Walt" came with a resume of having scored more than 300 goals in his career, 50 or more in two seasons, and lots of time in the box. The thought was that the big man (at 6-foot 2 and 235 pounds) would add scoring depth, toughness, and a large backside that could not be easily moved from in front of the net - critical in tight-checking playoff games. In time Walt would add his name to the sensational number 7's in Blues' history.

And management was not through with its tinkering. The Blues added another big winger and leader-type in the Florida Panthers' Scott Mellanby for much the same reason. Certainly, two positive additions to help bolster the team's Cup chances.

But instead of stopping there, the Blues also decided to send center Craig Conroy to the team's favorite trading partner, Calgary, for skillful winger Cory Stillman, Calgary's top scorer, in an attempt to add more scoring depth. The problem was that

Conroy was our best defensive center who had the unique ability to neutralize the other teams' best players and was also the team's best penalty killer after Pronger.

As luck would have it, the Blues once again drew San Jose in the first round. This time the Blues got redemption and dispatched the elasmobranch fish in six games. In the second round the Blues would face their long-time rival the Stars who had defeated the Edmonton Oilers in six games.

Brimming with confidence, the Blues crushed the Stars in four straight games to advance to the Conference Final for the first time since 1986, and only the second time since the 1970 Stanley Cup Final. But waiting for the Blues was the team with the most talent not named Detroit - the Colorado Avalanche - with the dual center superstars Joe Sakic and Peter Forsberg, additional scorers Milan Hejduk, Alex Tanguay, and Chris Drury, star defensemen Adam Foote, 40-year-old legendary defenseman Ray Borque and the best goalie at the time, Patrick Roy. The Avalanche had been the top team in the NHL during the year with 118 points and looked every bit as devastating as their team nickname.

We had played Colorado relatively evenly during the regular season, beating them once and tying them another in four tries. Although Colorado had swept Vancouver in the first round they had a surprisingly difficult second round series with Los Angeles that went the full seven games. Perhaps the well-rested Blues could take advantage of that?

The Blues promptly lost the first two games in Denver. But then we rallied to win Game 3 in Double Overtime at home to cut the Avalanche's series lead to 2-1. In critical Game 4, the Blues fell behind 3-0 in the first period. But with two goals from Turgeon in the second period and a goal by Jamal Mayers in the third, the Blues had pulled off a great comeback and tied the game and it went to Overtime. Just four minutes into the extra session, however, Colorado's Stephane Yelle scored, causing me and my fellow Blues' comrades to yell many expletives.

And Game 5 in Colorado would be similar: The Blues erased a 1-0 lead to tie the game and force Overtime. This time, it only took 24 seconds: Joe Sakic scored on a power play (which was rarely given in Overtime in those days) to win the game and the series. Naturally, Colorado then went on to win the Stanley Cup over New Jersey.

I have always wondered how the Blues might have fared in this very close series had we had Craig Conroy to check Joe Sakic and kill power plays. Colorado scored seven power plays in the series, and Sakic personally scored four goals, including the game winner, in the deciding Game 5. Stillman was largely a non-factor in the series, with no goals, though he did have two assists. It might have been the Blues' best opportunity to capture the Cup in the team's long history and we fell short - perhaps because of the one trade too many.

The next year (2001-2002), the Blues remained a very solid team, though slightly less spectacular, finishing with 98 points. On April 25, 2002, the Blues would finally defeat the Chicago Blackhawks in a playoff series, much to the delight of the local fan base (since beating a Chicago team is worth double the points). But then we once again had to get by our more talented nemesis, the Detroit Red Wings, to reach the Final. After dropping the first two games in Detroit, the Blues crushed the Red Wings 6-1 in Game 3. And we had the early lead in Game 4, when our most crucial player, Pronger, was badly injured on a freak play chasing Steve Yzerman along the boards and was out for the rest of the game and the series. That put a quick end to the talented Blues' season for yet another year. Remarkably, the team the Blues lost to in the playoffs went on to win the Stanley Cup for the fifth time in six years. Not exactly good luck or great timing for the Blues.

In the following year (2002-2003) the Blues had to play essentially the entire regular season without the team's best player as Pronger was limited to only five games due to injury. At the same time a new young defenseman, 21-year old Barret

Jackman, burst on the scene. Jackman had been selected by the Blues in the first round of the 1999 draft and with Pronger's absence was slotted to assume a significant chunk of his duties. He was not especially big but, like Pronger, played with a tough edge to him. And indeed, Jackman had an excellent rookie season, no doubt aided by having MacInnis as his partner. In fact, his play was considered so outstanding throughout the League that he won the Calder Trophy for Rookie of the Year beating out two future superstars in Detroit's Henrik Zetterberg and Columbus' Rick Nash (Florida's Jay Bouwmeester, who would a decade later become an integral part of the Blues, finished seventh in the voting.)

Jacks would be the first to admit that he had limited offensive skills - he never scored more than four goals in a season and had a rare complete goose egg in 2010-2011. But he was very solid defensively and played with smarts, heart and moxie, much in the old-school mold of Barclay Plager and Brian Sutter. He was also loved by his teammates and was a great representative of the Blues in the community.

Al MacInnis replaced Pronger as the Blues' captain and led the team to another very solid 99-point season. Many thought that this team could make some serious noise in the playoffs, especially with Pronger back. The first-round opponent was a significant challenge in the 104-point Vancouver Canucks, led by Markus Naslund, Todd Bertuzzi, Brendan Morrison, Trevor Linden and two young twins from Sweden named Sedin. But the Blues' team was loaded as well. With Demitra, Tkachuk, Weight, Mellanby, Boguniecki, Drake, Rucinsky and Valeri Bure up front; Pronger, MacInnis, Jackman, Salvador, and Khavanov on defense; and two-time Stanley Cup Champion Chris Osgood in goal (the same Chris Osgood that broke Blues' hearts playing for Detroit in the famous Gretzky series) the Blues were a formidable opponent for anyone and appeared to have a legitimate shot at the Cup.

Indeed, the Blues dominated the explosive Canucks 6-0 in the first game at Vancouver. And we won two of the next three games as well to hold a commanding 3-1 series lead. But that only magnified the torture when we managed to drop the last three games in succession. What few knew at the time, however, was that several Blues had collected a bad case of the flu around Game 5 (and when flu hits a locker room it can become an epidemic). While excuses are generally taboo in hockey, there were guys taking I-Vs and even throwing up between periods.

And there was the crushing blow that MacInnis took separating his shoulder in Game 2 (I believe that thug Bertuzzi was responsible - the same guy who was charged criminally for attacking Colorado's Steve Moore from behind and ruining his career and life during a game two years later). MacInnis was out after having played less than two minutes and was unable to suit up for Games 3, 4, 5 and 6 as well. Although he forced his way back into the line-up for Game 7, knowing how badly his team needed him, he could barely even grip his stick for that game. Chalk all of that up to more bad timing and bad luck. It would be the Blues' 35th season without a Stanley Cup.

The Blues attempted to soldier on in 2003-2004 with many of the same cast of characters that had been so successful during the regular season. No team in the NHL had a better record than the Blues over the prior six years except for Stanley Cup powerhouses Detroit and Colorado. But the Blues were suddenly not as sharp. Perhaps it was the weight of so many playoff disappointments. Perhaps repeated suggestions by some in the media and fan base that the Blues were chokers come playoff time were taking their toll. The loss of MacInnis (who suffered a serious eye injury and was only able to play three games the entire year) and Jackman, (who suffered a shoulder injury limiting him to fifteen games) certainly didn't help. Nor did the fact that many of the core players were getting older.

In any case, the fan base and the ownership were getting edgy after so many good teams that had failed to deliver when it mattered most. Two thirds of the way into the season - and despite a winning record (though not nearly at the same pace as prior years) - the Blues surprisingly dumped their longtime coach, Joel Quenneville. Under Coach Q's leadership the Blues had been a force in the League every year. Indeed, Coach Q's Blues' teams never had a losing season, and for his six full seasons from 1997-1998 through 2002-2003, the Blues *averaged* a whopping 100 points per season. As Adam Sandler might say, "not too shabby."

But as consistently successful as the Blues were in the regular season, the results in the playoffs were characterized by consistent failure and disillusionment. Coach Q was at the helm for twelve playoff series during his tenure, and the Blues won only five of them. More importantly as far as most Blues' fans and ownership were concerned, the Blues never won the Cup, and never really even came close to competing for one - never making it to the Final and only making the Conference Final once, where we only won one game.

A lot of that candidly had to do with the quality of their opponent. But perhaps the nail in the coffin in the assessment that Q was not a great playoff coach was the crushing loss to a mediocre San Jose team in 2000 when the Blues had the best record in the NHL and had expectations of grandeur. It was enough to make a grown man cry at the time and may have been enough to get Quenneville fired. Though that trauma had happened years before, the memories and wound were lasting.

Coach Q, of course, got his sweet revenge, and showed that he WAS a great playoff coach, by going to the rival Blackhawks and winning not just one, not just two, but THREE Stanley Cups with Chicago. *The torture is unrelenting.*

With a new coach at the helm for the 2004 playoffs, the Blues fared no better. The Mike Kitchen-led Blues made the playoffs but promptly lost in just five games to a now much more talented and first place San Jose Sharks' team.

And then came the biggest blow to Blues' fans and hockey fans everywhere: there was no hockey to be had. The NHL owners wanted a hard salary cap to contain costs and ensure that the profitable teams, of which they claimed there were only eleven, would not take all the best players, and the unprofitable ones would not go out of business. The players knew that a hard salary cap would greatly restrict their salaries and cause some older, more expensive players to be out of a job.

Both sides dug in and with no end to the impasse, the NHL announced in February 2005 that the entire 2004-2005 season was cancelled - the first major sports league in North America to cancel a full season due to a labor dispute. For the first time since I was eight years old, there would be a winter without skating and checking, no hockey version of "the thrill of victory and the agony of defeat," and no Stanley Cup awarded. It was a sad day throughout hockey land - many in Canada undoubtedly went on suicide watch.

With the lockout, the NHL teams naturally lost a lot of money. The Blues in particular were bleeding cash and reportedly had lost $60 Million in the last two seasons. The Lauries could naturally afford that as billionaires but were tired of losing money with an underperforming team and a fan base that was growing weary and not showing up to games as regularly. Bill Laurie was not really a hockey fan anyway - his desire to own an NBA team was still paramount in his mind and he wanted to refocus his energies in that direction. So, the Lauries decided to sell the team.

More disconcerting, they sought to greatly reduce payroll and dispose of the best (most costly) players; somehow the very wealthy sophisticated businessman didn't appreciate that by getting rid of your best assets you were actually diminishing interest and the value of your team.

Indeed, the Blues traded the team's most valuable asset, Chris Pronger, to Edmonton for Eric Brewer, Jeff Woywitka and Doug Lynch. Needless to say, it was a total salary dump. Only Brewer was a meaningful player - Woywitka scored 6 goals total in four years and Lynch never stepped foot on the ice for the Blues. As for Brewer, in parts of five injury-riddled seasons, he scored a total of 30 goals and had a cumulative net minus rating of 75 at even strength. By contrast, Pronger played seven more quality years of his Hall of Fame career leading three different teams to the Stanley Cup Finals - Edmonton, Anaheim and Philadelphia, and winning the Cup with Anaheim in 2007.

And the other great warrior on defense with the biggest slap shot west of the Atlantic Ocean, Al MacInnis, decided to hang up his skates due to advancing age (now 42) and his bad eye injury, though the extended layoff didn't help. Perhaps Al also knew that this team was going to struggle. Several other players had their illustrious careers end unceremoniously by virtue of the cancelled season, including the two most important Blues who got away: Scott Stevens and Adam Oates.

To further add to the frustration of fans, the Blues lost another one of their most dynamic players as a result of the cancelled season. During the 2004–2005 NHL lockout Pavol Demitra went back to his native Slovakia to play for a team there. When he returned to the NHL the following year, he signed as a free agent with the Los Angeles Kings, as the Blues had no interest in incurring his high salary.

Like Turgeon, Demitra was one of most underrated players in Blues' history; he was elusive and creative with the puck, had good speed, played hard at both ends of the ice, and was a great passer and reliable goal scorer. He played for the Blues from 1996-2004, scoring at least 30 goals three times, was a three-time All-Star, and, like Turgeon, was the rare player who averaged essentially one point a game - 493 points in 494 games with the Blues. He also won the Lady Byng Memorial Trophy in 2000 for the player with the best sportsmanship combined with a high level of play - one of the best awards in hockey; even if the name might suggest that the player is "soft." Pavol was actually one of the stronger guys on the team and could lift more weight per pound than most of his teammates. He finished his career with the Blues fifth in points, third in plus/minus and second in game-winning goals.

So, when hockey returned in 2005-2006 the Blues were clearly not the same. With no Pronger, MacInnis or Demitra, and no Quenneville running the show, the team fell completely off the Zamboni. And just to make sure: during the year, management traded the team's leading scorer, Mike Sillinger, and top center and assist man Doug Weight. Management gave coach Mike Kitchen no chance in his first full year in charge.

Not surprisingly, the Blues went from a team that regularly registered points in the high 90's and above, and always at least made the playoffs, to a mere 57 points and watching the playoffs at home. The team tried hard but was terrible - at one point dropping thirteen games in a row! Remarkably it was the first time that the Blues had missed the playoffs in a quarter of a century and the first time in Blues' history that the team had finished dead last in the standings.

The sale of the team to a group headed by Dave Checketts (the former president of Madison Square Garden with a great name for a hockey owner) helped apply a tourniquet to the bleeding Blues. He brought in former Blues' goalie and broadcaster John Davidson to serve as general manager.

The one benefit of a horrendous season on the ice was that the Blues got to choose the first draft pick in the entire NHL for the first time in history. It's a rare opportunity to potentially get a player that can define your franchise for a decade or more. And you had better capitalize - you need to make a great choice and ideally try to find the next Gretzky, Lemieux, or Connor McDavid, or at least, a regular All-Star. Blues' coaches, scouts and management grappled with the decision, finally deciding upon Erik Johnson a big 6-foot 4 225-pound defenseman who could skate well and had a big shot. In the process they passed on a fellow named Jonathan Toews, another named Niklas Backstrom and a third named Jordan Staal.

Johnson would prove to be a decent player with the Blues but certainly not worthy of the number one overall pick. It didn't help matters that after his first season he was badly injured while playing golf! How is a young big tough hockey player that endures punishing checks at high speeds night after night injured playing an old man's game? As it turns out he was apparently not even *playing* the game, but rather allegedly *driving* the golf cart when his foot got caught between the accelerator and the brake, tearing ligaments in his knee and causing him to miss the entire 2008-2009 season.

The rest of the decade was unfortunately not much to write about. The Blues improved from the horrendous 2005-2006 season to reach about 81 points in 2006-2007 and 79 points in 2007-2008 but didn't make the playoffs either year.

Despite the disappointments on the ice, the team remained close off of it. Hockey players' appetite for golf and beer (and sharing it together) persists in good times and in bad. When there were night games on the road which would result in returning to the hotel late, the Blues' players ordered ahead of time to make sure that they had filled a bathtub (or two) of iced beer to enjoy as a team after the game and into the wee hours.

In 2008-2009 the Blues improved to the 92-point plateau, ending the season on a run winning 16 of the last 23 games - finally good enough for a taste of playoff hockey. But it was more like an appetizer or a small salad as the Blues were swiftly eliminated in four games by the Vancouver Canucks.

In the final year of the decade (2009-2010), the Blues nearly mimicked the regular season record of the prior season, finishing two points shy at 90 points. But the small drop-off was just enough though to miss the playoffs. Thus, in four of the last five years, the Blues had gone home for the summer without the financial or emotional benefit of a single playoff game. The Blues weren't a bad team, but we now played in a good division. It was payback for the 1970's when the Blues made the playoffs many years with a losing record - the yin and yang of hockey.

During this difficult stretch, Andy Murray was the coach - he was known as a psychologist who liked to surreptitiously find out what players were thinking. One of his classic maneuvers was to enter a crowded weight room at one end, find a player he wanted to send a message to and then leave the room. He would then subtly enter the room through one of the other two doors in another part of the room to hear what the players were saying among themselves about what he had just said.

The Blues captain during this period was Eric Brewer, apparently a strong leader who was liked by his teammates. But he was always known as the guy traded for Chris Pronger and was unable to fill his massive skates. He did, however, play an important (inadvertent) role in helping the Blues' march to the Stanley Cup this year. In February of 2011 he was traded to Tampa Bay for a package that included their third-round pick in the 2011 draft. That pick just happened to be Jordan Binnington.

Despite the paltry playoff participation, the Blues' teams from the late 2000's had some good players and engaging personalities. Chief among them was T.J. Oshie, the creative, charismatic and popular player with the boyish looks. He would later wow the nation as a member of the U.S. Olympic team with his four successful shootout/penalty shots to defeat Russia in the 2014 Winter Olympics (putting the Oshie in Sochi).

There was also his good friend and sidekick David Backes - not the most talented player but another guy who worked hard to improve and would run through a wall to win. Thus, he made the perfect captain type to replace Brewer - basically, Brian Sutter in a bigger body and a right-handed shot.

There were a few veterans as well: aging greats Paul Kariya and Andy McDonald - not the players they were in their prime, but each possessed world class speed and had pizzazz to their game; and "Big Walt" Tkachuk, no longer in his hey-day but still a tough net presence with a sarcastic wit. As for goal production, Brad Boyes surprisingly pumped in 76 goals over a two-year span. And for steadiness, work ethic and leadership there was Alexander Steen and Barret Jackman. Budding youngsters David Perron and Erik Johnson, each only 21 at the time, offered some hope for the future.

Recap of the 2000's

The decade of the 2000's was clearly the worst in Blues' history. Surprisingly, the team actually won more games than we lost in the decade, *if* you were to ignore the aberrational 2005-2006 horrendous season. And yet, the team missed the playoffs half of those years, and only had a total of three playoff series wins for the entire decade. Indeed, as the decade ended the Blues' last playoff *game* win was in 2004 against the San Jose Sharks – a series we lost four games to one. The last playoff *series* win was in 2002 against Chicago back when Coach Q running the show and Pronger was manning the blue line.

Goaltending was certainly a contributing factor to the team's disappointing results. The Blues tried eighteen different goalies in the decade (seven in one season: 2002-2003). Brent Johnson was the best statistically and by my eye test (he played 127 games, won 69, lost 42 and tied 8, with a very solid goals against average of 2.26 and a save percentage of over .900), but he never seemed to get much love from the coaches or fans.

Poor coaching may have also contributed; Andy Murray was fired as the calendar turned to 2010, replaced by Davis Payne, a first-time NHL coach, who would be gone soon thereafter and never again serve as head coach in the NHL (however, he won a Stanley Cup after he left - as an *assistant* coach with the Los Angeles Kings - of course he did!) But it was perhaps mostly a case of the whole being less than the sum of the parts.

With the turnover of personnel and especially the lack of playoff hockey (the heartthrob of the NHL) excitement for the team had waned - never good for a sport that depends heavily on attendance. Once again, issues arose about the future of the Blues in St. Louis as financial woes of the team mounted.

The 2010's

The decade of the 2010's started where the last decade left off. The Davis Payne-coached team of 2010-2011 finished the season with a few more wins than losses, good for 87 points, and fourth place in the Central Division. But, once again, there were no playoffs to be had for the diehard Blues' fans. Making the playoffs and ideally winning a series or two is the bread and butter of an NHL team. It is by far the most exciting part of professional hockey and keeps the base interested and buying seats. It is also critical for the financial success of most organizations, not named Toronto or New York, as the extra attendance revenue often means the difference between red and black ink on the income statement in a sport with small margins and lacking a lucrative national television contract. Conversely, missing the playoffs six out of seven years, as the Blues had, causes great fan and financial strain to a club.

A big development during the season was the decision to trade Erik Johnson, the Blues only first pick in the entire NHL draft in our history. Johnson was traded to Colorado as part of a deal that included Kevin Shattenkirk and Chris Stewart. It showed just how far and quickly his star had fallen in management's eyes. The kid was only 22!

The trade was especially upsetting for my better half. In an effort to get her more excited about my favorite sport, I suggested buying her a Blues' Jersey with a player of her choice at the beginning of a game against the Los Angeles Kings in late January. *(Besides Valentine's Day was approaching and what screams love more than a Blues' hockey jersey?)*. She wisely pointed out that players get traded and retire and inquired who was the safest player that she could be *assured* would be with the Blues for a long time. After all, who wanted an expensive hockey jersey with a *former* player on the back, especially one still playing on an opposing team?

I boldly predicted Erik Johnson was the safest play - not because I was especially enamored with him or because he was a star yet, but because as the Blues' first overall pick, management would be especially reluctant to trade him and acknowledge their failure in drafting him as the overall number one pick in the first place. Plus, he was still very young and had many years ahead of him and would presumably get better.

So, she went with Johnson and by the end of the second period her spanking brand-new Blues' jersey with Johnson's number 6 emblazoned on it was ready at the Blues in-game store. She put it on proudly and, almost on cue, Johnson scored the game-winning goal in the third period to defeat the Kings 2-1! *How's that for timing and a good omen?* And then, only a few weeks later, the Blues announced that Johnson had been traded!

Before the start of the new 2011-2012 season, the Blues family received some horrific news. Long time Blues' great Pavol Demitra died in a plane crash on September 7, 2011. He had joined the Russian team Lokomotiv Yaroslavl of the Kontinental Hockey League and was on its way to Minsk, Belarus to start the 2011-2012 KHL season. The entire team, including another former Blue Igor Koralev, perished.

Pavol was one of my favorites. I have always had a special fondness for the smaller athletes who not only manage to survive but thrive among the increasingly larger and more dangerous creatures in sports. Whether it is Isaac Bruce or Marshall Faulk, Curt Flood or David Eckstein, or Doug Palazzari or Demitra, these smaller men have to have speed, elusiveness, guts and inordinate skill to overcome the size bias of coaches and general managers just to make it to and play in the bigs. And then in the rare cases when that happens, they have to avoid the one bad collision, especially in the heavy contact sports, that could easily end their careers.

Pavol will be remembered as one of the greatest Slovakian players of all time. It was no coincidence that the team experienced our worst season of all time the very year after Pavol left the Blues. Pavol followed in the footsteps of the great Peters - Bondra and Stastny, the latter a Hall of Fame player who played for the Blues at the tail end of his career, stayed in St. Louis and raised two boys who played in the NHL (both for the

Blues at some point) as well as a daughter who won the Missouri High school state Tennis Championship four years in a row. Pavol also helped pave the way for other great players with Slovak roots like Zdeno Chára, Marián Hossa and Marion Gaborik.

The very humble man with the likeable personality was survived by his wife Maja and his two children, Lucas and Zara. Following his death, the elementary school which he attended, and the ice hockey stadium where he started his successful career were named after him. The Blues honored both Pavol and Igor Korolev in a special ceremony before the November 8, 2011 game with the Blackhawks that I attended. The date was chosen so that the coach that gave Pavol his first real chance, Joel Quenneville, and his best friend, Marian Hossa, could be there. The Blues wore Pavol's Number 38 on the team's uniforms for the game but, in my view, the team needs to retire his number.

On the ice, the Blues' fortunes were about to change considerably. Only thirteen games into the 2011-2012 season, management determined that the Blues' performance was causing too much discomfort and sought to eliminate their pain - specifically Coach Payne - replacing him with Big Ken Hitchcock (the moniker more attributable to his girth than his height). "Hitch" had the reputation as a great cerebral hockey mind, was a good friend of General Manager Doug Armstrong, and had led the Dallas Stars to that franchise's first (and only) Stanley Cup. Perhaps the Blues could hitch this wagon all the way to the Cup themselves. Most great Blues' coaches had won their Stanley Cups only *after* they left the Blues. Management tried to go the other way this time around; hiring someone who had actually accomplished the deed *before* he became a Blues' coach (ignoring the fact that the team had tried this with the hiring of Mike Keenan who proved to be a disaster).

And then just a few months later, the Blues had a new owner - the team's eighth. A group of prominent local businessmen under the catchy name SLB Acquisition Holdings, LLC (*it just rolls off your tongue*) acquired the Blues and associated assets and liabilities for $130 Million. The leader of the group, Tom Stillman, was the CEO of a St. Louis-based beer distributor (*What is it with booze and sports in St. Louis?*) More importantly, he was a lifelong hockey guy - having been born in Minnesota and played hockey in college. In addition, many of his fellow partner/members (which included James Cooper, Christopher Danforth, John Danforth, Jim Johnson III, Jim Kavanaugh, Jerald Kent, Jo Ann Taylor Kindle, Donn Lux, Steve Maritz, Scott McCuaig, Edward Potter, John Ross, Jr, Tom Schlafly, David Steward, and Andrew Taylor) were themselves huge hockey fans and some, even as adults heading into the more senior ranks, still played the game recreationally.

Stillman announced to the relief of many in town: "We're 100 percent committed to the Blues and the City of St. Louis." It sounded like a great potential marriage. The owners' resources collectively were significant, they were passionate about hockey and this team and most importantly, they truly understood how badly the Blues' fan base (which included *them*) wanted a Stanley Cup, and were determined to get it for them.

Hitch completely turned the team around. He took a squad that was just 6-7 when he arrived and went 43-15-11 the rest of the way, good enough for first place in the potent Central Division. He did it with a strong emphasis on defense, relentless forechecking and accountability all over the ice, and he got his players to buy into his system. It wasn't the most entertaining brand of hockey and goals were often hard to come by. Indeed, despite the stellar record, the Blues finished 22nd out of 30 in offense. Oshie and Backes tied for the team lead in points for the season with just 54 in 82 games.

But it worked in the win column, as the Blues gave up the least number of goals in the League. It was a throw-back to the very first years of the Blues, where the team thrived and died on defense. Young talented defensemen Alex Pietrangelo (age 22) and Kevin Shattenkirk (age 23) joined Barret Jackman and Roman Polak in keeping other teams at bay, and Jaroslav Halak and Brian Elliott splendidly split the goaltending duties, recording a League-leading 15 shutouts, a combined minuscule goal against average of 1.78 and combined save percentage of .932. It was *almost* like Hall and Plante.

The question in some Blues' fans minds (*like my own*) was whether playing such a defensive style with so little offense could be successful in the playoffs? And what if the Blues were to fall behind in games: Could the team effectively change its style of play and generate enough offense to win?

The answer at least to the first question was "yes" in the first round of the playoffs, as we beat the San Jose Sharks in five games, even though the Blues averaged less than three goals per game and four of the five games were decided by one goal (if you ignore empty net goals).

The answer against better competition in the second round and a hot goalie in Jonathan Quick of the Los Angeles Kings was a resounding "no," to both questions as the Blues got swept in four games, only scoring a total of six goals in the entire series! Once again, a great regular season gave way to a very disappointing, though in my mind somewhat predictable, playoff performance.

Nevertheless, the Blues stuck with the program the next year (2012-2013). At first, there was no next year as the owners and players' union once again could not reach a Collective Bargaining Agreement, leading to a lock-out that lasted for nearly half of a season. When the season resumed again in January, the Blues essentially continued with the philosophy that focused primarily on defense. In fairness, the offense improved some - from bad to average while losing only a little bit in defensive prowess. The results were solid, with the team finishing second in the very difficult Central Division.

As the Blues headed to the playoffs, I confess I had a concern. For 45 years, I had been hoping, wishing, and even occasionally praying (*and I'm not an especially religious person*) that the Blues would win the Stanley Cup. But I have to say that there was also a part of me that didn't want the Blues to win it *this year*. If the team were to pull it off in a strike-shortened year, it would be somewhat tainted and to some in the hockey world, an asterisk perhaps, and arguably not quite as meaningful. It would be akin to getting a hole-in-one in golf on a very short hole. If I'm ever going to get one (and unlike my dad who has done it three times I never have) I want it to be on a 200-yard hole (ideally over water and surrounded by an array of sand traps) not from 100 yards with a pitching wedge.

I needn't have worried about such ruminations and preposterous thoughts, though, as the Blues lost again to the same team, the Los Angeles Kings, and the same goalie, Jonathan Quick, with the same defensive approach. The Blues managed to light the lamp a paltry ten goals in six games, with every single game a one-goal game. I understand that Hitch is reportedly a great hockey mind, but after two years of this same approach, someone needed to explain that you need to be able to score more than 1.67 goals a game to win the Stanley Cup. His tendency to scream throughout the game, and in his trademark high-pitched voice - was also starting to rub some of the players the wrong way.

The good news was that some significant offensive help was on the way for the 2013-2014 season with the arrival of 22-year-old Russian sharpshooter Vladimir Tarasenko, and the emergence of 21-year-old skilled and hard-working winger Jaden Schwartz. Schwartz, in particular, was proving himself to be a strong two-way player who always gave his all and led the team with a plus 28 at even strength. With Steen, Oshie, Backes, Pietrangelo and Shattenkirk coming more into their own as well, the Blues now had a lot more depth to the offense and jumped to the seventh best offense in the NHL, while maintaining a first-rate defense - third overall in the League. That combination led to a great regular season with a franchise record 52 wins. Nevertheless, the 111 points was still only good enough for second place in the highly challenging Central Division.

Would the new-found offensive punch make a difference in the playoffs this year? To attempt to buttress the chances and overcome a perception that we were not as good as the elite teams in the area of goaltending, the Blues added former all-star goalie Ryan Miller with about 25% of the season left. Miller had won the Vezina trophy as the best goalie in the NHL in 2010 and was also the starting goalie for the U.S. Olympic team that captured the silver medal that same year.

But that was a couple of years ago. And Miller had been playing for a poor team in Buffalo and was used to seeing over 40 shots a night and where giving up three goals was considered a job well done. But the Blues were a far different team - a lot less shots against and far less action which can actually be disconcerting to many goaltenders. Further, with the Blues' style of play and limited offensive output, we often needed the goalie to surrender only one or two. In the nineteen games Miller started at the end of the regular season for the Blues in 2014, he was really no better than Halak or Elliott, and actually had a higher goals against average and lower save percentage.

Still, the conventional thinking was that because of his greater experience at age 33 and having played in the pressure of the Olympics, he was the kind of goalie who could put a team on his back and lead it to the Promised Land when it mattered. *I wasn't so sure from what I had seen but suppose you can't fault the Blues for trying.*

Unfortunately, the Blues ended the season in a funk on a season-worst six game losing streak which cost the team first place by one point. Worse, it meant that the Blues' first-round opponent in the playoffs was the 107-point Chicago Blackhawks, the top offensive team in the League. The Hawks were a star-studded team still coached by ex-Blue Coach Joel Quenneville and led on the ice by the dynamic duo of Jonathan Toews *(the guy we somehow thought Erik Johnson was better than)* and Patrick Kane *(arguably the most exciting player in hockey)* along with such other stars as Marian Hossa, Patrick Sharp, and Duncan Keith. It was not an ideal first-round match up for either team as both were among the best in the NHL. The teams had played each other very closely during the season with the Blues winning three games (two in a shootout) and the Blackhawks winning two games.

It looked like it would be a monster series between two powerhouse teams and coaches and it was. In Game 1, Jaden Schwartz tied the game with less than two minutes left in regulation to make it 3-3 and Alexander Steen scored the game winner in Triple Overtime - the longest playoff game in Blues' history. The teams combined for 94 shots on goal. I was worried that Miller, a beanpole of a man at 6 foot 2 and only 168 pounds, might evaporate from the nearly six hours of hockey and heavy pads.

If that wasn't enough hockey and excitement, two nights later they did it all again. And it was a remarkably similar outcome. Tarasenko scored with only 6.4 seconds remaining to tie the game and the Blues once again won the game in Overtime. The goal was scored by the unlikeliest of players and in a highly unlikely way.

The game winner was by Jackman, he with merely three goals in the entire 82-game season. He directed a wrist shot toward the net from a distance with the hope that someone might tip it or get a rebound and yet, instead, it somehow found its way through Corey Crawford's legs. Jackman had no idea that he had scored until he saw a teammate raise his arms. (It would bear some resemblance to what would later prove to be most important goal in Blues' history - the first goal in Game 7 of the Stanley Cup Finals).

In any case, the Blues had a second straight Overtime win by the identical score: 4-3. We now had two huge wins on home ice and a great start. This Blues' team seemed potentially magical. We would merely need to win two of the remaining possible five games to advance against a very dangerous team.

But, put the genie back in the bottle. The Blues never won another game in the series, although we were able to take two more of the games into Overtime. It didn't help that David Backes missed Games 3 and 4 due to a concussion from a brutal hit from Brent Seabrook. Or that we, once again, only scored 14 goals in the entire series. Miller started all six games in goal for the Blues and was fine but clearly wasn't a difference maker.

If there was any silver lining, four Overtime games and the valiant effort by the Blues may have taken its toll on Chicago and cost them a Cup (as the Blackhawks eventually succumbed two rounds later in Overtime of Game 7 to Los Angeles). But that did little to satisfy me or most Blues' fans. Another great team and another playoff failure. *I needed a new mantra.*

On to the 2014-2015 season with essentially the same guys, though with Miller now out of the picture the goaltending duties fell to Elliott and a young goalie the Blues were very high on, Jake Allen. Tarasenko had now emerged as a legitimate star with 37 goals and a team leading plus 27 at even strength. The Blues once again replicated their fine regular season and had a very balanced team; fifth in offense, fourth in defense, 109 points and a first-place finish. But how could the Blues finally convert their great regular season into an equally great post-season?

Once again, an analysis of the potential shortcoming or weakness, at least compared to other top teams, was the goaltending. Specifically, it was felt by the powers that be that Blues' goalies had never come close to winning the Cup before and lacked the experience many felt that it takes to "go deep" into the playoffs. *Don't tell that to Jordan Binnington!*

So, in another bold move, the Blues decided to bring in Marty Brodeur, one of the greatest goalies ever who had won 691 games (the most of all-time) in his long and storied career, including 113 playoff games, and three Stanley Cups. The problem was that Brodeur was 42 and hadn't played all year. Perhaps the Blues thought he could rekindle the magic of his youth for one more epic playoff run like the great Jacques Plante? Or perhaps the Blues just wanted him around to serve as a mentor and provide guidance to the Blues' less experienced tandem. After playing portions of seven games with the Blues, where Brodeur looked like a mere shell of himself, it was pretty clear that his role in the playoffs would be strictly limited to that of a mentor.

As the first-place team, the Blues avoided the Blackhawks and drew instead the Minnesota Wild, a team that was essentially a clone of the Blues as a top defensive team. Indeed, the Wild and Blues gave up the exact same number of goals for the year - tied for the fourth best in the League. The Blues had a little more offensive firepower but the Wild's style of play, coached by a young Mike Yeo, made scoring goals very difficult even for more explosive teams. *At least there was no Toews or Kane to deal with, right?*

It turned out not to matter whether we were playing an offensive or a defensive team; the result was eerily the same. Like the previous year, despite having the superior record during the season and home-ice advantage, the Blues lost the first-round in six games. And like in the previous year the Blues scored a total of exactly 14 goals in those six games - far below what would be required to actually win this thing.

And so, what did the Blues do to address the offensive woes in the playoffs over the past several years and attempt to make 2015-2016 different? Management traded T.J. Oshie, one of the Blues' best offensive players, and also probably the single most popular player among fans, to the Washington Capitals for Troy Brouwer. Brouwer was a veteran player who played hard and was a "gamer" and wound up scoring 18 goals for the Blues, and one especially big one in the playoffs, but he is and was no Oshie. The trade made little sense to most of the fan base, and still doesn't, but there was a sense that perhaps there were non-hockey factors that played a role in the decision. (A recurring theme in most of the Blues' bad trades: *See* Gilmour, Mullen Shanahan and Pronger).

The Blues also bid adieu to Barret Jackman after 13 years and over 800 games, the second most of any Blue all-time. Like all-time games' leader Federko, Jackman joined a Blues' Central Division rival (the Nashville Predators) for his swan song. It was surreal for him at that first encounter with the Blues to look across the ice and see the Blue Note - the only professional jersey he had ever worn while he was draped in mustard yellow. And it was a bit awkward to take a shot at Tarasenko and receive one from his friend Backes that first game - when he had just them and most of the team over for dinner at his place in Nashville the night before.

Like Federko, Jackman only played one season in a color other than Blue. In a class move, the Blues signed him to a one day contract the next year so that he could officially retire as a member of the St. Louis Blues.

In an effort to re-load for the 2015-2016 season, the Blues got a boost from two emerging youngsters: a 22-year-old giant defenseman with lots of skills in Colton Parayko and a 20-year old speedster with promising talent in Robby Fabbri, the team's first-round draft pick the year before.

Nevertheless, with the loss of Oshie and with Jaden Schwartz sidelined with an injury for most of the year, it was no surprise that the offense often sputtered, finishing 15th out of 30 teams. Still, the reliable defense remained stellar - once again 4th best in the NHL in goals allowed. The combination was good for another outstanding 107-point season and a second place finish this time. The Blues' award? Another date with the third place Chicago Blackhawks, who had just won the Stanley Cup the previous year.

Once again, the Blues had the better regular season record and home-ice advantage, and once again the Blues had won the regular season series against the Blackhawks 3-2. And yet the Blackhawks sure *felt* like the heavy favorites. They had won the Stanley Cup in two of the last three years. The Blues had never won the Stanley Cup, hadn't been to the Final in 45 years, hadn't been to the Conference Final in 15 years and hadn't won a playoff series at all in four years.

Similar to two years previously, the Blues won Game 1 at home 1-0 in Overtime, despite being outshot nearly two to one, 35-18. David Backes was the hero this time, but it only took one Overtime. While the Blues lost Game 2 at home, we shockingly won both Games 3 and 4 in Chicago, only one game from eliminating the reigning Stanley Cup Champs.

But then in Game 5, after the Blues rallied from a two-goal deficit in the third period to tie the game - only one goal away from advancing - Patrick Kane scored in Double Overtime to force a Game 6. The Blackhawks went home and took care of business, setting up a Game 7, back in St. Louis. The experienced clutch team loaded with prior Stanley Cup Champion players versus the playoff choke team. *I could hardly watch, but naturally I was there.*

It was a very close and tight checking game. And when Troy Brouwer, Oshie's replacement, broke up a 2-2 tie in the third period with the series-winning goal (a lucky awkward rebound goal that Brouwer conceded was the ugliest goal he had ever scored) it put a huge smile on my face and that of most of the 19,935 in attendance. A couple thousand of the fans were from Chi-Town. And, I am a little ashamed to say that I was kind of hoping that most were openly weeping all the way back home on Highway 55. *Not to be vindictive or a poor winner.* Finally, ding-dong the Blackhawks were dead!

It was just one year and one series, but it felt cathartic. To win a playoff round against anyone at this point was great. To do so against your biggest rival whom we had a terrible record against in the playoffs was that much sweeter.

But on a grander scale, the goal here was to win the Cup, and all we had really done was eliminate one team, though perhaps the most feared team in hockey. Still there were hopefully three more rounds to go. Next up on the slate was the Dallas Stars - a most familiar foe, whom the Blues had some success against in the past (except that 1999 season where the Hitchcock-coached Stars beat the Blues and won the Cup). Now, ironically, Hitchcock was coaching the Blues against his old team in the playoffs for the first time.

Although the Blues had dominated the regular season against Dallas (winning four of five games), Blues' history had painfully shown that doesn't really matter come playoff time. And the Stars were a very solid team. In fact, Dallas finished in first place ahead of the Blues for the season.

The Stars took Game 1 in Dallas. The Blues won game 2 in Overtime with David Backes once again getting the game winner. After yielding the first goal in Game 3 back in St. Louis, the Blues scored six straight to blow out the Stars 6-1. Dallas then won Game 4 in Overtime to even the series. The Blues responded with a win in critical Game 5 in Dallas, but with a chance to close out the series at home, the Blues lost Game 6. So it was down to a deciding Game 7. With the season on the line, the Blues turned in a remarkable performance scoring early and often with three goals in the first period and cruising for a 6-1 win in Texas. The Blues were heading to the Conference Final for the first time in 15 years!

But the glass half-empty guy in me couldn't help but notice that after two long and grueling series we were still only half way there. The next opponent was another old Blues' nemesis - the men in teal from the Bay Area who had eliminated our President Trophy squad in a huge upset in 2000, and then again in 2004. Like the Blues, the Sharks had never won the Stanley Cup, though they had been at this thing for a lot less time. But one of these teams would be heading to the Final with a chance to win their very first Cup.

The Sharks did not have as a good a record as the Blues during the regular season but were a deep and experienced team - likely the most experienced in hockey with numerous thirty plus star players: Joe Thornton, Joe Pavelski, Brent Burns, Patrick Marleau and Joel Ward to go along with a rising star in Logan Couture and a great young stud in Czech Tomas Hertl.

The Blues captured Game 1 at home with the game winner from Jori Lehtera but were shut out in Game 2 at home. The Sharks shut the Blues out yet again in Game 3, but the Blues rebounded with a six-goal outburst in Game 4 (two goals each from Brouwer and Kyle Brodziak) to win 6-3 and even up the series. It was now just two out of three games to decide the winner. Put another way, we were just two wins away from being in the Stanley Cup Final!

In the biggest hockey game in St. Louis since 1986 - thirty years before - the Blues took a 2-1 lead into the first period intermission. Deep into the second period the Blues held a 3-2 lead. But with about a minute and a half left in the period, Joe Pavelski tied the game on a power play, with assists from Joe Thornton and Logan Couture. With one period to play in critical Game 5 the Blues and Sharks were tied. *If I didn't have intestinal problems before, I certainly did now.*

The tie didn't last long. Once again Joe Pavelski was the villain, scoring the go-ahead goal just 16 seconds into the third period. He was no ordinary Joe. And that goal would hold up. The Blues couldn't score again, and the Sharks added two empty netters in the final minute to finish the scoring.

Game 6 in San Jose began as it had pretty much ended, when Joe Pavelski scored the first goal of the game to give the Sharks the lead. *Say it ain't so Joe.* The Sharks would add three more goals for a 4-0 lead before Tarasenko finally scored a pair of goals late in the third to cut the lead in half. But it was way too little, too late, and the Blues were done. The Blues' primary downfall once again was the inability to score; like a broken record, only 13 goals total in the six-game series.

The good news for Blues' fans was that it was a rare and significant playoff push. But, at the same time, it felt like a wasted opportunity. Yes, the Sharks were a very good team. But they were not like some of the other great teams that the Blues had lost to in years we had a legitimate chance - the Chicago Blackhawks, the Colorado Avalanche, the Detroit Red Wings or the Montreal Canadiens. This Sharks team felt beatable (they only had 98 points for the season and ultimately lost in the Stanley Cup Final in six games to Pittsburgh). In short, it seemed unlikely that the Blues would have an easier path to the Stanley Cup for a long time, if ever.

Coming closer to tasting the Cup in 2016 (though getting only essentially half the way there) just increased the fervor of Blues' fans to get there and "get 'er done." But how? There were so many great teams out there - teams just as dedicated and determined as the Blues, who were not about to feel sorry for us because we had never won a Cup. Toronto has been waiting even longer than St. Louis, though they had won several Cups in their much longer history. Frankly, some teams just had more talent than the Blues and many teams had a better goaltender. It just didn't seem like this would be happening for a very long time, if at all in my lifetime.

One significant change in the off-season was that the Blues let long time popular Captain David Backes walk and sign as a free agent with Boston. Backes had played his entire ten-year career with the Blues and was a great leader. But his skills had diminished, and it undoubtedly was the right move given the money he would command and salary cap considerations. Still, it was hard for some of the fan base that worshipped him (not just on but off the ice) and hadn't accepted that he was no longer among our best players.

On the plus side, the vacancy allowed highly regarded Alex Pietrangelo to assume a greater leadership role and serve as the Blues' 18th captain in history.

With better performances like the Blues finally had in the 2016 playoffs also came greater expectations. And thus when, in the next season, the Blues got off to a less than ideal start in the first 50 games (a slight winning record but in 8th place and far below what we had been achieving for the past five seasons) the Blues fired Ken Hitchcock in a surprise move and replaced him with his assistant Mike Yeo, the former Minnesota Wild coach who had upset the Blues in the first round of the 2015 playoffs. It was an emotional call for General Manager Armstrong to make, given his close friendship with Hitch and the fact that he had more regular season success than any coach in Blues' history - his career average of 1.3 points per game is surprisingly *numero uno* among all of the first-rate coaches who have led the Blues.

Moreover, the Blues were arguably the best team in hockey during the regular season in the Hitch-era. Nevertheless, one continual criticism of Hitch's style of play was the consistent lack of offense, and an apparent unwillingness to change his approach. And when it mattered most, the playoffs, the team was not able to match the regular season success.

Hitch's replacement, Yeo, was considered a bright hockey mind but also a guy who focused heavily on defense. So, it seemed like the Blues were simply replacing an experienced cerebral defensive style guy with his younger, less experienced (and thinner) clone. That said, the Blues did respond well to Yeo and complied a solid 22-8-2 mark under his leadership, finishing with a respectable 99 points, good for third place.

Certainly, a highlight during the year was St. Louis hosting its first Winter Classic against the rival Blackhawks on January 2, 2017 at a sold-out Busch Stadium. It was a surprisingly warm day for January and a wonderful scene with the Arch in the background and a bit of fog just to enhance the unique atmosphere. And for the cherry on top, the Blues won the game 4-1 behind two goals by Tarasenko.

Even the Blues' alumni prevailed in the old-timer's game versus their Chicago counterparts 8-7 (though it didn't hurt that the Blackhawks had to endure Blues' announcer and former goalie Darren Pang in their goal). Surprisingly, none of the

Blues' incredible starting five - Hall of Famers Gretsky, Hull, Oates, Pronger and MacInnis - scored. But Turgeon scored twice and Federko, Tkachuk, Stastny, Patey, Jackman and the Chaser each added a goal. Tkachuk touchingly wore the jersey of his beloved fallen "little brother" Pavol Demitra.

Come playoff time the Blues drew Mike Yeo's former team, the Wild, in the first round who with 106 points had finished second in the division. This time around - perhaps aided by Yeo's knowledge of his former team - the Blues defeated Minnesota in five games. Not surprisingly, all of the games were low scoring affairs. Indeed, the Blues only scored ten goals in the entire series and yet somehow won four of the games.

The Blues tried to repeat this formula against the next opponent - the far more skilled and offensive-minded Nashville Predators. We were able to dictate the style of play and keep the Predators' big scorers largely under wraps. But in six games, the Blues only scored 11 goals total - and lost four of the games. *Some things never change.*

I understand that playoff hockey is tighter, that the effort in checking and back-checking is much greater and that there isn't a lot of open space on the ice to maneuver. But other teams had found ways to score, by taking more shots, hunting ferociously for rebounds, and paying the price in front of the net by screening the goalie. The Blues' repeated inability to score many goals in the playoffs for years on end had become a systemic problem. It's either the system, the players or both. The tendency was always to blame the Blues' goaltender for our ills, but the real Achilles heel was lack of scoring. Until the Blues corrected that problem, we would never be able to win the Cup.

The 2017-2018 season presented another opportunity to become Stanley Cup Champions after 50 years of futility. To break this streak at the half-century mark would be pretty cool and provide a certain symmetry and magic.

The Blues had a fairly typical season with their usual strong defense (sixth in goals against) but struggled even more than usual with scoring (indeed, only seven teams in the NHL scored fewer goals). The Blues ultimately won twelve more games than we lost and finished the season with a reasonably respectable though not overwhelming 94 points.

It wasn't a dramatic difference from the prior season, but unfortunately it was just enough to miss the playoffs by a single point in arguably the best division in hockey. But for a poor ending - losing five of the last six games - the Blues would have made the playoffs. Indeed, if we had simply won *one* more Overtime or shootout (the team had six such losses during the year), the Blues would have been in the big show. But it was not to be. It had been six years since the Blues last missed the playoffs and it didn't feel very good.

The natives were growing restless and the ownership group - astute and loyal hockey fans who were determined to not only make the playoffs but actually compete for the Cup - was not pleased. It would be a long early summer for the boys in blue and management had a lot of time on their hands to see if there was a way to dramatically improve this talented but stagnant hockey team.

The Cup- Starved Blues Fans

The Blues had now played 50 full seasons in the Gateway to the West in search of Lord Stanley's Cup and come up with bupkis. The photo of the grand trophy on the opening night program on October 11, 1967, suggesting that it was a realistic goal to strive for, seemed like simply a tease and a cruel joke to those of us who had borne witness to the last five decades.

There had been several other sport franchises that had gone a half of a century without a championship before. But I would contend there had never been a franchise quite like this one; that had a better opportunity to win a championship for more than five decades and failed to come through even once.

For starters, the Blues made it to the Stanley Cup Finals each of the franchise's first three years - undoubtedly something that has never been done in sports history (or ever will be again). Granted the Blues were decided underdogs in each series as an expansion team, so the chances of winning in any one of those years was not great. But we were only four games away from Cup glory three separate times.

And it wasn't as if we didn't have numerous chances after that. The Blues made the playoffs an astounding 41 times in these 50 seasons - at one point 25 years in a row! This consecutive playoff streak has only been eclipsed by the Boston Bruins (29 seasons) and the Chicago Blackhawks (28 seasons) and each team has won several Stanley Cups, six and three respectively, since the Blues have been in existence.

Aside from the sheer quantity of opportunities we had, are the quality of those opportunities. So many of the greatest players ever to don a pair of skates have worn the Blues' sweater. Admittedly some were for only brief periods, like the greatest player of all time Wayne Gretzky and Hall of Famers, Glenn Hall, Jacques Plante, Doug Harvey, Dickie Moore, Scott Stevens, Glenn Anderson, Dale Hawerchuk, Phil Housley, Marty Brodeur, Peter Stastny, Guy Lapointe, and Paul Kariya. But others wore the Note for extended periods of time, like Hall of

Famers Brett Hull, Adam Oates, Bernie Federko, Chris Pronger, Al MacInnis, Brendan Shanahan, Joey Mullen, Grant Fuhr and Doug Gilmour. Beyond Hall of Famers, the Blues had many other all-star caliber players over the years: Barclay Plager, Red Berenson, Garry Unger, Curtis Joseph, Pierre Turgeon, Keith Tkachuk, Pavol Demitra, Rod Brind'Amour, T.J. Oshie, and current players Vladimir Tarasenko, Ryan O'Reilly, Jaden Schwartz and Alex Pietrangelo.

Naturally, all of these players were not on the Blues' roster at the same time - if they had been, they would be the greatest team ever assembled. But several were on the Blues together. One team had *seven* players who would make it to the Hall of Fame!

And they were not just talented guys who could never bring home the championship bacon; almost all won one or many Stanley Cups with *other* teams. Perhaps most galling and disheartening to me and my fellow comrades who bleed blue were the guys who played several years for the Blues searching valiantly for the big prize, only to eventually leave and then win their Stanley Cups with another team - Hull, Oates, Pronger, Shanahan, Mullen, Gilmour and Oshie to just name a few. There have been 39 of them!

Perhaps the statistic that makes the Blues' Cup futility entering the 2018-2019 season most unique, surprising and infuriating of any team that had never won a Championship was that ALL FOUR of the winningest coaches in NHL history spent extended time coaching the Blues, and three of the four got their starts coaching in St. Louis! No other team in any other sport in history can say that.

Scotty Bowman, the winningest coach of all time, coached the first three years in St. Louis before winning his NINE Stanley Cups with Montreal, Pittsburgh and Detroit.

Al Arbour, at one time the second winningest coach (now third) became a coach for the first time for the Blues on multiple occasions before leaving and winning four Stanley Cups at the helm of the dynasty New York Islanders.

Joel Quenneville, who eclipsed Arbour as the second winningest coach of all time, also began his head coaching career in St. Louis where he repeatedly produced some of the team's most successful regular seasons. But, like his legendary predecessors, Coach Q couldn't get the Blues over the finish line, like he did for the rival Blackhawks on three separate occasions after he left.

Ken Hitchcock, the fourth winningest coach in history, won his lone Stanley Cup with Dallas before he got to St. Louis (thanks in no small part to Blues' legend Brett Hull). Although Hitch also produced a lot of really good winning teams in St. Louis, he also wasn't able to pull a rabbit out of the Cup.

Even Jacques Demers who coached several years for the Blues led the Montreal Canadiens to Lord Stanley's place only *after* he severed ties with St. Louis.

Moreover, hockey has more parity than any other major professional sports, such that *any* team, including the eighth-place team who squeaks into the playoff on the last day of the season, stands a legitimate potential chance of upsetting the best team in the League. The Blues remember that all too well in 2000 when the eighth-place Sharks took down our President Trophy-winning team in the first round. And just this year, the Columbus Blue Jackets stunningly swept the Tampa Bay Lightning - one of the best teams to ever hit the ice. That virtually never happens in other sports. The likelihood of the New England Patriots or Golden State Warriors (the one with a healthy Curry, Thompson *and* Durant) dropping a first-round series is so much smaller. So, with 41 tries at this one would expect that the chances the Blues would have hit the jackpot at least once by now would have been extremely high.

In fact, not only had the Blues not won the Cup in 41 playoff chances, but we hadn't even *reached* the Final since those first three years. Only three times in 38 did the Blues get to the *Conference* Final (i.e. won two playoff rounds) - against Calgary in 1986, Colorado in 2001 and San Jose in 2016. And only in 1986 did we win three games in the Conference Final, close enough to even get a whiff of playing for the Stanley Cup.

The Blues' best teams and best chances in my view were in the Q era of 1997-2002, with Pronger and MacInnis on the back line, and some combination of Hull, Turgeon, Demitra, Courtnall, Young, Tkachuk and Weight up front and Fuhr and then Turek or Johnson in goal. But in five of those six years the Blues incredibly ran into the eventual Stanley Cup Champion early in the playoffs - be it Detroit, Dallas or Colorado. Most of those series were close, and there was a sense each time that if we had just been able to get past that team, we could win it all. But it was not to be.

So, as the Blues entered the 2018-2019 season, we were the only original expansion team without a Stanley Cup (directly or indirectly).

The Philadelphia Flyers were the first expansion team to win the Cup in both 1974 and 1975.

The Pittsburgh Penguins followed suit in 1992 and 1993, and then again in 2009, 2016 and 2017 after acquiring the game's then biggest star, Sidney Crosby.

The Minnesota North Stars, who became the Dallas Stars, finally accomplished the dream in 1999, thirty-one seasons after they began operations.

Even the Los Angeles Kings, not exactly a hockey haven, got a chance to experience the wondrous joy of winning the Stanley Cup in both 2012 and 2014.

While the only other 1967 expansion team, the California Seals/ Cleveland Barons did not technically win a Cup, they merged with the Minnesota North Stars in 1978, which became the Dallas Stars. So, one could say that at least some legacy of that Seals/Barons team also went on to win the Cup.

Since that time, numerous clubs have been added to the NHL and many have had a chance to drink from the Cup - the New York Islanders, Edmonton Oilers, New Jersey Devils and Colorado Avalanche have had an embarrassment of riches, each winning multiple Stanley Cups in their short existence by comparison. Indeed, Denver was treated to a Championship in the Avalanche's very first year of existence after moving there from Quebec. *That's just not fair!*

Even traditional non-hockey cities like Tampa Bay, Carolina and Anaheim have had the privilege of hoisting the game's greatest trophy. And last year the Washington Capitals finally broke their much publicized "long awaited" drought to capture glory – after a mere 43 years.

It was surely *our* turn for the Cup by now. But just because you had been waiting longer, deserved it or craved it more didn't give you a better shot.

The 2018-2019 Season
(A new year and a reason for optimism)

As the Blues entered the 2019-2019 season, management once again decided it was time to go "all-in" to try to win the Stanley Cup. Prior custodians of the team had tried this before several times with the best of intentions but it had often produced less than ideal results: the trade of Courtnall, Ronning, Momesso and Dirk for Butcher and Quinn in late 1991 to attempt to buttress the first place team's playoff chances but which instead harmed the Blues' mojo; the signing of Scott Stevens that led to the loss of five first round draft picks; the signing of Shanahan that led to the loss of Stevens and more draft picks; the hiring of Mike Keenan fresh off of his first (and only) Stanley Cup followed by the acquisition of the game's best player and biggest star Gretzky, which led to tremendous turmoil, including the loss of Gretzky and ultimately Hull; and the trade of Conroy for Stillman (no offense to the current majority owner with that name) that limited our ability to defend against the power play and the magnificent Joe Sakic in 2001.

But the Blues had missed the playoffs the previous year by one lousy point and had several key players approaching the age and stage where there would need to be a decision made whether to sign them long-term or let them go. Management appropriately felt the time was now and that the squad needed a few critical additions and a jolt to give us a legitimate shot.

In a monumental trade the Blues acquired Ryan O'Reilly, a first-rate cerebral center who played "a 200-foot game" (attention to sound defense as well as offense) and was great on face-offs (critical to controlling the puck). In exchange, the Blues gave away two overpaid players past their prime that we were likely looking to dispose of anyway (Patrik Berglund and Vladimir Sobotka - the former would shockingly walk away from the game and his $12.5Million contract during the year); a youngster in Tage Thompson who was considered to be very promising (though I saw little to get overly excited about from what I had seen so far); and two first round draft picks. It seemed like a great deal for the Blues. Buffalo fans - some of the more astute hockey fans from a city that has also had more than its share of sports suffering - were and still are outraged.

When O'Reilly first became a St. Louis Blues he had a phone conversation with General Manager Armstrong. Army welcomed him to St. Louis and O'Reilly expressed how excited he was to be with the Blues and promised: "I won't let you down." And when O'Reilly was introduced to legendary long-time Blue Bobby Plager, who told him how much he wanted - no *needed* - his Stanley Cup parade, O'Reilly didn't flinch over the lofty and arguably unrealistic expectations but rather told Bobby that he was "going to get him one."

We Blues' fans are hardly naïve - we had been through 51 seasons of trials and tribulations and high expectations, and we come from the "Show Me" not the "Tell Me" state. We are aware that platitudes and promises don't equate to performance. We have learned that bringing in new players and coaches, however talented, determined and well-intentioned, has never before been a cure for our Cup ailment. And we know from personal experience that one player - even the greatest of all time - does not assure a Stanley Cup or even a deep playoff run.

But, at the same time, there was something about O'Reilly's sincere manner that just generated confidence. If we weren't going to win the Cup, you knew that he was at least going to give everything within *his* power to *try* and make that happen.

To further improve the team down the middle - one of the big keys to a team's success - Armstrong acquired another veteran two-way center in Tyler Bozak as a free agent. He then inked former Vegas Golden Knight and twice former Blue, David Perron, to a free agent contract to add some veteran leadership and scoring punch. The signing was a surprise to many as the Blues decided to pay him a lot of money and lock him in for four years - the same guy management had (mistakenly) left unprotected in the draft only one year before.

And the Blues procured the services of the big local kid Patty Maroon for some muscle, net presence and additional leadership. The "Big Rig" was a free agent and closer to the end of his career than the beginning of it and was not commanding the offers that he liked. The Blues had less money to offer than some other teams as we were bumping up against the salary cap. But Maroon was hankering to play for his hometown team that he had grown up supporting and, more importantly, he wanted to spend more time with his young son who lived here. The opportunity to enjoy a year of living in the same town as his family is a rare one for most athletes and, to his credit, Maroon sacrificed a few dollars and likely an additional year of commitment, for that chance; he decided to sign a one-year year deal for what the Blues were offering.

The first game against Winnipeg would serve as a good barometer of how good a team we were, and if the Blues had made any meaningful strides from our one-point playoff miss the prior season and our four new significant acquisitions. Winnipeg had made it to the Conference Final the previous season, had young, talented and big-time scorers, an agile defense, and a first-rate goalie, and was primed to be one of the teams to beat for the Cup this year.

The game was at home and the crowd was pumped up after several months away from hockey and excited about a new season and an improved team. The house was packed with 18,292 dressed in their best Blues' gear with even NHL Commissioner Gary Bettman in attendance. *Did he know something we didn't - that this Blues' team was the real deal?*

And then the Blues went out and promptly laid an egg. As high as expectations were to begin the game and the season, they couldn't have been deflated sooner. Just four minutes into the game the Jets had a lead, one that they would never relinquish.

The Blues were competitive in play and even dominated for a good portion of the game, outshooting the Jets 42-25, but the quality of chances and the ability to convert them to goals as all hockey fans know matters far more than the total shots taken.

The Jets knew how to put the puck in the net and scored in every conceivable way: the first goal on the power play, the second goal short-handed, the third, fourth and fifth goals at even strength, before the Blues finally added a mercy goal late in the third to lose by a highly disappointing score of 5-1.

It was just one game in a very long 82 game schedule, but it left a bad taste in your mouth that this team may not be as good as advertised. When the Blues lost their second straight game at home to rival Chicago, a team not expected to even be a playoff team, there were immediate early concerns.

Fortunately, the Blues secured their first win of the season in Game 3 against a much-improved Calgary team since it would have been disastrous to start out the year by dropping the first three games - all at home. But the Blues then proceeded to lose the next three games in a row, dropping their overall record to an underwhelming 1-5. While six games represented only a little more than 7% of the season, falling behind early in the NHL is never wise, where there is great parity among teams and where it is more difficult than in most sports to make up a deficit in the standings due to the "Overtime loss" rule. Playing from behind in the standings in the Blues' Central Division is even more problematic since it is the deepest and most balanced in the NHL. Indeed, by year end the Central was the only division in hockey where every single team had a winning record.

In response to the less than stellar start, the team leaders and Coach Yeo said all the right things: the team understood their mistakes, were committed to rectifying them, and were confident in their process (after all, the team had shown good potential at times and for long stretches of games). There was nothing to panic about we were told.

And then a mere nineteen games in, the panic was in full bloom. At 7-9-3 and sitting in last place in the division after having just been shut out in Los Angeles against a Kings' team that was dead last in the conference, the Blues needed something to stop the bleeding. Often the victim in these scenarios in sports, rightly or wrongly, is the coach, and the Blues gave Mike Yeo the boot. He was gone about the same time that Lynn Patrick voluntarily turned over the head coaching reigns to Scotty Bowman in the Blues' very first year.

Yeo had been seen as a rising star coach in his early tenure with the Blues compiling a very credible 66-40-8 record in his first two years. But now he was out - just like that - less than 20% into the season. The Blues' ownership had seen enough to know that this team was not playing like a playoff team, much less like a serious Cup contender. And to ownership's credit, they wanted and expected to win now, especially after all they had invested.

That said, the likelihood of a new coach dramatically changing the fortunes of the team was very limited mid-year. Indeed, six other teams were sufficiently frustrated with their team's performance during the season to fire and replace coaches; none of those teams even made the playoffs.

Moreover, to be honest, the replacement coach was hardly someone that ignited a groundswell of excitement in the fan base. Few folks except the most hard-core following knew much about Craig Berube. Those who did, remembered him as a hard-nose player whose greatest contributions generally involved spending time - LOTS of it - in the penalty box. Indeed, he racked up more than 3,000 penalty minutes in his career. That's more than Barclay Plager and Brian Sutter combined! In fact, it's the 7th most penalty minutes in NHL history.

On the surface spending inordinate amounts of time in the penalty box is hardly an attribute you want to pass on to your team. But at one point in the NHL having a lot of penalty minutes was widely regarded as a positive thing because it meant you fought a lot, which demonstrated character and that you would stand up for and protect your teammates. That in turn, it was believed, would enable your star skill players to do their thing with more freedom and less harassment for fear of retaliation from the Berube "enforcer" types.

It's always been hard for me to reconcile the message that legalized fighting in hockey sends to kids, or to see much of a logical connection between how two enforcer "goons" fighting each other really serves to protect the skilled players who often aren't even on the ice at the same time. Yet, every Canadian-born hockey player and fan that I have ever spoken to swear that fighting is an essential part of keeping the sport "honest"- i.e. to reduce flagrant slashes to the hands and ankles often designed to injure star players. The great Mario Lemieux once called the NHL a "Garage League" for not sufficiently disciplining players who take such "liberties." The Canadian hockey "justice system" contends that fighting prevents this kind of behavior. If that's true, hockey has become a lot more dishonest since Coach Berube's day. Back in the 1980's and 1990's there was a better than even chance if you went to a hockey game you saw a fight break out as part of the package. In 2018-2019 the number of games with fights for all teams was down to 213 or 16% of all games. By comparison, the Detroit Red Wings alone once engaged in 154 fights in a single season!

Although Berube was widely thought of as a good man who had transitioned nicely into coaching, it would be fair to say that he was hardly someone that those "in the know" considered to be a top line coach, or even someone being groomed for prime time. He had a brief stint with the Philadelphia Flyers - taking over in 2013-2014 for a struggling team and leading them to the playoffs (and a first-round loss) and then being fired after the Flyers failed to make the playoffs the next season. In short, he had never coached an NHL team to a single playoff series win.

The Blues first hired "Chief" (the nickname derived from his unique Cree "First Nations" heritage) as a minor league coach with the Chicago Wolves in 2016. (*Does anyone else think it's odd that we had a minor league affiliate in the same city as our arch rival?*) In 2017, the Blues added him as an assistant coach to the big-league team. But if Berube was considered a coaching protégé it was a secret to the 31 other teams. It had been more than three years since Berube last had even a sniff at head coaching in the NHL.

When Armstrong announced Berube as the new coach and that he "was excited to work with Craig," he made it quite clear that this was purely on an "interim basis." And it was likely intended to be just that - to get the Blues through this season. Armstrong needed a change to shake things up and Berube was already there and knew the personnel. Further, as a guy who had been an "enforcer" as a player, perhaps he could add some toughness and motivate a talented team that was greatly underperforming. I suspect it also didn't hurt from a financial perspective that he was not an expensive hire since they were already obligated to Yeo and the year was looking like it would be a tough one at the box office.

If we could have hooked up Armstrong to a lie detector test on November 21 I suspect he was *hoping* that Berube could turn things around, but likely felt that the chances he could do so appreciably - enough to make this team into a playoff team, much less a Cup contender - was slim. Further, the likelihood that Berube would be the Blues' head coach to start the next season (assuming Armstrong wasn't fired himself if the Blues once again failed to make the playoffs) was also slight.

Berube's initial statement to the press reflected a very modest goal: "We've got to move forward, and we've got to get better." Behind the scenes, he sought a tough work ethic and to build up the team's dwindling confidence, a good instinctive reaction to where the psyche of the team stood. Early on in his tenure, he famously ripped down the standings that were routinely posted in the locker room in order to focus the guys on one game and one shift at a time, rather than the numerous teams between the Blues and a playoff spot.

The beginning of the Berube-led Blues' era hardly began in an auspicious manner. In the Blues first game with Chief running the show, the Blues lost soundly to Nashville 4-1 in the

Music City. But on the positive side, the team responded well in the next game against these same Predators winning handily 6-2 at home. It was perhaps our best game of the year to that point and our second-best goal output. *Was this a sign of things to come?*

Any thought that the Blues had turned the corner, however, was quickly dispelled as we were thrashed at home the next night by Winnipeg 8-4. And then we dropped three of the next four games to lowly Detroit, Arizona and Edmonton, the loss to Arizona by an embarrassing 6-1 margin - one of the Blues' worst outcomes in a year replete with bad outcomes.

After 26 games, nearly one-third of the season, the Blues had lost 17 of them. Someone forgot to tell the guys that winning wasn't illegal. The guys looked defeated before they stepped on the ice. The frustration level among fans had reached a crescendo; the loyal folks who bled blue were about to bleed *out*.

And then in the next game, the Blues extinguished the Winnipeg demons. We not only beat a Jets' team that had crushed us three times but blanked this offensive powerhouse in their own building, where they hadn't been shut out all year. And the star of this effort? The much maligned and frequent scapegoat for everything bad in Blue at the time, Jake Allen, who stopped all 26 Jet shots in a brilliant 1-0 effort.

Could this finally be the confidence and momentum swing that we had been lusting for? The Blues returned to home ice against a relatively weak Vancouver Canuck team to prove that the win over the Jets was no fluke… and we were unceremoniously demolished 6-1. In my entire career of following the Blues, including some pretty poor seasons, I can't remember a season or time where the Blues lost so many lopsided games, often against weaker competition and mostly at home. In a sport where the vast majority of games are close with rarely more than a goal or two separating the teams, the Blues had already lost seven of their first twenty-eight games by three or more goals, five of them on home ice. And we had lost two of the last three games by a combined ten goals to two of the worst teams in the NHL!

What made this particularly maddening to Blues' faithful is that the guys would often intersperse such cataclysmic failures with a few fantastic games and outcomes: we defeated a star-studded Toronto team in their own building, were the first team to shut out Winnipeg in The Peg, beat a Calgary team that would ultimately lead the Western Division with 107 points, annihilated talented San Jose and Nashville and possessed two early wins over the Stanley Cup runner-up Vegas Golden Knights.

The Blues were clearly a team that could play with and beat the best, even on the road. And yet, we were also capable it seemed of losing to a minor league team. Yes, there is a lot of parity in the NHL and the margins between winning and losing can be small and luck can play a factor, but the disparate results the Blues were getting from game to game, night to night, were unlike anything I had witnessed in my five decades of following this team.

Was it a lack of motivation, effort or discipline against the less skilled teams? A bad "system" or the inability of certain players to adhere to that system? The inability to play well if we got behind? Overconfidence? Under confidence? It was likely some or all of the above. But whatever the reason(s), it was perplexing and frustrating to fans and undoubtedly to the coaching staff, ownership group and the players themselves. Time was clearly running out to have a reason to believe in and care about this season.

At this point in the schedule, the Blues had thirteen games to play before reaching the halfway point of the season - 41 games into an 82-game grueling schedule. If the Blues were going to make a significant dent in the point deficit and show that we still had the potential to go on a big run and get into playoff potential position, now was clearly the time to do it. Everyone knew the importance of this stretch. Not only would it likely determine the team's chances to compete for a playoff spot, but it could well impact the future of certain key players and indeed the Blues' franchise for years to come.

If the Blues were clearly not in the playoff hunt, it would suggest that the chemistry of this team was not one likely to make a deep playoff run in the future and, thus, that it may be time to dispose of certain expensive assets and trade them for younger talent; to regroup and plan for the future - the common plan these days for unsuccessful teams. Everyone who did not own a full no-trade clause (Tarasenko) was conceivably on the trading block, especially those making a lot of money or who would be in the near future. There was talk about trading Pietrangelo, Schenn, and others. The players knew it. It was a stressful time for them and for General Manager Armstrong. Many in the Lou were calling for his job. Thirteen games to turn things around or at least provide a direction to turn.

But the next thirteen games provided no clear answers. The team clearly started playing better and for longer stretches during games and looked more like a competitive team. Even in games that we lost, in some cases badly, we appeared to have the better of the play for much of the game - in particular, back to back losses to the Pittsburgh Penguins and New York Rangers at home. And yet the results continued to be underwhelming: 7 wins, 6 losses. It was nowhere near enough to make a meaningful move into playoff contention, but not so bad as to suggest that this team couldn't be pretty darn good at their best. But was it already too late?

The oddsmakers sure thought so. I was at a casino in Biloxi, Mississippi where I took my Dad for his 89th birthday, and there was a spanking new legal sportsbook thanks to Mississippi law and the Supreme Court's decision in <u>Murphy vs. the NCAA, NFL, MLB, NBA, and NHL</u>, affirming the rights of states other than Nevada to have legal sports wagering without federal interference.

The Mississippi sportsbook listed the odds of the Blues winning the Stanley Cup on January 14, 2019 at 300-1. I have great admiration and respect for oddsmakers. I believe that they generally know a lot more about the probability of a sporting outcome than former players, coaches and so-called "expert" commentators. They use sophisticated modeling and actual math and have resources not necessarily available to the world at large. They have to post thousands of lines, often on fairly short notice, and they generally do their job extremely well. They have millions of reasons to do so: it's *their* money on the line.

A 300-1 proposition is not just a long shot; it borders on the impossible. To put this number into some kind of sports' perspective, the biggest longshot in Super Bowl history is generally considered to be the New York Jets' upset win over the Baltimore Colts in 1969. Despite Broadway Joe's bold prediction that the Jets would win the game, the AFL (the Jets' League) was widely considered at the time to be greatly inferior to the NFL (the Colts' League). The NFL's Green Bay Packers had demolished the AFL's Kansas City Chiefs and the Oakland Raiders in the first two Super Bowls, not unlike what the Montreal Canadiens did to the expansion Blues in our early years. Indeed, the Jets were an 18-point underdog and I understand that Jet bettors on the money line (a bet to win the game outright without any points) were reportedly given 7 to 1 odds (though that seems really low for an 18-point spread in my experience).

When Buster Douglas shocked the world and beat the seemingly invincible Mike Tyson for the heavyweight title the odds of that occurring were an astounding 42-1.

And when an unheralded horse with a great hockey name resemblance, Giacamo, upset a field of great horses in the Kentucky Derby in 2005, having never even won a race before (and only once since), it paid a hearty 50-1.

The oddsmakers were essentially saying that my Blues' chances of winning the 2019 Stanley Cup at this point of the season was deemed at least SIX times less likely than any of those events.

The likelihood of the Blues winning the Stanley Cup in 2019 was no doubt exceedingly small - and I had no illusion that it was actually going to happen. But I felt the oddsmakers had made a rare mistake and that the Blues' true odds were considerably lower than 300-1 given the talent on this team, the ability to defeat the best teams, and the parity of the NHL in the unlikely event that we were to make the playoffs. It was, nevertheless, a huge long shot - probably at least 100-1. I don't ever play the lottery and I don't make a habit of betting on 100-1 propositions either, even if someone is offering much greater odds, since it means that I should still lose 99 out of 100 times.

The logical mathematical side of my brain that usually wins any debate was wrestling with the emotional side which made a compelling argument: Wouldn't it be incredible if after all of these years of great players, coaches, and teams that could have *legitimately* won a Stanley Cup but never did, that it would be *this* Blues' team that was in last place in the entire League at the half-way point who pulled it off? It would be beyond magical; it would be legendary and one for the ages.

I was also acutely aware that St. Louis' sports teams had a long tradition with miracle championships. I was just five years old in 1964 when the St. Louis Cardinals baseball team trailed the Philadelphia Phillies by 11 games on August 23 and stood in fourth place. Despite a big winning streak, the Cardinals remained six games back with only twelve games to play. But thanks to the "Philly Pfold," the Cardinals were able to eke out winning the National League by one game over the Phillies and the Cincinnati Reds and then go on to win the World Series against the New York Yankees. What were the odds of that? *Perhaps that's why Philly fans are so bitter.*

And then almost fifty years later the Cardinals were 4 ½ games behind the Atlanta Braves for the National League wild card spot with 15 games left in the 2011 season. Then Atlanta collapsed, and the Cards went 11-4 and made the playoffs. After defeating the Philadelphia Phillies and Milwaukee Brewers in two very close playoff series to advance to the World Series, the Cardinals found themselves down three games to two against the Texas Rangers. Worse, they trailed in Game 6 by two runs in both the 9th inning and 10th innings and were down to their last strike on each occasion. And yet somehow, miraculously, they prevailed: the local boy David Freese hit a game tying triple in the 9th and Lance Berkman produced a game-tying single in the 10th before Freese hit a homerun in the 11th inning to win the game. The Redbirds then won Game 7 the next night. The odds of all of that happening had to approach if not exceed 300-1.

And then there was the 1999-2000 St. Louis Rams. They had years of futility and finished in last place the previous season. In an effort to improve their fortunes, the Rams made a splash by signing free-agent Quarterback Trent Green. But in a meaningless pre-season game against San Diego (which I attended with my daughter) Green suffered a devastating season-ending injury, ending even the remote hope of fans that the Rams might have a competitive year.

Without any meaningful alternative at that late date, the Rams turned to a former college quarterback from Northern Iowa who had not even been drafted and had spent most of his football days since playing Arena League and in Europe when he wasn't bagging groceries for Hy-Vee. The Rams took him out of the grocery aisle and put him into the huddle, where naturally the young man, Kurt Warner, led the Greatest Show on Turf and catapulted the Rams to the Super Bowl. I was told that the odds of the Rams winning the Super Bowl after Green's injury that year were posted *at exactly 300-1*! Now that's spooky.

And so, I decided to make an uncharacteristic wager on a long-shot. I looked to see what cash was still remaining in my wallet from a day of less than impressive wagering and all I saw was a $10 and a $20 bill. I stared at Alexander Hamilton and at Andrew Jackson - neither could offer much guidance when it came to hockey. I instinctively reached for Mr. Jackson and was soon was the proud owner of a $20 ticket on the Blues to win the Stanley Cup that would pay $6,020 (if only I had sacrificed both or, better yet as my wife admonished later, gone to the damn ATM machine and put a couple hundred down!)

As the Blues entered the second half of the season, the coaches and management sought to identify why the team's performance fell so short of expectations. There are always lots of factors and excuses when teams underachieve. Some espoused the argument that there were several new players and that they just had to adjust and get acclimated to playing with each other. It was understandable there could be a transition period before players got use to each other's tendencies and developed important personal bonds, but it had been 40 games and it was hard to believe that this was a material factor in the significantly underachieving performance of the Blues. After all, these are professional hockey players who were used to playing with different folks throughout their careers. Further, all four of these new additions were seasoned veterans.

Others pinpointed a lack of confidence - the Blues had lost many close games and after a while that can mess with your head. Some contended that this team just lacked the right chemistry; sometimes even the best laid plans just don't pan out the way you thought.

And there were plenty of standard "on-ice" factors to highlight, including a propensity to take bad penalties at inopportune times, mental mistakes and poor decision-making leading to way too many odd-man rushes, and a weak power play. Perhaps the biggest of these factors may have been poor shooting: some combination of failing to shoot often enough (an obsession with passing the puck and trying to make the perfect play), failing to shoot quickly enough (before the shot gets blocked), shooting right into the goalie's pads (unable to lift the puck or put it in the corner) and completely missing the goal.

But the overwhelming reason many ascribed to the team's poor record was goaltending. Jake Allen, a very talented goalie who at times and for stretches in a game could play at an elite level, routinely gave up soft goals where he was overcompensating, out-of-position or screened - which he seemed to be a disproportionate number of times. In a position where confidence is huge, he often looked demoralized. In fairness to Jake, the team seemed to play its worst when he was in goal, leaving key players uncovered, getting routinely caught on odd-man rushes, and failing to clear the net to give him good sight lines, the area of the game where Allen seemed to struggle the most.

In any case, there were undoubtedly serious questions and ruminations going on in Doug Armstrong's head about whether the Blues ought to be sellers - dispose of some of the high-priced valuable talent to teams more in the running and accumulate young talent and rebuild for the future. Army undoubtedly received numerous inquiries and offers for players which must have been tempting as the Blues' chances of making the playoffs, much less a serious run for the Cup, were diminishing and near extinct. How close he actually came to pulling the trigger remains buried in the recesses of his cerebellum, but for whatever reason he decided to stick with the plan at least a little while longer. Perhaps it was faith in the players he had assembled and his initial decisions, or his "gut" instinct. Perhaps it was recognition by him that his job was every bit on the line as well and would not likely be enhanced if the team traded key players and the team did even worse.

The team and coaching staff also finally bought into the narrative that fans were espousing - that a change was needed in goal. The problem was that we had no one really to turn to. The Blues stellar back-up from the prior season, Carton Hutton, was now with Buffalo, unable to commit to two starting goalie type salaries in the salary cap-conscious NHL. Chad Johnson, the back-up goalie hired to start the season, made Jake Allen look like Patrick Roy and had to be released. The Blues' third-string goalie - highly regarded but young and untested Ville Husso - was injured.

So, the job for the moment essentially fell by default to the man fourth on the totem pole - a rookie goaltender playing in San Antonio, Texas who few in the Lou had ever even heard of, named Jordan Binnington. By rookie, it didn't mean that he was super young. He was 25 years old. The fact that he had wallowed around in the Blues' organization for more than 200 minor league games from the Owen Sound Attack to the Kalamazoo Wings to the Chicago Wolves to the Providence Bruins to the San Antonio Rampage for the last seven years, getting all of twelve minutes of NHL action under his belt in 2016 in relief of Brian Elliott, is testament to how little the Blues actually thought of him. The fact that 31 other teams likely could have acquired Binnington at the beginning of the year for a little more than a low-level prospect and perhaps a few Budweiser's and some toasted ravioli is pretty indisputable.

For anyone in the Blues' organization to say that they *knew*, or even had much of an inkling, that this kid was good enough to play in the NHL, much less start, much less lead a team to the playoffs, much less win playoff round after playoff round and then ultimately the Stanley Cup is hogwash. It shows frankly just how difficult it is to assess talent and potential and how wrong the "experts" can be. For every Jordan Binnington out there, who ultimately does get his chance to prove his mettle, there are undoubtedly numerous others, in every sport, who never get the chance, and are glossed over because according to the assessment of a scout or a coach they weren't big enough, strong enough or fast enough. Or they were simply a late round pick and did not secure a large signing bonus and thus were not deemed worthy of a full and fair unbiased opportunity.

Binnington got his first NHL start on January 7, 2019 in Philadelphia. Some athletes start their professional careers with a whimper and others with a bang. One game doesn't define who you are or what you will become. But there isn't anything much better for a young athlete making a professional debut than to get off to a good start. It proves to you (should there be any internal doubts circulating) that you can do this and that you belong, and it inspires confidence in your teammates and coaches as well.

Binnington's first effort was a clear bang. Facing 25 shots on goal, he stopped all 25 in a 3-0 victory. "Binner" had his first career shutout in his very first NHL start, something only accomplished by 35 goalies in NHL history - and none of them named Hall, Plante, Brodeur, Hasek or Roy.

The night before this game, as legend now tells it, five Blues players (Schwartz, Steen, Edmondson, Bortuzzo and Fabbri) paid a visit to a private club (not technically a "bar") in South Philly called Jacks. It was a Sunday and the hometown Eagles were battling the Chicago Bears in an NFC playoff football game, so the place was hopping with excitement. The players were mingling well with the regular patrons, as hockey players are famously good at with a few beers in the gut. And they were enjoying the exuberant atmosphere of the place - it didn't hurt the celebration that the Eagles pulled off a big upset when the Bears' field goal kicker hit the crossbar and missed a game-winning field goal with ten seconds left.

The Blues' players became particularly amused and enamored with one Jacks' member who insisted that the DJ play Laura Brannigan's 1982 hit "Gloria" after every break in the action when the game was muted for commercials. The obsessive fan would repeatedly shout out to "Play Gloria!" and the DJ would accommodate him with the upbeat song. The tune stuck in their heads and the next night, after the Blues' victory, the guys who attended Jacks decided to play Gloria in the locker room. It soon became the Blues' anthem played after every winning game.

When the Blues embarked on a winning streak and later the playoffs, the whole Gloria thing metastasized. It was a fun story, especially given that many of the Jacks' members were loyal Philadelphia Flyers' fans. But given their fondness for the Blues' players they met, and the Flyers increasing ineptitude, they adopted the Blues as their own team come playoff time, holding huge parties wearing Blues' jerseys and being visited by Blues' fans and ex-players from as far away as the Lou. Naturally, commercialism entered the fray and with it lots of t-shirts, money, and legal trademark disputes. Good old classic American capitalism at work.

    The Blues were naturally pleased with Binnington's first effort but no one (from Armstrong to Coach Berube to the other players) likely thought this young man was going to be the team's salvation or even the starting goalie the rest of the season. The prevailing view undoubtedly was that he would get some more chances and hopefully progress, and perhaps help get Jake Allen get back on track with some competition. Binnington was not slated to be a starting goalie this year, if ever, much less a star. But Binnington wasn't buying it. And he was not done with his heroics - not by a long shot.

    The Blues played the next night in Dallas with Allen in goal and lost 3-1, with Jake allowing three goals on just 17 shots. So, in the next game vs Montreal, Binnington got his second chance and the team won again - though his streak of perfection ended when he gave up his first goal, the only one in 29 shots on goal. Berube decided to put him back in the pipes for the next game against Dallas on the road and Binner secured yet another win and fine performance: 3-1. The Blues then went back to Allen against the powerful Washington Capitals on the road and Jake responded with one of his best games of the season - a 4-1 win over the reigning Stanley Cup Champs. Apparently, competition was a good motivator. It also meant that the Blues had now won three games in a row for the first time all season.

    The problem with a modest three game winning streak at this point in the season was that it felt bitter sweet; the sobering reality was that the Blues were not about to make the playoffs barring something extraordinary. And by adding points at this juncture we were just moving down in the draft pecking order and reducing our chances to get some great young talent, ideally the purported next superstar in Jack Hughes, who would become available at year end and who might just revolutionize a team for the next decade.

And there was also part of winning a few in a row that actually made fans feel *more* frustrated - showing the team's talent and potential at a point of the season when it was nearly mathematically lost just highlighted what *could have been* had we just gotten it together sooner.

The Blues fell back to reality the next night with a 2-1 Overtime loss to the New York Islanders and their stellar young goalie Robin Lehner. It was Binnington's first loss in the NHL, though he played very well and once again limited the opposition to only one goal in regulation. That was followed by another loss at Boston behind Allen, a win against Ottawa with Binnington and another loss against last place Los Angeles in Binnington's worst start of his career - allowing four goals on 29 shots.

Unfortunately, it appeared that order had now been restored to the Blues' topsy-turvy season. Despite the earlier modest winning streak, the playoffs were now even less likely with the recent losses and with more games having ticked off the schedule - we were now already up to Game 48. I could confidently use my Stanley Cup wager ticket as kindling for the fire. Or perhaps I would buy a similar ticket each year and make a collage of them and frame them to display the Blues' futility.

But an unlikely lucky charm was on the way. In addition to the odd warm fuzzy coming from Philly of all places (the same place whose cops mercilessly beat the Plagers and other Blues with billy clubs), the Blues had another heart-warming story in the legend of this season. This one came from an 11-year old St. Louis girl with an extremely rare auto-immune disorder in need of a bone marrow transplant. She was a huge Blues' fan, egged on by her father's obsession with the sport as a young boy himself in Minnesota. As hockey players are prone to do, because they are truly the nicest professional athletes *off* the ice, some of the Blues' players were visiting Children's Hospital where they met Laila and heard of her predicament. The team hosted a "Be the Match" event at a home game inspired by her.

Little Laila Anderson got her bone marrow transplant and through the long ordeal was befriended by many of the players. She developed a particularly special bond with the Blues' biggest man Colton Parayko and he would regularly visit and stay in touch with her. Laila alternated between her time in the hospital and her home but was not allowed by doctors to go out in public because of the risk of infection.

As the Blues were trying to emerge from the doldrums of this very difficult season, Laila provided inspiration to the team - they knew she was going through a lot more than they were and handling it with dignity, grace and an incredible fighting spirit. Indeed, while she tried herself to stave off infection, her optimism was infectious. On a visit with her on January 18, 2019 Parayko tried to encourage her in her recovery by telling her that he hoped to see her at some games later in the year. According to the St. Louis Post Dispatch, her Dad piped up: "Well, if you make it to the Stanley Cup Final, Laila might be able to go - no pressure." Parayko smiled widely and promised: "I'll see what we can do."

And then, sure enough, the Blues started winning: First a win on the road at Anaheim, then at Columbus and then at Florida, rallying from a 2-0 deficit in the third period to prevail 3-2. The next few games would surely bring the Blues back to reality. After all, the next team on the schedule was the best team in the NHL: Tampa Bay. The Lightening were the highest scoring team in the NHL and also one of the best defensive teams, and on pace to break the all-time record for points in a season. And we were playing them in Tampa where they had only lost five games all year to that point. It would be a test for the Blues and their new netminder to even keep the game close.

The Blues played a very solid game and even outshot the Lightning but couldn't score on their star Russian goalie, Andrei Vasilevskiy. But Binnington matched him save for save as the game headed to Overtime tied at zero. Shortly into the extra session, the Blues' Vince Dunn took a bad penalty, but the referee decided to also issue one to Tampa's Brayden Point as well for "embellishment." (I never understood how a player could be called for a penalty based upon the way he reacted to an *actual infraction*; if he was embellishing a *non-infraction* to try and earn a penalty that would be different. But I will take off my logical lawyer hat and put on my Blues' one and just be happy that the Blues got a break this time.)

And I was especially happy when less than two minutes later, the Blues' own Braydon (Schenn) scored the game winner, producing a shocking 1-0 win and the team's fourth straight victory. It was not only the first time that Tampa Bay had been shut out all year - it would be the *last* time as well! To further show how impressive a win this was, Tampa proceeded to reel off ten wins in a row thereafter scoring 45 goals in the process, a whopping 4.5 per goal average. The win solidified any doubt that Binnington, now often referred to by fans as "**Winning**ton," should be given the chance to be the team's Number 1 goalie.

After the game, Binnington was swarmed by the media, some of who were mesmerized by the play of someone who had never played at this level. He was asked by one reporter whether he gets nervous out there, playing in so many tight games. Binnington calmly shrugged off the question and famously asked one of his own: "Do I look nervous?"

But there was no time to rest on the best accomplishment of the year. Despite the win and the four-game winning streak, the Blues still stood in 5th place in the Central division and meaningful distance from a playoff position.

Moreover, the rival Nashville Predators were next up on the schedule, arguably the most talented team in the Western Conference who had had their way with the Blues the previous year. And the Blues would have to play them back-to-back home and away games. Regardless of the opponent, the number of sweeps in the NHL's beloved back-to-back games is very small, so at minimum that would presumably end the streak.

Once again, the Blues defied the odds. The Blues defeated the Predators 3-2 in St. Louis with Binnington back in the net stopping 29 shots. The next day, with Jake Allen in goal, the Blues were in Nashville and won 5-4 in Overtime, with Vladi Tarasenko scoring a hat trick. He also tallied perhaps his best goal of the year in the first few seconds of Overtime (the "Josi-Juuse"). Tarasenko gathered the puck from O'Reilly on his backhand and raced past Predators speedster Viktor Ardvidsson into the Predators zone, where he was confronted by all-star defenseman Roman Josi. He then sharply cut back to his left sneaking the puck through his skates to his forehand and completely undressed Josi. He was now all alone on Preds' backup goalie Juuse Soros. As Juuse came out of his net, Tarasenko quickly fired the puck past him into the corner, stick-side for the game-winner. Allen was also spectacular, stopping 40 shots on goal. Clearly, Binnington's great play was raising Jake's game as well.

Winning six in a row stirred the blue blood in the faithful - maybe we still had a chance after all. We were now in 18th place overall in points - we had made up considerable ground but still had a way to go to secure a playoff berth. Nevertheless, after beating two of the best teams in the League (one of them twice in a row) some were starting to believe that this could actually happen. And if we could get in, anything was possible. Indeed, if the Blues could just make the playoffs we could be a handful for any team, given the team's performance against the top teams in the NHL and what we had been through to get there. But first things first. There was a lot more winning that needed to take place between now and the end of the season.

And the Blues accommodated. We blasted New Jersey at home for our seventh in a row, won our eighth in a row at Arizona, our ninth in a row at Colorado, our tenth in a row at Minnesota and our eleventh in a row, back at home and in dramatic fashion against Toronto with O'Reilly scoring the game-winner 34 seconds into Overtime. Binnington carried the bulk of the load during the streak but Allen contributed as well with a stellar shutout win at Colorado. Indeed, the Blues' goalies combined for three shut-outs in a row and a scoreless streak of over 213 minutes during the streak. Step aside Glenn Hall and Jacques Plante!

As a result of the record eleven-game win streak - the longest in Blues' history - the Blues now had the 13th best record overall and would make the playoffs barely if the season ended right now. Incredible! But there was a long way to go and lots of teams in close contention. The Blues could hardly afford to sit on their laurels.

The winning streak ended in the next game against the Stars in Dallas. But it showed the Blues and the rest of the NHL what this team was capable of. For fans, the winning streak was a drug; once we tasted the addictive high of victory we wanted more - a lot more.

The Blues bounced back from the loss to the Stars with a big home win over Boston in a shootout, with Binnington stopping 31 of 32 shots and five of six shootout attempts, before Sammy Blais won it for the Blues on our fifth shoot-out attempt. A good sign and omen for things to come.

Then the Blues went into a little bit of a funk. We won a couple of big games - against Nashville yet again and on the road against Sidney Crosby and the lethal Pittsburgh Penguins. But the team also sprinkled in a few stinkers against lowly Arizona, Ottawa and Buffalo. Fortunately, some of the competition for a playoff spot began to struggle, especially the Minnesota Wild and Anaheim Ducks.

And as the season hit the home stretch, the Blues recaptured the mojo and ran off victories in eight of the last ten to not only make the playoffs but finish third in the Central Division with 99 points. The Blues actually finished tied with second-place Winnipeg but were behind them due to the tiebreaker rules. Indeed, had the Blues merely gotten one more point we would have finished first in the division since we owned the tiebreaker over first-place Nashville that finished with 100 points.

In looking back, the Blues lost a point we easily could have won in the third to last game of the season, with an Overtime shootout loss to sixth place Chicago. Had the Blues won the shootout instead, the Blues would have finished in first place. That would have created a totally different dynamic - the Blues would have drawn Dallas in the first, not the second, round and if we advanced, played Winnipeg or perhaps Nashville in the second round - starting the series at home rather than on the road. Given the Blues far better play on the road in the playoffs and great start to the playoffs, the result could well have been completely different and less favorable under that scenario. In short, it's crazy to think that we may have never have been talking about the Blues' first Stanley Cup in five decades had Bozak, O'Reilly or Tarasenko scored on their shootout attempts against Cam Ward, or if the Hawks Jonathan Toews had missed his attempt against Jake Allen - the lone shootout goal. It was all possibly a great blessing in disguise - and yet another inadvertent gift from our friendly rivals from Illinois.

In any case the Blues were back in the playoffs after a one-year hiatus. It was an amazing roller coaster ride to get there. It was expected at the outset, then increasingly less expected, then "unlikely," then "definitely not," then "perhaps just maybe" and then, "I can't believe we're in the playoffs."

Regular Season Wrap-Up

The Blues were a total enigma and had one of the strangest regular seasons ever produced by a hockey team or any sports team. Yes, we were actually the worst team record-wise for the first half of the season and actually the best team record-wise for the second half. But even that doesn't really begin to describe the strangeness and how Jekyll and Hyde this team was. Even within the forgettable first half when we had a terrible record, we had some monstrous wins. And even within the memorable second half when we were winning at a pace not seen in the Lou, we had some bad losses.

In fact, there was one odd consistency throughout the season: the better the opponent, the better we played; the worse the opponent, the worse we played. The Blues' record against most of the best teams in the League was nothing short of incredible. We beat Tampa Bay, the best team in the NHL by far and one of the best teams ever in the regular season, in *both* games we played them. The Blues were the only team in the League to go undefeated against the Lightning. The Blues also beat the 2018 Stanley Cup Washington Capitals *both* times we played them. And we won all three games against the Stanley Cup runner up Vegas Golden Knights and clearly one of the best teams in the NHL. The Blues also went undefeated against the high-powered and talented 100 point plus Toronto Maple Leafs. And against the rival Nashville Predators, arguably the most talented team from top to bottom in the Western Conference, we won 4 of the 5 games. Thus, against five of the premier teams in the NHL the Blues' record was a mind boggling 13 and 1!

However, when it came to weaker teams - teams that did not even make the playoffs - it was a completely different story. The Blues went a dreadful 1-4 against the rival Chicago Blackhawks, 1-3 vs Minnesota, 0-2 against the New York Rangers, 1-2 against the lowly Arizona Coyotes, and 1-2 against the last-placed Los Angeles Kings. That's a combined 5-15 against five of the worst teams in the League. Go figure!

The good news for Blues' fans, therefore, was that we would only be playing good teams in the playoffs. And, by definition, there would be no *non-playoff* teams on the schedule from here on out. Unfortunately, however, one of the only top teams that we did not play well against was our first opponent, the Winnipeg Jets.

The tremendous turnaround to the season clearly coincided with the emergence of rookie Jordan Binnington as the starting goaltender. How good was Binnington? In the 32 games he had played he won a startling 27 of them - his 81.7% winning percentage was the best of any of the approximate 70 goalies to play a game for the Blues in history (and that includes Glenn Hall and Jacques Plante). And his 1.89 goals against average was number one among any goalie in Blues' history playing more than four games in a season. It was also the best average in the entire NHL this year.

The transformation of the Blues was not solely attributable to much better goaltending. The team also developed a more sustained and vicious forecheck, especially in the opponent's zone, cleaned up many of the errors that had repeatedly led to breakaways and odd man rushes, and learned to do a better job of staying out of the penalty box. But perhaps most importantly, you could sense that the Blues now really believed in themselves. And when you come from last to first in only a few months and win 11 games in a row and beat the best teams in the NHL it breeds confidence. At the end of the day, confidence (not to be confused with arrogance or lack of respect for the opponent) may be the most underrated component of any successful athlete and team.

But the regular season is one type of game and style of play and the playoffs is another version of the sport. Sure, the game is played hard during the regular season and the players and basic objectives are the same. But the intensity, physicality and the effort expected and given in the playoffs is off the charts. So focused on the team and the game during this special time in the season for the 16 teams privileged to compete for the Cup that none of the players pay particular attention to facial hygiene!

Although there are no weapons involved (other than rudimentary sticks) playoff hockey is akin to warfare. It is certainly treated as such by the men who coach and lead these squads with constant admonitions to "fight hard," "be aggressive," "hit them all over the ice," "take no prisoners," "win the wall battles, the blue line battles and the net battles" and "win the war of attrition." Almost all of these instructions are accompanied by an F-bomb - the favorite adjective and adverb used by coaches, especially of Canadian descent, to show the players that they *really* mean what they are saying!

The Winnipeg Series
(Who will win the battle of the Gateway to the West?)

It seemed especially befitting that the Blues' quest for the Cup should begin against the team where the season began and where the Blues had previously failed - the Winnipeg Jets. The Jets had solidly beaten the Blues at home on Opening Night which, while only one game, had deflated many of the lofty expectations going into the season.

The first game of the season was hardly a fluke. Just to make sure the Blues got the message from the Jets' about their superiority; they beat the Blues the next time in Winnipeg, 5-4 in Overtime, after trailing the Blues 2-0 in the game. And in their third matchup back in the Lou, the Jets completely dismantled the Note 8-4 with Jets' star Patrik Laine scoring FIVE goals.

The Blues were able to eke out a lone victory in the teams' final contest, an exceedingly rare 1-0 shutout win in Winnipeg, to salvage some pride. But the Jets clearly had the Blues' number for the year; in four games the Jets had outscored the Blues 18-10. Moreover, the Blues had shown no ability to stop Winnipeg's top guns of Laine, Mark Scheifele and Blake Wheeler, who combined for a ridiculous 19 points in the three games they won against the Blues.

However, the Jets had not yet faced the new-look Blues - with the unflappable rookie goalie Binnington, a rejuvenated heavy forechecking bunch, and a team brimming with self-confidence. At the end of the day, despite being manhandled by the Jets early in the season, the Blues finished with the exact same number of points as the Jets and owned a better record in the second half of the season. As Jets Coach Maurice astutely acknowledged and cautioned his players "we haven't played *that* team yet."

At the same time, most knowledgeable hockey people knew the Jets were among the best teams in the League, having made it to the Conference Finals the year before. Indeed, one could make a strong case that they were *the* best team in the Western Conference. They had explosive talent with some of the best young players in the game (Laine, Scheifele and Kyle

Connor) to go along with their veteran leading-scorer Wheeler, top defensemen in Dustin Byfuglien and Jacob Trouba, and a highly-regarded goalie in Connor Hellebuyck. And the Jets had tough character guys like Adam Lowry (who was born in St. Louis), a mammoth 6-foot 8 defenseman in Tyler Myers and five other regulars who were 6-feet 5 along with a 6-foot 4 goaltender. This team was big, fast and intimidating.

And the Jets had home ice advantage. Playing at home may be overrated, and it certainly turned out to be in this year's playoffs, but in the case of Winnipeg it appeared to be a huge advantage. The Winnipeg fan base is downright religious about hockey - the equivalent of football in Texas - with their "True North Whiteout," and everyone dressed like clergy, screaming their lungs out. For the year Winnipeg had only lost 12 of the 41 games played at home. Further, the Blues' struggles against the Jets were no aberration; the Blues had won just three of fourteen encounters with their rivals over the past three years.

So, this would be quite a challenge for the Men in Blue and an opportunity to see how much the team had improved since the early part of the season. Could we somehow lasso the seemingly uncontrollable top line of Laine, Wheeler and Scheifele? Solve Hellebuyck enough to match the Jets' scoring prowess? Manage to win at least one game in Canada? It seemed like a daunting task. But if this Blues' team was truly different, and the last half of the season was no fluke, then this opponent and series would be a good indicator of how well we could compete with the big boys on the biggest stage.

Both teams' cities call themselves the "Gateway to the West" in their respective countries, as both are located in the often neglected middle of the country. The historian in me thought back to the Blues' very close encounter with Saskatoon. Had the Blues actually moved there, naturally few folks in St. Louis would have been glued to the tube watching this series. But at the same, neither would perhaps many of the wildly exuberant fans of Winnipeg. It seems unlikely that the NHL would have placed another team in the middle of Canada from a small market, had there already been a Saskatoon Blues.

Game 1 (Season Opener "Take Two")

It was clear from the outset that Winnipeg's plan was to disrupt, torment, haze and generally make life miserable for the freshman goalie Jordan Binnington, playing in his first ever playoff game. Word was spread throughout devoted Jet-land about trying to rattle the rookie. Seizing upon his deadpan sound bites during the season, the boisterous gathering of folks dressed in their Wimbledon all-whites cleverly serenaded him with loud chants of "Are you nervous?"

And then to really put an exclamation point on their effort to intimidate Binnington, Winnipeg's colossal star forward Mark Scheifele (he of 6-foot 5, 225-pound frame) crashed into Binnington just 34 seconds into the contest, when he simply went behind the net to clear a puck. Scheifele knocked the netminder flying, sending his goalie stick ten feet into the air. It was a clearly calculated maneuver to let Binnington know that he was in hostile territory now and that all the success he had experienced in the regular season meant nothing in the playoffs. The Blues were furious and went after Scheifele, but Binnington remained perfectly composed - the best possible sign of a man who was not overwhelmed by the occasion.

The Jets next tried the more traditional form of intimidation - throwing puck after puck at him. There were a couple nice saves on the Jets' Nik Ehlers, including a point-blank shot on a 3 on 2. There were shots from the point, close in, rebounds and screened shots. Throughout the barrage, Binnington stood tall. The man was clearly NOT nervous.

The Jets ultimately did break through late in the first period, taking the lead on a goal by whom else but Blues' nemesis Patrik Laine. Laine received a quick feed from Bryan Little and with a rapid-fire release exquisitely picked the top corner of the net to Binnington's left. The young goalie had no chance.

And that's where the score stood for a long time. Tarasenko had a breakaway in the second period that was barely stopped by Jets' goalie Hellebuyck (indeed, the puck was fluttering behind him after the save and about to cross the line when Jets' defenseman Byfuglien steered the puck away). The Jets had a breakaway of their own, while shorthanded no less, when Adam Lowry sent Par Lindholm alone on Binnington. But he thwarted the backhand attempt with a clean glove save.

So, the teams entered the third period with Winnipeg ahead by the lone goal; the Blues had hung close enough that the critical first game was still up for grabs. But could the Blues sneak one by Hellebuyck? It looked like Ryan O'Reilly might when he received a nice pass from Brayden Schenn to spring him down the left wing. With a step on the Winnipeg' defender O'Reilly took a slap shot that cleanly beat Hellybuyck. But it clanged off the goal post. Soon thereafter, the puck gods returned the favor as Laine hit the goal post behind Binnington.

Finally, the Blues got on the board in an unlikely manner. The crafty veteran David Perron snapped a shot from far out at the right point that somehow managed to make its way through a maze of players, and a helpful screen by Oskar Sundqvist, into the left corner of the net, eluding the perplexed Hellebuyck and knotting the game at one a piece.

The Blues' first goal of this Stanley Cup run was the 1,000th playoff goal in Blues' history. Fittingly, it belonged to a guy who bleeds Blue through and through. Perron was drafted by the Blues and played with the team for six years. After being traded and playing for three different teams over the next three years, he longed to return to St. Louis and signed as a free agent. But in 2017 the Blues chose not to protect him in the draft and he was selected by the Las Vegas Golden Knights, playing an important role in the expansion team's remarkable run to the Stanley Cup Final in their very first season. Perron's love for the

Blues remained though, and despite the slight of not protecting him, he re-signed with the Blues for the 2018-19 season and three more years. It was nice to see his loyalty rewarded.

With the score now tied, and less than a period to play, the tension was mounting. Back and forth the action went. Each team had some Grade A chances - most notably two great opportunities by Tyler Bozak, and a close-in shot from the always-dangerous Mr. Laine. But both teams remained stymied by the goaltenders. The next goal felt like it would surely be the winner. The only question for restless fans on both sides was: "Who would break through with a great play, a tipped deflection or a rebound "garbage collection" goal? Alternatively, which stellar goalie would uncharacteristically relinquish a "softie?"

With only 2:05 left to go in regulation play, the answer came. In a scrum behind the Jets' net, Pat Maroon gained control of the puck and quickly sent a backhanded pass past several Jets toward the front of the net and right on to the stick of a charging Bozak who quickly wristed one into the upper corner, stick-side, just under the bar. Bozak got his redemption for his earlier missed chances and, more importantly, the Blues now had the lead!

The last two minutes, however, would prove to be exasperating to watch as the Jets mounted a furious rally pinning the Blues in our zone and not letting us out. Around and around the net they circled with the puck it seemed, looking and finding open shots at the point and slot and taking them and then gathering rebounds and doing it all again. It didn't help that the Jets had pulled their goalie and had an extra attacker, nor the fact that Alexander Steen had broken his stick and had to try and defend and chase without one.

But on each occasion Binnington was up to the task. With less than twenty seconds remaining, there was a big face-off down at the Blues' end. The Jets won the draw and controlled the puck, and the Blues were scrambling to defend. The puck came back to the point to their big defenseman Byfuglien as

O'Reilly converged. Pietrangelo moved toward the front of the goal to serve as an additional blocker. But in the process the Blues' captain inexplicably left the sharpshooter Scheifele wide open to his side of the goal. Byfuglien fed Scheifele the puck perfectly and he rifled a blistering one-timer from close range to the right of Binnington headed for a dramatic last second game-tying goal. But with 14 seconds left on the clock the rookie netminder quickly maneuvered to his right just in time to block the attempt.

Yet another potential opportunity presented itself directly in front of the Blues' net with less than two seconds remaining when the Jets' Little was left unmarked and got the puck but appeared to tip it just wide. FINALLY, the horn sounded, and the Blues had escaped with a win in Game 1, and primarily because of their "nervous" goalie Jordan Binnington.

One down and only 15 more wins to go! *If they are all going to be this difficult, I wasn't sure if I was going to survive to the end - assuming by some wild stretch of the imagination* we *could get there.*

Game 2 (Let's do this again!)

Conventional wisdom says that when you are the lower seeded team and start a playoff series on the road, the goal is to try and "steal" one of the first two road games. The Blues had already done that. But great teams and championships teams are never satisfied with a split when they win Game 1. They want to "put the hammer down," the "nail in the coffin," and any other cliché the coach can think of to motivate the team to another road victory. Aside from the win itself that gets you only two away from a series victory, it serves to discourage the opponent and perhaps take some "fight out of the dog." It also potentially means more rest and less aches and pains if a team can somehow win a shortened series. So, it was incumbent on the Blues to put forth their best effort in Game 2 and perhaps even pull out another one.

And the Blues came out like a team that was determined to do just that. Just five minutes into the game, Jay Bouwmeester tipped a puck away at center ice to emerging star Oskar Sundqvist creating a two-on-one and Sundqvist buried it in the corner midway stick-side for the first goal of the game. The lead was short-lived, however, as Winnipeg's Captain Wheeler found an open space in the slot and got a perfect feed behind the net from Scheifele and buried his chance.

In the second period, the goals would come fast and furious. The unstoppable Laine gave the Jets the lead on the power play on a great cross-ice feed from Wheeler. But Maroon responded with a goal of his own, jamming in a rebound on a backhand attempt from Robert Thomas after a speedy maneuver around the goal. It wouldn't be the last time in the playoffs that Maroon helped clean up the garbage from a great move by Thomas.

Sundqvist then gave the Blues the lead just before the halfway mark of the game, scoring his second goal of the game on a nice pass from Perron. But with time winding down in the second period, and the Jets once again on the power play, Scheifele scored the equalizer on a hard wrist shot from the deep slot. Three goals each after two periods of play.

On to the critical third period! The Blues stood in the enviable position of having a legitimate chance to leave Winnipeg with two victories and take a commanding lead in the series. Very few teams in NHL history have dropped the first two games at home and gone on to win the series (less than 20%). The Jets were fully aware of this reality and were what the hockey world likes to call "a desperate team."

The Blues would soon add to the Jets' feeling of despair by scoring less than four minutes into the third with the help of two long break-out passes: First, Parayko from deep in his zone to Bouwmeester near the blue line, and then Bouwmeester to O'Reilly who was racing down the right side. With a defender closely on him, O'Reilly let go a long wrist shot from his off-wing which somehow managed to beat Hellebuyck up high to his stick-side. The Blues now held a 4-3 lead!

There was still three-fourths of the period to play but the Blues seized the opportunity and put on a defensive clinic from that point, clogging up the middle, forcing the Jets to the outside, limiting chances, and cleaning up any rebounds. The Blues also aided their cause by putting pressure on the Jets in their own end, smothering them there and not giving them many chances to get the puck into the Blues' zone where their big guns, Laine, Wheeler and Scheifele, are so dangerous.

As the buzzer sounded with the score Blues 4 Winnipeg 3, the Blues implausibly were able to leave Winnipeg with an impressive two game lead and appeared to have the series solidly in hand.

Game 3 (It's not going to be easy)

The Blues were surprisingly, ok shockingly, up two games to none over a great Winnipeg team, having beaten them twice in the land of "big muddy waters" (*Winnipeg derives from a Cree word as the Chief could presumably attest)*. If the Blues could somehow manage to capture Game 3 at home, while we had the momentum, we would likely take away any chance of Winnipeg winning the series. But as a Blues' fan, especially one who has been in the trenches for 51 seasons, you know there is no such thing as the Blues having a "stranglehold" on *any* series.

The Blues started out Game 3 in fine fashion in front of an exuberant home crowd, playing the inspired Jets evenly and closely for most of the first period. And then we finally capitalized on a power play goal with less than a minute left in the first period - Pietrangelo made a slick pass to Perron who scored on a beautiful wrister. It was another high stick-side goal, clearly a spot the Blues were targeting.

But five minutes into the second period, a long seemingly innocent shot from the point took an unlucky bounce off of the Jets' Kevin Hayes in front, hit the goal post and then went in, tying the game. And then the floodgates opened as the potent Winnipeg attack scored two more goals in less than four minutes to take a 3-1 lead (Laine was somehow left completely alone in front of the net to gather a rebound for his third goal in three games, and Connor scored on a four on three power play).

It was a lead the Jets never relinquished. Tarasenko scored his first goal of the playoffs to cut the lead to 3-2 in the third period, but the Jets responded with two quick goals of their own. The teams exchange two more largely meaningless goals before the game ended 6-3. It was a disappointment to Blues' fans that had unrealistic visions of this being an easy and quick series.

The Jets were now guaranteed another date up north, and if they could somehow pull out Game 4 as well on the road, they would be back in control of the series. For the Blues, one loss was not a huge deal. But we needed to win Game 4 to maintain our advantage in the series.

Game 4 (The same old Blues?)

Both teams understood the importance of Game 4 and played from the outset with purpose and special attention to defensive responsibilities and trying to stay out of the penalty box. Both teams badly wanted to seize the first goal but both goaltenders were clearly on their games, especially the rookie Blues' netminder who didn't have his best outing in Game 3.

Neither team was able to score in the first period. And neither team was able to score in the second period, despite some great chances on both sides. Binnington stopped the Jets' Brandon Tanev on a clear breakaway. Hellebuyck responded by robbing Thomas who was in all alone after a nice steal by a forechecking Maroon, and a quick pass by the pinching defenseman Joel Edmundson to the 19-year old speedster.

This hugely important game and possibly the series would come down to the third period. And merely 35 seconds into the third period, with the Blues on a carry-over power play from the second period, the team's biggest offensive weapon Tarasenko put the Blues ahead - a strong wrist shot from his favorite left side position on a feed from the point by Pietrangelo. Finally, a goal and the lead!

But seven minutes later, the Jets' big stars struck back on a great passing display from Wheeler to Conner to Scheifele all alone in front of the net - and the game was now tied at one. Both teams would press hard for the game-winner; the best chance a nice move by Perron with less than seven minutes left in regulation that sprung him in all alone on Hellebuyck. But the big goalie was up to the task. And with one-minute left, Scheifele got briefly in all alone for the potential game-winner but was denied by Binnington.

The game headed to Overtime. And six minutes into the extra session, the same Winnipeg trio who scored the first goal were responsible for the game-winner - this time it was Connor scoring from Scheifele and Wheeler, after the latter had made a great charge into the Blues' end with Parayko draped all over him. The Jets' top players were simply electric.

The result was a backbreaker. In classic Blues' form, the boys had turned an overwhelming advantage from two surprising victories in Winnipeg into, at best, an even series with the Jets regaining home ice advantage. The Blues seemed determined to impose the maximum frustration on their fans. Or perhaps the Jets were just the better team?

An ominous feeling fell over many Blues' supporters. Some delusional types who had not suffered for 51 seasons expressed unrestrained optimism; the Blues had stolen two games in Winnipeg already in the series, so the y would simply do it again. Others (like me) needed a narcotic to ease the pain. Yes, we *could* beat the Jets three in a row in Winnipeg but were the chances of that? The proud Jets would be flying high in Game 5 to show their loyal fan base that they were not about to get skunked at home in a playoff series.

Game 5 (The most important win in the playoffs?)

The team that wins Game 5 in a playoff series tied 2-2 is far more often than not the team that wins the series. The historical statistical odds are 78.8%. Both teams clearly understood how critical this game was. The Jets were determined to get off to a big start, get the crowd behind them, score first and never let up. The Blues were hoping to keep an energized Jet team at bay for the first several minutes, play hard all over the ice and eventually get a turnover or break, score first and hold on for dear life.

But the Blues could not have gotten off to a worse start. The Jets' Lowry won the face off from O'Reilly, and the puck was quickly shot down into the Blues' end by Winnipeg, where the Jets' Andrew Copp and Brandon Tanev raced after it. Copp won the puck, gave it quickly to Tanev who without hesitation took a bad angle shot on goal from the corner. Binnington was alert and blocked it but the rebound found Lowry all alone in front of the goal. And Lowry put the puck in the net a mere 12 seconds into the game. *Are you kidding me?* It might have been the reliable O'Reilly's worst 12 seconds of play with the Blues, losing the face-off and then showing up late to cover Lowry in front of the net, only proving that nobody's perfect (*though where was the weak side defenseman?*).

The Jets and the crowd naturally went crazy and it seemed as this might be a tough night for the Blues. Undeterred, the Blues pushed hard for the equalizer. Sundqvist had a glorious chance at the midway point of the period with a clear breakaway but shot wide. Pietrangelo had a shot that Hellebuyck seemed to struggle with briefly but the Blues could not secure the rebound.

And then the Jets scored another goal later in the period to go up 2-0, when the 6-foot 5 Hayes powered around Edmundson and poked one in while barreling down on top of Binnington. Things were now looking doubly bad in this crucial game.

The Blues desperately needed a goal and couldn't afford to give up another Jets' goal or it would undoubtedly be lights out for this game. Jaden Schwartz raced in all alone down the left side but Hellebuyck was able to get a good piece of his shot as it trickled wide. Schenn looked like he had a wide-open net but tripped (or, more accurately, was hooked down without a call) and was not able to get off a shot.

Then, midway through the second period with the score still 2-0, Robby Fabbri turned over the puck trying to exit the Blues' zone. Winnipeg's Mathieu Perreault willingly accepted the gift and closed in on Binnington who came out of his net to reduce the angle. Perreault took a shot that was tipped by the Jets' Hayes. Binnington was able to get a piece of the puck but it squirted past him and was heading slowly into the net.

Hayes was now behind Binnington watching the puck moving toward the goal line. Colton Parayko was rushing back to try and rescue the ominous situation, but he was going to be too late. Apparently wanting to make absolutely sure that the puck made it over the blue line, and with inches to go, Hayes tried to help the puck faster into the net. In the process, his stick became entangled with the goal post and somehow, miraculously and inadvertently, Hayes' own stick swept the puck *out* of the goal. It would have been a certain goal if Hayes had done nothing, in which case the Jets would have had a likely insurmountable 3-0 lead. But thanks to some incredible luck, the Blues were saved by the Jets' own player, and were still "only" down by two goals. Hayes and the Winnipeg faithful were beyond disbelief when they watched a replay of what happened on the video scoreboard.

Hayes' frustration would be compounded just moments later when he was sent in on a clear breakaway and was stuffed by Binnington - without any help this time. The Blues were being outplayed and generating little offense, but Binner was doing his level best to keep them in the game.

And then very early in the third period, with just seconds left on a Blues' carry-over power play from the second period, O'Reilly gathered a rebound on a shot by Schenn (helped by Perron) and scored to break the ice and pull the Blues to within one goal. The Blues now had about nineteen minutes left to try and get the equalizer and force Overtime.

But the number of quality chances for the Blues were small as time was rapidly winding down. Then, with just over six minutes left in the game, Sundqvist made a great power move down the left side after tipping the puck between the legs of Jets' Defenseman Byfuglien. Using his superior speed, he gained a step on Byfuglien and protected the puck using his body as a shield. Sundqvist was charging forward on his backhand with the mammoth defenseman holding and pushing him and trying to prevent him from breaking in all alone on Hellebuyck. As Sundqvist got very close to the goal, Hellebuyck moved toward him slightly to cut down the angle. With a final push and trip by Byfuglien, Sundqvist crashed into the goalpost slowly dislodging the side to Hellebuyck's right from its moorings.

In the process of falling, Sundqvist managed to push the puck toward the goal crease. It went through the legs of Jets' defenseman Dmitry Kulikov and right to a fast-charging Schenn - the first skater to the other side of the net. Schenn quickly jammed it over the line and into the partially dislodged net.

Goal!!! Or was it? The referee behind the net (whose arm was up because of a delayed penalty on Byfuglien) called it a goal. But the play was being reviewed. I wasn't sure of the rule but had a bad feeling - one side of the goalpost was clearly off *before* Schenn scored, even though the reason for that happening was the Jets' own player. The TV announcer confidently declared that this was NOT a goal "within the strict letter of the rules." The fact that it was in Winnipeg and a riot might ensue if the goal was upheld wasn't likely to help matters either. And this was the Blues, after all - the team that rarely got a break when we most needed it.

And then the decision came down - the call on the ice of a goal was confirmed. The Blues had tied it! What a relief! At least now we had a chance. Nevertheless, the way the game was going, and it being in Winnipeg, I wouldn't have exactly considered the Blues the favorites.

From that point on, both teams played conservatively, determined not to give up any meaningful chance. As the clocked ticked down to the last thirty seconds before what appeared to be certain Overtime, the Blues shot the puck deep into the Jets' zone and tried to retrieve it. Schwartz, a master at winning pucks in the corner despite his smaller stature, dug in behind the goal fighting with two Jet players. Steen came in to help and the puck found his stick as he was fighting with a third Jet, Scheifele, for the puck. Steen was just barely able to direct the puck along the sidewall where Bozak was now stationed.

Bozak got the puck along the side boards to the left of Hellebuyck. And as a fourth Jets' player quickly converged to challenge him, and with limited time on the clock, Bozak just wheeled and fired the puck to the front of the net. It's not clear whether he was trying to shoot the puck or pass it to Schwartz who had smartly moved from his position behind the net to the front of the goal. Schwartz was closely guarded by Jets' defenseman Trouba with Hellebuyck fully engaged on him as well. Bozak's pass (or shot) was heading toward Schwartz a couple of feet above the ice. Schwartz stuck out his stick and it magically careened off of it past both Truoba and Hellebuyck into the goal with 15 seconds left in the game. *Un-Hellebucking-believable!*

It was the second latest game-winning goal in Blues' playoff history - eclipsed only by Gino Cavallini's game winner vs. Chicago in 1990 in Game 3 with nine seconds left. Incredibly, Bozak was not even supposed to be on the ice at the time but had quickly jumped on when Schenn had to leave the ice unexpectedly, apparently for some repairs. Had Schenn been there instead the goal undoubtedly could not have transpired since, as a left-handed shooter, he would have been on his backhand along the right boards when the puck came to him and, thus, would not have been able to shoot the puck toward the goal from that position.

And it was the unlikeliest of goals - an innocent pass from a bad angle above the ice to a player who was closely guarded, with little room to get the puck past both a large defenseman and goalie. And the player in front, though a great player, had struggled mightily to buy *any* goal over the course of the season, even when he had a great chance or an empty net. And yet the goal happened - I only believe it because I saw it.

It was the greatest goal of Schwartz's fine career, the biggest goal of the season to that point and, one could argue, the biggest goal in the entire playoffs. While it was certainly possible that the Blues could have still won that game in Overtime, the odds of that were statistically less than 50-50, and Schwartz's miraculous goal ensured that instead of the Blues potentially trailing 3-2 in the series and having to win the next two games, including a Game 7 in Winnipeg, we now only had to win one more game - ideally the next one in the Lou.

But for a great save by Binnington on a breakaway and by the Jets' own Hayes on his own shot, a favorable ruling on a very close call on the Blues' tying goal, an unexpected change by Schenn, a smart play by Bozak and great hands (and some luck) by Schwartzie, the Blues likely lose that game and, if so, I suspect the series. Perhaps the hockey gods were finally looking favorable upon the Blues. Miraculously, in three playoff games up north there had not been a single *Winner*peg for the home squad.

Game 6 (Home Sweet Home - Finally!)

After five games, the home team in the series had, shockingly, won ZERO games. That had only happened four times in NHL playoff history! At the same time that had to give Winnipeg at least some comfort as the road team after losing a Game 5 that they thought they should have won. But the Blues were determined not to make that six wins in a row for the visitors.

And to emphatically make that point, the Blues gave the Jets some of their own medicine. With the game having barely begun, Schenn aggressively skated with the puck into the Winnipeg zone along the right side, hounded by two Winnipeg players with a third in front of the goal for extra measure. Undeterred, Schenn took the puck right to the net for a close-in backhand shot. Hellebuyck was able to stop the high shot but it bounced straight down. Schwartz had rushed to the front of the net and was waiting, apparently anticipating the forceful move of his Saskatchewan buddy (the two had grown up and had played hockey together since they were ten-year old's in the same Canadian province).

Before Hellebuyck could contain the loose puck, the last-second hero of Game 5, quickly jammed the puck into the goal, just 23 seconds into the game! It was the Blues' second goal in the very first minute of play in this series. Moreover, the Blues' player who was unable to score for long stretches of the season had just scored **two goals** - and the two most important in his entire career - **in 38 seconds** of combined time.

The Blues continued to play with a vengeance. O'Reilly made a great defensive back-check to prevent Wheeler from being in all alone on Binnington. Fabbri took a pass from Steen in his skates, was able to skillfully kick the puck to his stick and with a sonic burst propel himself past both Jets defensemen Byfuglien and Trouba to put himself all alone on Hellybuyck. But his backhanded attempt was caught after it popped up into the air. Shortly thereafter, Fabbri used his exceptional speed to create a clearer full-scale breakaway. Again, Hellebuyck denied him with an arm save. David Perron also had two excellent chances and was unable to convert them into goals.

But this was Schwartzie's night. Not content with having scored the last two goals, he scored the Blues' next goal as well in the second period on the power play to make it 2-0. And then, just to make the story more miraculous, he did it again in the third period, holding the puck patiently while deking and dusting off a sliding Byfuglien and then all alone, scoring on a wrister, naturally stick-side - a natural hat trick. Talk about being in the zone! A guy who couldn't seem to score all year if his life depended on it, suddenly had scored the team's last *and only* four goals in the span of 3 periods and 15 seconds.

I have been privileged to see my fair share of hat tricks over the years, but I never saw one more glorious than that one - given who scored (my favorite player), the way he scored (the only Blues' goals in the game and no empty-netters, which I don't think should even count as goals for the player) and the circumstances (game and playoff series-winning goals).

And I have never witnessed more hats - and expensive hats at that - raining down onto the ice at a hockey game. The sheer jubilation of the fans was off the charts. If the tradition had been to throw wallets and purses instead of hats, I am confident that many folks would have obliged in the elation of the moment.

As it turned out, Winnipeg scored two more goals before it was over, including a shorthanded goal with less than a minute remaining to make the score 3-2. The Blues were apparently determined to squeeze every last bit of emotion and suffering out of the adoring fans before the celebration could begin.

Recap of Winnipeg Series

Even though this series did not go the full seven games, in retrospect, it may have been the most difficult the Blues played. Five of the six games were decided by a single goal, with the Blues winning four of them. The Jets scored the same number of goals as the Blues in the series, and according to the data geeks, the Jets had a higher expected goal rate in four of the six games. The Blues had to win three games in Winnipeg to win the series, one of the places where home ice advantage was considered to be the greatest and did so - each by the slimmest of margins and twice coming from behind. In short, Winnipeg could have easily won the series. And if they had, we would have never been treated to the magic and the miracles that were just beginning.

Given the way the Blues won the Winnipeg series, this team just felt different and seemed special. Perhaps this was actually a team of destiny.

The Dallas Series
(Will the stars be aligned with the Blues?)

Defeating a very tough Winnipeg team in the first round was huge. But there were still three more excruciating rounds to win if the Blues hoped to reach hockey nirvana. The next opponent who stood in their way was the Dallas Stars, the team with whom the Blues had the longest and greatest history.

The Stars were the first team the Blues had ever played, the last team who played the Blues at the Old Arena, and the team that we had faced more than any other in the playoffs - thirteen previous times, with the Blues winning seven of them. Further, we had three of the best moments in Blues' history against the Stars: The Double Overtime win in Game 7 in 1968, the Overtime win in Game 7 of 1972, and the deciding Game 5 win in 1986 in a series that preceded the Calgary Monday Night Miracle. The Stars were also responsible for two of the Blues' more painful moments in history: the Overtime Game 7 loss in 1984 and the second-round loss in 1999 when we had one of our best teams in history and lost a close series to Dallas with four Overtime Games, and then the Stars went on to win the Stanley Cup with Brett Hull - *our Brett Hull*- scoring the Game 7 winner in the Final.

And the Blues and Stars had other significant connections. The Stars' most important player - their 6-foot 7 giant of a goalie, Ben Bishop - grew up in St. Louis and attended Chaminade High School (he still lives here, and his parents own a very successful business in the Lou). One of his teammates on his youth hockey team, the Kirkwood Stars (naturally it was the "Stars") was Maroon, who attended high school at Oakville twenty minutes away. When Bishop was not *playing* hockey as a kid, he was attending and watching Blues' games and rooting against the goalie for the opposition. Now that was him.

Bishop was scheduled to live the dream of many kids – playing for his home team squad. He was drafted by the Blues but for some reason, which was a mystery to me and many fans, the Blues' coaches did not view Bishop particularly highly - or at least as highly as other goalies in the organization, like Brian Elliott and Jake Allen. So, he played very sparingly with the

Blues, starting only eight games in four years from 2008-2012. Ultimately, he was traded him to Ottawa for a second-round draft pick which traded him to Tampa Bay, which traded him to Los Angeles, which finally traded him to Dallas. It was enough to give the big man a giant chip on his shoulder. And, sure enough, he became the biggest star on the Dallas Stars. In 2018-2019 Bishop finished second in the Vezina race for the best goalie in the NHL with a goals against average under two and a save percentage of 93.4%.

Bishop was undoubtedly looking forward to playing the Blues; nothing quite like giving a great player extra incentive to beat the team that didn't believe in him and let him go.

In addition, one of the Stars' defensemen, Roman Polak, was drafted by the Blues and played eight seasons with the Note. He was a hard-hitting rough and tumble guy who was not very fast or skilled offensively but who always gave his all for the team. Polak would be traded for Carl Gunnarsson, who would later have some pretty big heroics of his own to come. Furthermore, the Stars' Coach Jim Montgomery, was drafted as a player by the Blues, wore the Note, married a local girl from the Lou and had a baby born here - a naturalized Blues' citizen.

And, on a personal level, I attended the University of Texas where the majority of my friends were from Dallas. While most were not huge hockey fans - some hardly knew the rules or even how to skate - they relished the opportunity for payback after the Cardinals beat their beloved Texas Rangers in heartache fashion in the compelling 2011 World Series.

In some respects, the Blues seemed to have received a break by playing the Stars. Dallas had upset the Nashville Predators, the first-place team in the division. The Preds were the far more skilled team in my book with their invasion of European talent: Swedes Forsberg, Arvidsson, and Ekholm, Swiss Fiala and Captain Roman Josi, and Fins Granlund and goalie Pekka Rinne to go along with a couple of Canadians of note, leading scorer Ryan Johansen and tough offensive defenseman P.K. Subban. The Predators were clearly the scarier offensive team. But the Blues had played better against them than probably any team during the regular season, winning four of the five games, including the last four. While the regular season's success did not guarantee similar success in the playoffs, the Blues seemed to thrive against more talented offensive teams who played an upbeat style.

Dallas, on the other hand, was a very different team than both Nashville and the Winnipeg team we had just faced. Like Winnipeg and Nashville, they had a top scoring line that could be explosive in Tyler Seguin, Jamie Benn, and Alexander Radulov and two very impressive offensive-minded defensemen in John Klingberg and the young speedy Miro Heiskanen. But they were 29th out of 31st in the NHL in scoring goals. The Stars' success was predicated upon very solid defense, much like so many of the successful Blues' teams of the past. With Big Ben in goal, they employed a tight checking defensive system that played things very close to the vest and waited for their opportunities and then counter-attacked. As a result, the Stars gave up the second least goals in the NHL. They were a team far more similar to the Blues than Winnipeg or Nashville.

And unlike with Nashville, the Blues had really struggled against the Stars recently; having dropped six of the last seven games over the past two years. So, while the Blues had the home ice advantage (to the extent one could call that an advantage after the first series) and the Blues were the slight favorites in this series in Las Vegas (the only series that we would be favored in) the games were expected to be very close, tight checking and low scoring.

Game 1 (Blues take care of business)

The crowd was pumped up at the Enterprise Center for the start of Round 2 hoping to propel the Blues to a good start to the game and the series. And sure enough, just five plus minutes into the game, Fabbri used his superior speed to get to a puck first along the side boards in the Stars' zone and beat a surprised Bishop on the first shot of the game - a relatively weak wrist shot right through his legs. It would be the only goal (and point) that the former first-round draft pick would register in the entire playoffs for the Blues, and one of the few softies that we would get from Ben Bishop the rest of the way.

The Stars tied the game in the second period on a goal by Jason Spezza on a strong charge into the Blues' zone after a great set-up by Stars' defenseman Klingberg. Tarasenko answered later in the period on a power play goal, receiving a cross-ice pass on the left point from Schenn and skating in close before rifling a shot between Bishop's legs to put us up 2-1.

But the Tank saved the best for last early in the third period. Powering around the Stars' highly-skilled defenseman Heiskanen to break in on goal with the young defenseman hanging on him, he moved the puck from his backhand to his forehand and flipped a shot into the top opposite corner to put the Blues up 3-1 - an absolute highlight-reel goal. And the Blues held on for a 3-2 win.

Candidly, it was a relatively lackluster performance by the Blues - we only took 20 shots on net for the entire game, and Dallas arguably outplayed us, registering 29 shots of their own. But Binnington was solid in goal and the important thing was that the Blues had won and gotten off on the right foot in the series. Still, the boys would have to play a lot better in my judgment if we hoped to advance.

Game 2 (And then we don't)

The Blues have rarely made it easy throughout the team's 42 playoff runs by seizing a series lead and then putting a vice grip on the opponent. We did win Game 2 in Winnipeg after winning Game 1, which was exceedingly rare for the Note, but then made up for it by dropping the next two games at home.

The Blues have been a team that has always seemed to struggle with success and make things as hard as possible.

So why should it have been a surprise to ardent followers when the Blues came out and fell flat on their faces early in Game 2, up one game to none in the series? The Blues yielded a goal to Dallas one-third of the way into the first period (to the young Finnish speedster with the cool name, Roope Hintz), then another two thirds of the way in (to even younger Finnish Heiskanen on a beautiful between the legs pass from Hintz), and after the Blues' Parayko had scored, a third goal only 26 seconds later (from Swedish forward Mattias Janmark). *Enough with these damn Scandinavians!*

Giving Dallas and Ben Bishop a two-goal lead after one period (1/3 of the way to the end) was like giving Texas' Nolan Ryan or the Cardinals' Bob Gibson a five-run lead after three innings. They are rarely going to relinquish a lead like that.

The Blues attempted to apply heavy pressure but struggled to get anything by Bishop. At one point a shot by Perron right off the face-off was only partially blocked by Bishop and rolling toward the goal and about to go in when the 6-foot 7 bear of a man reached back behind him, and with his outstretched giant paw swatted the puck away just before it crossed the red line. It was going to be one of those nights.

The Blues eventually got a goal from the rejuvenated Schwartz early in the third period to cut the lead to one. But that was as close as we would get. The Stars added an empty net goal (another one for Hintz) for the 4-2 victory and headed back to Dallas with the series tied at one game each.

Game 3 (Back and forth we go until Maroon ends the show)

The Blues had developed two really good habits in the young Berube and Binnington era. First, the team had far more often than not scored the first goal in games, often very early.

Scoring first naturally enhances a team's confidence - especially a team like the Blues that doesn't score a lot of goals - and also often causes the opponent "to chase" the game, which can result in further errors and opportunities. A team's statistical chances of winning a game is also greatly increased by scoring the first goal - 67% on average, though the Blues' percentage in the playoffs was a whopping 76% when we scored first.

Second, the Blues had a tremendous knack for rebounding from losses with wins since Binnington took over. Indeed, during the regular season, Binnington, incredibly, *never* lost two games in a row! And in the playoffs thus far, Binnington had only lost one game after a loss - Game 4 against Winnipeg.

It was paramount that the Blues got off to a good start and ideally scored the first goal. And once again, that man named Schwartz (the same surname as my sister's family) came through only 1:27 minutes into the game, deflecting a blast from the point by Parayko to give the Blues the lead.

Binnington then made a great save on the Stars' Heiskanen who was in all alone to preserve the lead. But he could not stop Alexander Radulov's top shelf shot on the power play soon thereafter which evened the score after one period.

In the second period, the Stars applied heavy pressure initially and Binnington was forced to make several excellent saves. But midway through the second period, the slick stickhandling defenseman Vince Dunn took the puck at the right point and with Dallas forward Janmark pressuring him, skillfully spun around him along the boards into the corner with Janmark in hot pursuit. Once he had drawn the attention of the Stars' defenseman who began to move toward him, Dunn passed the puck to a wide-open Robert Thomas. Thomas took a stride and then a shot from close in. Bishop stopped the puck, but it dropped at his feet and Tyler Bozak quickly cleaned up the mess and stuck it in giving the Blues the lead. *Perhaps a foreshadow of a huge future goal?*

From that point on the pace was fast and furious with far less attention to defense. Alexander Radulov had a clean breakaway but was snuffed by Binnington. With the Stars pressing forward to tie the game, O'Reilly had a breakaway of his own as did Bozak, though in each case there was a player hounding them from behind and minimizing the threat. After a hectic second period, the Blues headed to the dressing room holding a narrow 2-1 lead.

In the first half of the third period the Blues played tight and smart with lots of energy. The guys were also determined not to take a penalty and give the scoring-challenged Stars a heightened opportunity to score on their solid power play. With the clock ticking down close to the eight-minute mark, and the Blues successfully clinging to their small margin, former Blues' defenseman Polak took a high-sticking penalty.

If things went well, the Blues would take advantage of the opportunity and score a power play goal and take a commanding two-goal lead. But even if they didn't, it would at least kill two minutes of time and bring the game clock down to only six minutes remaining. Good news all around!

Not so fast. One minute into the Blues' power play, the Stars' Andrew Cogliano knocked down (i.e. tripped) Schenn to the ice in the Stars' defensive zone creating a break out by Janmark and ultimately a two-on-one with only Dunn back. Janmark skated the puck deep into the Blues' zone before shooting toward the goal. Binnington blocked the shot but Cogliano - the player who created the break-out with an arguable penalty - was able to find and punch in the loose rebound as Dunn unsuccessfully scrambled on the ice for it. *(Keep that in mind come Game 5 of the Stanley Cup Final.)* Giving up a "shortie," is never good. Doing so in the third period of a game you are leading by one goal - and a playoff game no less - is simply inexcusable.

But the Blues had no time to sulk or regret. The game and potentially series were on the line, and the Blues needed to regroup. Alex Pietrangelo decided to take matters into his own hands. First, he took a hard wrist shot from medium range that Bishop stopped; then he took a wicked slap shot from the left side that beat Bishop but clanged off the goalpost; and then he got another clean opportunity from a similar spot on the left side. This time the Captain made good and buried the slap shot. The adage to shoot, shoot and shoot again had paid off and we had our precious lead back, with only five minutes left in the game. Happy days were here again!

And then they weren't. Only a minute and a half after Pietrangelo' s goal, the Stars' leading scorer Seguin answered with a goal of his own, directing a great pass from Heiskanen into an open net as Gunnarsson fell down trying to guard him. The score was now 3-3. Two of the best defensive teams with two of the best goaltenders in the League had just surrendered three goals in less than three minutes, late in the third period no less.

But the wild ride wasn't through. With just under two minutes remaining in a game that felt certain to be going to Overtime, the St. Louis kid, Maroon, gave the Stars' Esa Lindell a little "push" while battling in front of the net, knocking the 6-foot 3 defenseman down to the ice. Maroon then retrieved the puck behind the goal and emerged to the left of his buddy Bishop. From a very close and seemingly impossible angle to Bishop's left, he beat him high to his right side to give the Blues yet another one goal lead at 4-3. Surely this would do it.

The anxiety wasn't quite over yet. With 44 seconds left in the game, Parayko inadvertently cleared the puck over the glass giving the Stars a very untimely "delay of game" power play. Now, with the goalie pulled, the Stars had a two-man advantage. Fortunately, the Blues were able to hold the Alamo and win the pivotal third game.

Game 4 (Alternating wins continue)

While the Blues' propensity to rebound from losses was very encouraging, the team's inclination to follow wins with less than stellar performances was also becoming a pattern. Could the Blues break it with a compelling Game 4 performance and win their FIFTH straight game on the road in the playoffs and take a commanding 3-1 series lead?

Things were looking up for the boys in Blue when we got an early power play. Instead of passing it around for most of the time and rarely taking a shot (a great tendency of our unit) or, worse, giving up a shorthanded goal, Tarasenko did what he does best: Vladi shot the puck! And, better yet, he scored! The Blues led 1-0. Both teams generally played very well with the lead, so this sure seemed like a good omen.

But not this time. The Stars scored seven minutes later to tie the game - Jason Dickinson was the villain scoring after a funky bounce off the back boards came right to him in front. And then, just before the first period ended, the more likely Jason (Spezza) scored on a power play blast to put Dallas up 2-1. The early excitement gave way to the realization that this was not only going to be a hard game to win, but a very tough series as well.

Sure enough, once the Stars and Bishop had the lead they held on tightly, just as they had in Game 2. Dallas added a back-breaking goal at the midpoint of the second period on a terrific shot by Defenseman Klingberg and yet another goal near the end of the second period to essentially ice the game. The Blues got a meaningless goal from rookie sensation Thomas late in the third period when Bishop lost his goal stick to finish the scoring. Nevertheless, Thomas' goal was the first playoff goal of the 19-year old's career and perhaps would instill some confidence in him as the series and playoffs progressed.

The game was a rather feisty affair; at one point in the second period with Bishop behind the goal and his back turned,

Perron seemed to slash him in the back with his stick. Bishop went down like he had been hit with a sledgehammer and flopped about like a fish out of water or like most professional soccer players after being kicked in the shin. The contact by Perron appeared designed to aggravate but did not seem to be especially severe and certainly not enough to knock over the big man. Bishop clearly was not hurt and was looking for a penalty. The referee who was standing right there decided that it did not warrant one. That incident undoubtedly precipitated Stars' Captain Jamie Benn to slash the Blues' goalie in his mid-section soon thereafter after a stoppage of play, with Binnington boldly swinging back. Finally, and most surprisingly, Binnington swung his stick more ferociously at Bishop as they came together at center ice at the close of the second period - presumably upset that Bishop had "faked' or exaggerated an injury.

In any case, the series was now tied 2-2, a familiar spot for the Blues. It was now down to a two out of three series with Games 5 and 7, if necessary, on home ice. Despite the loss, I felt pretty good about the Blues' chances. But Game 5 would be critical; in the eight previous (seven-game) playoff series where the Blues were tied two games each and had won Game 5 we went on to win seven of those series (87.5%). Fortunately, the Blues and Binner had proven their ability to bounce back after tough losses, so I expected a huge performance the next game.

Game 5 (Bishop keeps Blues in check- will it be checkmate?)

There was anticipation and a quiet confidence in the building heading into Game 5. The Blues were determined to put on the team's best performance of the series and secure a victory in front of the home crowd. But the Stars would have something to say about that as well and one in particular, goalie Ben Bishop, was determined not to let that happen.

Contrary to the Blues' uncanny ability to start fast and seize the lead and the momentum early, it was Dallas this time that jumped on the scoreboard early with yet another goal by the veteran 35-year-old center Spezza on a great pass behind the net from Seguin less than three minutes into the game. This was huge not only because the Blues had difficulty scoring goals on Bishop, but because Dallas had an outstanding defense, especially once they grabbed the lead. Indeed, the Stars had not yet relinquished a lead in this series and didn't lose a game against Nashville in the first round when they had a lead after *any* period.

The Blues were determined to change that and came at the Stars and Bishop in waves. We took shot after shot, from the point, the slot, the sideboards and behind the net; slap shots, wrist shots, screened shots, deflected shots and rebound shots. Thomas had a nice tip on a give-and-go, Perron had several great chances out in front, and Tarasenko almost banked one in off the big goalie's own body. But no shots got past Bishop.

Binnington kept the Blues in it as well making several great saves, including two breakaways - one by Dickinson and another by Seguin.

But then the Stars scored again. Lindell scored his first goal of the playoffs gaining the zone as Steen was unable to keep up and then sending a medium range backhander that went off the leg of Bouwmeester and into the net. The 2-0 lead in the second period felt more like a four-goal lead the way Bishop was playing. The Blues received three power plays in a row but couldn't do anything with them.

Finally, Schwartz broke through and cut the lead to one about eight and a half minutes into the final period when Bishop uncharacteristically handed the puck right to him in front while being pressured by Thomas. The Blues then launched a full out assault on Bishop to try and even the score and dominated play thoroughly. The best chance came when Sundqvist made a nice power move to break in all alone on Bishop, but the big man stymied that opportunity as well. In the final seconds the pressure was immense, but not enough to score (though Tarasenko actually directed the puck into the net one second after the buzzer sounded). At the end of the day, the effort was there, but the result (due to less than great shooting, and a lot of Bishop) was not.

Despite 39 shots on goal, the Blues only scored once and were now down in games in a playoff series for the first time in the 2018-2019 playoffs. More importantly, we were only one game away from elimination and would have to defeat the Stars in Big D just to force a Game 7. Statistically, it did not look good. Teams with a 3-2 advantage in the Stanley Cup playoffs in a best of seven format had historically won nearly four out of five series. And as for the Stars specifically, in the eleven series in their history where they were tied two games each and had won Game 5 they were an astounding 10-1.

Game 6 (Desperate Blues produce huge win)

The tension was palpable in the Sophir household and around the Lou as the team we cared so much about was only one game away from going home for the season. To lose to the Dallas Stars would be disheartening and anti-climactic for several reasons. The team had come so far this season from dead last to make the playoffs and had upset a terrific Winnipeg Jet team - to have it end now just seemed way too early. Moreover, while the Stars were clearly a very good and well-coached hockey team, they were not, in my view, a great one. They finished in seventh place in the conference and were a team that the Blues could and arguably should beat.

If the Blues had lost to Winnipeg, I would have been very disappointed but not surprised and not overly upset. But to lose to a team that you are better than and that you had home ice advantage against would leave me with a bitter taste in my mouth.

I hadn't been this nervous before a game in a long time. I felt the inner Glenn Hall in me but avoided his regurgitation ritual. We needed a good start. We needed the first goal. And then we needed to hold it and never let it go - grab the Stars by the jugular, the cojones or any other part designed to achieve the mercy rule and never give them even the perception that they had a chance to win this game.

And the Blues responded. Just 63 seconds into the game - the Blues' potential last game of a wonderful season - Alex Pietrangelo, who was becoming more and more of an offensive force, scored a goal from Edmundson and Schwartz to put the Blues ahead. This team had an unbelievable ability to score early in games when we needed it. The Blues had both the good early start and the lead. Check and check! This really took some pressure off and I could ease up slightly biting down on my horse bit.

But the Blues didn't comply with my third wish - that we never relinquish the lead. Rather, midway through the period Dunn committed a slash that led to a penalty. On the power play, Pietrangelo got caught trying to chase Stars' defenseman Klingberg out high leaving Seguin alone in the front of the net, producing his fourth goal of the playoffs. And the first period ended at 1-1 despite six power plays, three for each side.

The second period was played very defensively with neither team wanting to make a big mistake and give up an odd-man rush. Each side was careful not to take a penalty and give the other squad a power play. Although the Blues were getting the better of the play in my estimation, there was a big difference between that and actually scoring a goal - especially on Bishop who was in a zone and playing at the height of his considerable height.

And then finally and thankfully, with a few minutes to play in the second period, Perron put the Blues ahead 2-1, assisted by two of the Blues most unheralded players Sundqvist and Ivan Barbashev. *Restrained jubilation though- there was way too much time left to celebrate.*

It would behoove the Blues, I told anyone who cared to listen *(frankly, no one),* not to try to sit on the lead with so much time left. We needed to continue to press Dallas heavily, make it difficult for them to get out of their zone or through center ice, get a few turnovers and shoot, shoot, and shoot every chance we got. Just maybe one would go in and the Blues could take that critical two goal lead. And, by all means, stay the heck out of the penalty box.

The Blues seemed to be following that plan well, bottling up the Stars for the most part. And then, with about one-third gone in the third period, the Blues had possession in the Dallas' end with a great chance. Parayko, the biggest man on the ice not named Bishop with a scintillating slap shot, was left alone at the point with the puck. He took a few strides forward to really get some momentum behind his upcoming blast. Bishop confidently skated towards him anticipating the big shot and to cut down the angle. And then with his best Al MacInnis impression, Parayko unleashed a rising howitzer of a shot from medium range. Bishop did not have sufficient time to react and the shot hit him hard in the lower portion of his face mask and collarbone.

The sheer force of the blast toppled Bishop over like a knockdown clown at a carnival. Bishop dropped his stick and glove and lay on the ice writhing in apparent pain. Steen smartly gathered the rebound, skated away with it briefly and with his back toward the net and in one motion swept the puck toward the vacated goal. Again, it wasn't clear if he was attempting a shot or passing, but once again this shot/pass found Mr. Opportunistic, Jaden Schwartz, who was wide open to the opposite side of the net. Schwartz, full of goal confidence these days, quickly fired it into the open net before the Stars could react (it was a shot Schwartz would no doubt have missed or more likely hit the goalpost with during this regular season).

The Stars cried foul - that Bishop was down on the ice injured and that the play should have been blown dead by the officials. But the rules state that the referees are not to blow a play dead if the opposing team still has possession (which thanks to Steen the Blues did at all times) *unless* in the judgment of the officials, the player or goalie is in essentially a serious or life-threatening situation. The on-ice officials had determined that (1) the Blues had always maintained possession and (2) Bishop may have been hurt but was not in imminent danger. *Perhaps they were cognizant of Bishop's Academy Award performance in Game 4 when Perron tapped him on the back with his stick?*

After some consultation and review, the call was upheld, and the Blues had their critical two goal lead. It clearly proved to be the right call because Bishop remained in the game and was not badly hurt - he would go on to play a lot more hockey.

And then less than a minute later, O'Reilly made a great play pushing the puck from center ice to lead Sammy Blais, a very welcome addition to the Blues' line-up, on a full out breakaway down the left wing with O'Reilly not far behind as a helpful decoy. Rather than skate the puck to the goal crease and then shoot or try to deke the goalie, the typical move in 99% of such cases, Sammy decided to unleash a slap shot from close range at Bishop. And he beat him right between the wickets: 3-1!

The decision to shoot a slap shot in retrospect was brilliant as Bishop was undoubtedly still feeling the effects of Parayko's blast and perhaps more than a little gun shy about slap shots from close range at the moment. According to Blais the directive to take a quick shot came from the veteran O'Reilly who while skating up just behind him told the youngster to "just shoot." *More kudos to O'Reilly's resume as a thinking man's player.*

In any case, Blais had his first playoff goal in his very first playoff game. *I had been calling incessantly to anyone who would listen since the start of the playoffs that Blais should be playing and felt vindicated by his admirable performance. Sammy never left the line-up thereafter and was an integral part of the team's future success.*

Following the Parayko and Blais knock-out punches, the Blues never let up on the throttle and won 4-1, sending the series back to the Lou for the always excruciatingly exciting, yet CPR-risking, 7th game. And this game would prove to be one for the cardiologists!

Game 7 (The Magic of 7)

Seven has been a special number since the beginning of time. In the Old Testament, the seventh day is the Sabbath and the basis for the seven-day week - the number 7 is also mentioned (I am told) 77 times. In the New Testament, there are the seven churches, the seven angels, the seven seals, the seven trumpets and the seven stars (*oops that could be a bad omen*). In Islam, there are the seven heavens; in Hinduism, the seven higher worlds and seven underworlds, and in Buddhism, the newborn Buddha takes seven steps after rising.

If that weren't enough, there are seven continents, seven colors of the rainbow, seven musical notes and the Seven Wonders of the World. In Vegas, slot machines routinely use the number seven, three of which in a single row, will often mean a big jackpot. And, similarly, nothing says blackjack better than three 7's. Studies show that seven is the number most often identified as folks' favorite and luckiest. And on a personal note, I was born in July, the seventh month, on the 21st day - the sum of three sevens.

So, when I saw that Game 7 against the Dallas Stars (the team that finished 7th in the Western Conference) would be played on the 7th of May, my first thought was well that's pretty magical. The only question, though, was which team it would prove lucky for?

Sevens have generally been pretty lucky for the Blues against the Stars. We had beaten the Stars seven playoff series in our history. And we had two splendid Game 7 wins against the Stars in 1968 in Double Overtime to advance to the Stanley Cup

Final for the first time and in 1972, winning in single Overtime. (We did lose a Game 7 to the North Stars in 1984, but they had the far better record that year and the game was in Minnesota). And no player number in Blues' history has played a more prominent role in our team's success: from Berenson to Unger to Mullen to Ronning to Emerson to Tkachuk. And the great Pierre Turgeon wore number 77.

When I entered the Enterprise Center very early on May 7 to watch the pre-game and get a vibe for the night, I saw that the seats were draped with rally towels bearing the name of our town's most recent Number 7, local boy Maroon. Somebody had clearly put some thought into that in advance.

And then naturally at 7 p.m. there was the puck drop. In a contest that most astute hockey experts expected to be very close checking with minimal penalties and great goaltending, scoring any goal, especially the first one, seemed huge.

The Blues came out flying but, as has been a problem for long stretches during this series, we couldn't get one past Bishop. The Stars also almost scored when Radek Faksa was in all alone on Binnington, but the man from Richmond Hill, Ontario made a great glove save. And then with a little more than *seven* minutes left in the first period, the Blues' young sensational defenseman Dunn (my wife's favorite player) scored his first career playoff goal to give the Blues the all-important first goal on the unlikeliest of shots - a high wrist shot from the point that made it through a maze of players with a helpful screen from Maroon (number 7). Who knew at the time how difficult it would be to get another one?

The Stars answered quickly - a little over two minutes later - on what can only be described as a terrible *unlucky* conglomeration of events. Perron had clear possession of the puck to the right of Binnington, and with two Stars converging upon him sought to reverse the puck behind the goal to the left where there were two Blues' defensemen available. But his pass inadvertently hit the referee behind the goal. The brave men in stripes are normally incredible at dodging pucks so as not to interfere in the game. But here the puck not only ricocheted off of the referee but also the side of the net and then came right out in front of the goal to the Stars' Mats Zuccarello.

To make matters worse, the Stars had gotten away with knocking the goalie stick out of the hands of Binnington moments earlier so that he was now playing without a stick. And to further compound the disaster, the Blues' defensemen closest to the puck and Zuccarello, Joel Edmundson, tripped over Binnington' stick in an effort to cover Zuccarello. In so doing he fell flat on his face leaving a wide open and unguarded skill player with the puck, no challengers and a goalie without a stick.

Binnington had little chance as Zuccarello scored to tie the game 1-1 with four minutes to play in the first period. To give up a goal like that in a game of this importance and where goals would likely be hard to come by was potentially devastating. If we only knew at that point just how hard goals would be to come by.

The score stood at 1-1 after one period. And there it stood. And stood. And stood. The Blues pressed and pushed and punched and took shot after shot. We were winning almost every battle, had constant zone time in the Dallas' end and had chance after chance. During one stretch the Blues had 17 of the 18 shots taken. Perron, Schenn, Dunn and Sundqvist all had excellent scoring opportunities.

But the night clearly appeared to belong to the local kid - not Maroon, but Bishop. He stood taller than his usual 6-foot 7 frame and seemed to be on a personal mission to win this series by himself against his hometown team whom he worshipped and loved as a boy and who abandoned him without giving him much of a chance, after we had drafted him. The Stars hung in there and counterpunched when they could. Seguin, in particular, had a great chance from the slot that Binnington got a piece of.

It remained 1-1 heading into the third period. Now it was pretty clear that whoever scored the next goal was likely to win the series. Every chance and near miss took on added importance and drew anxious "oohs" and "ahs" from Blues' fans and the few Stars' fans in attendance (including the two seated next to me, dressed very inconspicuously, who flew in on their private jet that day and were planning to leave right after the game regardless of the hour). The stress level was excruciating.

With less than a minute left in the third period, Dallas' rookie speedster Hintz sped swiftly down the left wing and had a step on Parayko. His speed carried him right to the goal. Binnington came out to meet him and cut down the angle of his shot. But seeing no room, the Finn continued past Binnington and around the net with an eye toward stuffing the goal in the other side - the famous "wrap around." Binnington was now out of the goal and scrambling to race to the other side to cover the shot. But he was clearly going to be late. *Oh no!* Despite his enormous reach, the 6-foot 6 Parayko was not in a position to prevent the goal either; Hintz had a step on him and with his big body Parayko was unable to squeeze behind the goal to knock Hintz off of his mission. For a millisecond, things look very bleak with the game and season in the balance.

But then 35-year old Jay Bouwmeester came to the rescue. Hustling hard from the other side, he was able to barely get his stick on the shot by Hintz, changing the direction of the puck ever so slightly and causing it to hit the goal post instead of going in the net, where it was then quickly cleared out by Parayko. Now *that* was a close call!

Despite playing their hearts out and thoroughly dominating the game and out-shooting the Stars 47-17 through three periods, and incredibly 31-4 in the final two periods, the Blues could only break through one time against the former St. Louisan, as the score stood at 1-1 after 60 minutes. The tension in the building was palpable as the teams headed to Overtime in Game 7 with the season and the hopes of 52 years in the balance.

Nothing more exciting and emotionally exhausting as a sports fan than that.

I was hopeful but also wary. I had seen a lot of disappointment in my 52 years as a Blues fan. I couldn't help but think: What unlikely bounce or other fluky goal was about to befall the team aptly named the Blues this time?

The Blues continued to have good chances in the Overtime period (many others were blocked or went just wide), but Bishop would not relent. Binnington had far less chances at the other end, but he also had to make a few huge saves, or the season would have been over. Indeed, it was arguably harder to be a goalie when there were long stretches where you never saw the puck and then suddenly had to face a significant chance. To his credit, Binnington remained highly alert and in each instance when tested, the rookie goaltender rose to the occasion and held the fort. The Stars' Radulov had a burst of speed down the right side and took the puck all the way to the net crashing hard into Binnington, but the puck stayed out. (*No goaltender interference?*) Jamie Benn then came very close on another wrap-around attempt but Binnington got over just in time to make the save.

The first Overtime ended with the game still knotted at one. The stress level was now off the charts. I had brought a rubber ball with me to help relieve some of the anxiety and had now squeezed the thing at least 7,777 times.

The second Overtime continued as much of the rest of the game had gone - the Blues had most of the puck possession and the better of the play, but the Stars kept looking to pounce and counter-attack. It only took one. But the way the goalies were playing and both teams' attention to defense it didn't look like anyone would be scoring anytime soon - after nearly 70 minutes without a goal by either side, I actually thought that this game could go on a LOT longer. Wouldn't it be something, it occurred to me, if this game made it to quadruple Overtime - i.e. SEVEN periods? I sure had hoped not, but if that meant a victory for the Blues I would have waited all night long. At the same time, I and my 18,000 comrades in Enterprise Center were fully cognizant that one little slip-up, missed assignment, deflection, or bad bounce could determine the Blues' and Stars' seasons. *I think I will take that epidural now!*

And then the game almost ended. Parayko had the puck in the corner to the right side of the Blues' net and inexplicably directed the puck right at the Blues' goal - fortunately Binnington was awake or it might have gone in the net. If the Blues had lost this series on an "own goal" in this manner after all the team had been through, that would have been a Cubs' Bartman-like moment and certainly would have added to the lore that we are a cursed franchise.

But there was no curse on the Blues this night. With nearly six minutes gone in the second Overtime, the Blues had a faceoff in the Dallas end to the left of Bishop - who was by this time undoubtedly significantly slimmed down from his normal starting game weight of 215. Tyler Bozak (lucky number 21 for the Blues) won the faceoff and the puck went to Maroon (lucky number 7) along the side boards, closely guarded by the Stars' defenseman Klingberg. Blues' rookie first-round pick Thomas - and one of the few players who did not appear exhausted perhaps due to his age and more limited ice time - smartly skated over from his left wing to assist and took the puck from Maroon as the better puck handler. Thomas initially looked as if he might skate down the right boards but then made a nifty move to the inside, freezing Klingberg who was also being screened by Maroon. Thomas was now free and all alone just past the face-off circle to the left of Bishop. Bishop dropped to his knees, still covering up much of the goal with his size, and Thomas took a rising wrist shot from close range. His shot beat Bishop, but like Hintz' earlier effort, it hit the goal post.

But for once the massive size of Bishop may have been a disadvantage for him as the puck careened off the post back at the big man, hitting him in the back of the head and then dropping immediately behind him, just short of the goal. Perhaps the ricochet eludes a smaller goalie, especially if in a crouch, or it hits a smaller man in a way that the puck comes out rather than just dropping and stopping. Further, the albatross of a goalie didn't know where the puck was, and before he could locate it, a charging rambunctious Maroon, sniffing his grand prize - the greatest goal in Blues' history on *his* Number 7 night - swooned in, and just before Stars' defenseman Heiskanen could arrive, simply pushed the round rubber into the net.

GOAL! GOAL! GOAL! GOAL! GOAL! GOAL! GOAL! The Blues had beaten the Stars and advanced to the Conference Final for just the fourth time since 1970 on their 54th shot on goal. The Blues' Number 7, one of only two kids on the ice from St. Louis, had scored against the other kid from St. Louis for the biggest goal in his life. He, I and all of Blues Nation were in Seventh Heaven!

Recap of Dallas Series

This series will clearly go down as one of the classics in Blues' history - yet another great series against the Stars of Minnesota and Dallas that ended in Overtime of a Game 7.

The Blues outplayed Dallas for the most part, but due to the great play of Bishop, came within whiskers of losing the series. In Games 5 and 7 Bishop played out of his mind. To the Blues' credit, after a devastating loss in Game 5 and facing elimination in Dallas, the Blues were undeterred and unrelenting and played like a highly determined and confident group.

And in a highly tense Game 7, after nearly four hours, and in Hollywood-like fashion, Pat Maroon, the team's resident St. Louisan, rammed in a rebound to beat his friend and fellow St. Louisan Ben Bishop! Simply incredible! Could this be the year?

The San Jose Series
(Will the third time be the charm?)

The Blues had now played thirteen additional gut-wrenching games over the course of a month. And yet, after all of this excitement and angst, we were still somehow only halfway there to our goal - eight wins in search of sixteen, a gargantuan task.

And the next obstacle in the path, the San Jose Sharks, were very talented and likely the most experienced team in the Western Conference. They had secured two miracle-like (some might say referee-aided) series wins of their own. Indeed, San Jose's win against Vegas in Game 7 of their first round was perhaps the most incredible comeback in NHL history: down three goals in the third period with about ten minutes to play the Sharks scored *four* power play goals on a single highly questionable major penalty. And against Colorado in the next round, the Sharks were able to overturn a game tying goal in Game 7 on a challenge that found the skate of Avalanche star' Gabriel Landeskog (who was getting off the ice and not even remotely involved in the play) still touching the ice and offsides by a millimeter. So, the Blues hardly had exclusive claim to any assertion that *we* were the team of destiny.

It was a match-up of two franchises that had never won a Stanley Cup and were desperate to do so. The Sharks had made it to the Final for the first time three years ago (after dispatching the Blues) but fell to Sidney Crosby's Pittsburgh Penguins. The Sharks' desperation was punctuated by the age of their team and specifically their long-time heavily bearded winger Joe Thornton, who at 39 and a 21-year career had played in more games than any other active player without having won a Stanley Cup - over 1500. (The Blues' Jay Bouwmeester was third among active players, having played nearly 1200 games without a championship.)

And the aging Sharks also had 34-year-old Captain Joe Pavelski – "Mr. Shark" - who had played all 13 of his NHL years with San Jose accumulating over 350 goals. He would be a free agent at the end of the year and would likely be gone. And there was 33-year-old Brent Burns, a toothless mountain of a man who scored more points than any other player on the Sharks and more than any defenseman in the NHL this past season. While the Sharks had several other great players who were younger, Logan Couture, Tomas Hertl and Erik Karlsson in particular, helping San Jose to the second most goals in the NHL, many astute observers felt that it was now or never for the veteran team in its current configuration.

To add to the drama, San Jose was a team that the Blues owed big-time after two of the most gut-wrenching playoff losses in team history. In 2000, the eighth-place Sharks eliminated the first-place President Trophy winning Blues in the first round of an exasperating series where the Blues had rallied from a three games to one deficit, only to lose at home in Game 7. And then, more recently, in 2016, the Blues made it to the Conference Final for the first time since 2001, only four games from our first trip to the Stanley Cup Finals in 46 years. But the Sharks once again put a dagger in our hearts winning in six games. Along with Detroit and Chicago, no team had given the Blues more heartache than the Sharks.

Game 1 (Not a great start)

The Blues wanted to get off to a good start in the series, winning Game 1 as we had done against both Winnipeg and Dallas. And we wanted to use a similar formula; get on the Sharks from the get-go, apply the team's patented pressure on the Sharks' defensemen, and score the first goal, ideally early, to set the tone.

But the Sharks were having none of that. Indeed, it was the Sharks that scored the first goal, and did so early - within the first few minutes of the game. It was Logan Couture, the player looking more and more like the potential Conn Smythe winner with his 10th goal of the playoffs who put San Jose ahead.

Blues' defenseman Edmundson answered back about halfway through the period with his first goal of the playoffs with helpers from Schwartz and Tarasenko to give the Blues some confidence and quiet the rambunctious crowd briefly. But then the obsessive goal collector Joe Pavelski scored on a power play to put the Sharks up 2-1 at the first intermission. It wasn't a great period for the Blues, but it could have been worse.

And then it did get worse - a lot worse. In the second period, the Sharks scored three more times to just one for the Blues, one on a spectacular move by Timo Meier around Bouwmeester, to take a commanding 5-2 lead. Although the Blues narrowed the score to 5-3 in the third period, the game was really never much in doubt, and Couture added an empty netter to record his 11th goal of the playoffs.

It was only one game, but each game at this point in the season was precious. More disconcerting, the Sharks looked pretty darn impressive putting up a six spot on the Blues, which tied the most goals that we had given up since Berube had taken over as coach and Binnington had taken charge of the goal. It was discouraging and mandated that the Blues rebound big time in Game 2 if we were going to finally get that long-awaited berth in the Stanley Cup Final.

Game 2 (Bobby Orr Bortuzzo)

The reason to feel confident about the Blues despite the lackluster showing in Game 1 was once again the team's uncanny ability to bounce back after losses and to start those games on a high with an early goal. Saying you would like to score early and actually doing it, however, are two very different things.

It ain't easy to score goals at any time in the NHL - the goalies are not only very good and sometimes great - but they are generally large, wear lots of padding, and occupy a substantial portion of the 6 x 4-foot net (a far cry from the 24 x 8 feet of a soccer goal). And scoring early, especially in the first few minutes of a contest, is especially hard - everyone is fresh, well-rested and keen to their assignments. And yet this version of the Blues seemed to have a knack for the early goal like nothing I had ever seen in my five decades of watching hockey, especially for a team that was not a huge goal scoring machine (finishing 15th out of 31 teams in goals during the season).

And sure enough, the Blues continued that terrific trend when Schwartz scored his 9th goal of the playoffs just two minutes into Game 2, with a great wrist shot into the top corner past Martin Jones glove, stunning the home team. The Blues were playing with intensity, colliding forcefully with everything in teal - Robert Bortuzzo had a monstrous hit as did Schenn, Edmundson and Maroon. Even little Schwartz pounded the much bigger Brent Burns. The objective clearly was to wear the Sharks down (or in Burns' case, dislodge the few teeth he had remaining and reduce him to an all-liquid diet).

In the second period Dunn added a goal on a long wrist shot through a maze of traffic to put the Blues up 2-0 and things were looking very nice. And then San Jose's Marcus Sorensen took an interference penalty giving the Blues a chance to go on the power play and potentially seize a three-goal lead. Instead, not only didn't the Blues score, but the troublesome power play actually yielded a breakaway and yet another shorthanded goal.

The extraordinary Couture blocked a pass from Pietrangelo from the point in the Sharks' zone and took the puck the length of the ice. Petro followed and harassed him the entire way, but the Sharks' superstar managed to score nonetheless to cut the lead to 2-1. And with that one play, the momentum completely changed. It was feeding time for the Sharks and they were hungry. Their appetites were satisfied just two minutes later when, yes, that same Couture fellow once again beat Pietrangelo down the left side and then Binnington as well on a wrist shot to even the score. *Logan Couture is phenomenal, but I am really getting sick of hearing his name.*

It didn't look especially promising for the Blues for most of the rest of the period until defensive-defenseman Bortuzzo made his play of the year. Bortuzzo had the puck at the right point guarded closely by the Sharks' Thornton. He released the puck to Bozak in the slot, and then surprisingly made a bee-line for the goal. Bozak had given the puck to Edmundson at the left point who saw the streaking Bortuzzo who now had the astonished Thornton beaten by several strides. Borts gathered a pass from Eddie on his forehand, and as he moved toward the net unmolested, went to his backhand of all things and then, for the trifecta of offensive skills, flipped a sweet shot high to Jones' stick side past the stunned goaltender.

He wasn't the only one shocked. The big tough-minded defenseman had only two goals *for the entire year* and had never before scored a playoff goal in nine years and 32 playoff games! Bortuzzo hadn't made a move or taken a shot like that in any game I had ever seen - and I see a lot of Blues hockey. *What an amazing time to break out his Bobby Orr imitation!*

Thanks to Bortuzzo's heroics, the Blues had that all-important 3-2 lead entering the third period. And we held it despite having to defend a power play mid-period from a hooking call on Robert Thomas. (We were also "forced" to go on the power play ourselves - we didn't score but at least we didn't let the Sharks score this time.) Sundqvist even added a late goal to seal the victory. The good guys had evened the series 1-1.

Game 3 (Give the refs a big hand)

Most of us expected Game 3 to be a great game and to play a critical role in who would have a major upper hand in the series. If we only knew just how big of a *hand*. It was a classic.

The Blues came out flying in front of the home crowd including their lucky charm 11-year-old Laila who was at her first playoff game having been given clearance by her doctors to attend. Sharks' goalie Jones stymied early great chances by Blais, Perron and O'Reilly. Determined not to let the Blues get off to their traditional quick start, and parlay that into a maddening crowd that might overwhelm them, the Sharks held the fort early and then scored not just the first goal (with six and a half minutes left in the first period), but a second one as well a few minutes later to put them up 2-0 after the first period. Not at all what the Blues and the faithful had in mind. The good news was that the Sharks' goalie was not Bishop or even Hellebuyck and the lead did not seem insurmountable.

The Blues started the second period with determination. Indeed, Steen scored a goal just over a minute into the period. Unfortunately, the roar from that goal had not yet subsided when Joe Thornton answered back 18 seconds later; his second of the game, to take the air out of the building and put the Sharks back up by two. *Urgh*!

But the Blues were far from done. Tarasenko scored a goal at the four-minute mark on a brilliant rush and shot to once again cut the lead to one, and then Perron, with about four minutes left to go in the period, scored to tie the game - a great response by the Blues.

And the boys didn't let up. They kept pushing, creating a hooking penalty by the Sharks' Burns. This time the Blues seized the momentum and the opportunity, as Perron scored a rare power play goal for the Blues with less than two minutes left in the period to put us up 3-2. The Blues had converted a two-goal deficit after one period into a lead after two periods. *Now the challenge was to hold it for 20 minutes.*

The Blues came out solidly in the third, employing their hard check, limiting the available "free" ice to the Sharks and avoiding the penalty box. The Sharks had a few chances but nothing that Binnington couldn't handle as the clock ticked away and as the Blues got closer and closer to taking their first series lead against the Sharks and being only two wins away from reaching the Stanley Cup final. The Blues had several good chances to take a two-goal lead, the most glaring an empty net opportunity for Schwartz after the Sharks pulled their goalie with a little over a minute left in the game. Schwartz had the puck cleanly just past center ice and shot to a wide-open net and yet managed to hit the goal post instead (a flashback to earlier in the season).

That miss would prove extremely costly. Shortly thereafter, Thornton had the puck in the corner to the right of Binnington. Bouwmeester went into the corner to challenge him. Steen was guarding the faceoff area and for some unexplained reason Pietrangelo was far away from the goal. *Was he anticipating a pass elsewhere?* That left no defenseman in front of the net and center O'Reilly alone to try to guard *two* Shark players - only their two most dynamic scorers in Pavelski and Couture. Thornton was able to get the pass through Bouwmeester and to the front of the net where Couture was able to collect it and quickly jam it in for his bleeping 14th goal of the playoffs, tying the game. For the Blues' captain to make such a huge positional gaffe, leaving the hottest hockey player in the world all alone in front of the net with only one-minute left in the game, was equally perplexing and maddening.

The Blues had turned what should have been a clear victory into an Overtime game - it was now truly anyone's game.

The Overtime went back and forth in the opening minutes with neither team having a great chance. About five minutes into the Overtime, the play was down at the Blues' end. Sharks forward' Meier took a shot from the face-off area to the left of Binnington which was blocked by the defense and in the process; Meier was knocked to the ice. The puck fluttered high into the air. In what appeared to be in a bit of frustration on Meier's part, he swatted at the puck with his glove from his knees and connected. The puck did not go far but it did go to the Sharks' Gustav Nyquist, who quickly passed the puck to Sharks' Defenseman Erik Karlsson, who had moved forward in front of the goal, and he put the puck in past Binnington.

My normal reaction in such a situation would have been something to the effect of "shoot" or "shucks," though likely with much saltier language and at a very loud decibel. But I was unusually calm about this development because I was confident that this was not a goal - anyone who follows hockey more than casually knows that you can't pass the puck with your hand to another player in the offensive zone, which he clearly did. Even if somehow the on-ice officials missed it, it would surely be reviewed, and the game would continue. Some of the Blues and even Binnington seemed to let up a bit assuming the play was dead.

The on-ice officials were conferring. This would all be over soon, and we could resume play. But wait - no - the officials were saying it was a goal and they hurriedly skated off the ice.

How was that possible? It was the hand-pass seen around the world. But the on-ice refs didn't see it - or at least were not certain. How could all four on-ice officials, including some of the most experienced refs and linesmen in the NHL, and any one of whom could have called it, fail to see what was plainly obvious to people at the game sitting in the upper deck and to millions on TV even without the benefit of numerous replays that confirmed it?

An excellent post-game analysis by the *The Athletic* showed that some of the officials were not in proper position. The "down low" referee was behind the goal away from the puck and his view of the hand pass was obstructed by the goal, the goalie and other players. The other referee was back at the red line, too far away from the play to get a good look. One linesman was on the right boards, precisely where he should have been, but also with an obstructed view, and the second linesman was on the other side of the ice, near the bench, and would have seemed to have had a decent view of the play but apparently didn't. In retrospect the first referee should have come out in front of the goal or worked his way to the other side, in order to have had his eyes directly on the puck.

That's not *my* opinion, but what former referee Kerry Fraser told the *The Athletic*. Frasier is only the person who has refereed the most games in NHL history (1,904 regular season games, 12 Stanley Cup Finals, and over 261 Stanley Cup playoff games). He also was one of the few referees that refused to don a helmet with pucks whizzing by his head, apparently unwilling to disturb his perfect hair - undoubtedly Ungie's favorite ref!

I certainly understand that mistakes and human error happen by even the best of them, especially in a very fast paced game where the refs have been skating for hours. And unlike the players, the refs don't switch lines but are on the ice for 100% of the action. But why wasn't the play reviewable? Because under the rules it just wasn't.

While it is surprising but understandable that four on-ice officials could all miss this infraction, the rule that precludes video review in this situation is not excusable. There is absolutely no reason that the NHL has a review system that allows review of all goals and even offsides calls but prevents review of something that was so easily discernible and correctable in less than thirty seconds and which would have prevented a terrible miscarriage of hockey justice that could well determine a team's season. To have the technology available that would definitively answer the question - and without delay - and not to use it is insane. (The NHL has now changed the review rule for the upcoming season to permit a video challenge to a hand pass in the offensive zone when a goal is scored. It's a smart move, though was too late to help the Blues.)

The Blues' players showed their extreme frustration at the non-call by slamming their sticks against the glass and yelling at the referees as they skated off hurriedly and helplessly with no opportunity to do anything to correct the blown call. The series was now 2-1 Sharks, instead of potentially 2-1 Blues (to be fair, there was no guarantee if the game had continued that the Blues would have won). How big a difference is that? Down 2-1 meant that the Blues (and not the Sharks) had to win three of the next four games, which is an extremely tall order against any team. *The NHL could drive someone to drinking (if I hadn't already begun).*

But Coach Berube's response to the injustice was about as mild-mannered as any I've ever seen in sports when a coach's team has been a victim of a critical outrageously bad call. When pressed in the post-game conference about whether he thought the play was a hand-pass, he simply asked the reporter what he thought. When the reporter responded that it *was* a hand pass, Berube calmly said: "Well, there you go," and refused to otherwise address the issue. In fact, he expressly told his team NOT to talk about it to the media or dwell on anything but the next game. It would prove to be sage psychological advice.

Game 4 (The Barber, the Bozer and the Binner)

It was back to the drawing board for Game 4 and it was critical that the Blues put the disappointment and the "screw job" of Game 3 in the trash receptacle and come out and win the next game. Berube undoubtedly felt more like a psychologist than a hockey coach in the 48 hours between these games, coaxing his guys to address the situation at present - the only thing the players could do something about.

And the Blues got just what the doctor ordered in the opening minute of Game 4 when Steen crashed hard into defenseman Karlsson - the "hero" of Game 3 - behind the Sharks' net. The pressure caused Karlsson to turn the puck over to Barbashev who quickly shot and scored his first ever playoff goal just 35 seconds into the game. The ability of the Blues to score early in games, especially in critical games in which we trailed in a series, was nothing short of remarkable.

And then later in the period, only nine seconds after the Blues got a second power play *(perhaps the union of referees felt a little bad about the last game's outcome?),* **Bozak** scored to put the Blues up by two to end the period on a high Note. It was a good thing we scored that second goal because it was the last goal we would score that night. The Blues were not able to mount much offense - only 22 shots on goal - but thanks to Binnington, the Blues held the Sharks scoreless until nearly seven minutes left in the game when talented Shark' Hertl scored his 10th of the playoffs on a power play. But Binnington shut the door from there and the Blues skated off with an essential 2-1 win. It wasn't one of the Blues' best performances by any stretch, and the Sharks seemed to have the better of the play, but a win is a win is a win.

For the third time in three series the Blues were now tied 2-2 in games, and down to a two out of three series, though unlike against Dallas, the Sharks would host Game 7 if necessary. First things first - let's win Game 5 and then come home and take the series - Winnipeg style.

Game 5 (The Blues' best game of the Playoffs)

Game 5 would be a Sunday afternoon game on national TV and I would be watching it from a small, dingy isolated bar along the coast near Pacific City, Oregon with my wife, my daughter and her boyfriend who were doing their best to accommodate my hockey obsession while undoubtedly preferring to explore the great outdoors. (*My daughter was living in Oregon and we had arranged to take this trip months ago but, always cognizant of the NHL playoff schedule, I had strategically selected days of travel that would not conflict with my ability to watch the Blues play, in the remote chance they would make it this far in the playoffs. Good thinking Sherlock!*)

The only other fellow in the bar, sitting alone at a table next to us, was a local elderly veteran who was disabled. It turns out that he had spent a good portion in his life near St. Louis and Scott Air Force base and was a huge Cardinal fan, especially of the old Gashouse Gang. It was a great coincidence and he would become a Blues' fan as well before the afternoon was through.

I didn't know what to expect from the Blues but can't say I was optimistic (*most who know me might say I never am*). The Sharks had been 7-3 at home in the playoffs thus far and were the clear favorites. Coach Berube seemed to appreciate the stakes and was especially animated in his pre-game speech. He encouraged his troops to get after the Sharks right away, to "go north" (straight at them), to get on the forecheck and make life miserable for their defensemen all day long, so that you wear them down and they turn the puck over.

Whether inspired by the coach's words and confidence, the Game 4 win and getting back even in the series or being in their favorite venue these days (*anywhere on the road*), the players came out with fire in their bellies. Schenn in particular was an animal, with two bone-crunching hits. Even Tarasenko got in the act with a punishing high hit on the Sharks' Meier.

As was becoming customary, the Blues scored first and early, though it took all of five minutes this time. Once again, the Sharks' Karlsson carelessly cleared a puck in front of his own goal with no pressure on him off the boards and right to Sundqvist. Like Barbashev in the previous game, Sunny wasted no time with the gift and promptly blasted a one-timer past the Sharks' stunned goalie.

And the Blues didn't let up. We had several quality chances - the best perhaps a great give-and-go from Perron to Blais to O'Reilly which gave him an open net, but he couldn't hold the puck. Not to worry: the playoff scoring machine, also known as Schwartz, scored early in the second period on a rebound from a Tarasenko shot to give the good guys a 2-0 lead.

Rather than sitting back and simply trying to protect the rare two-goal lead, the Blues continued to push. Bouwmeester made a long stretch pass to Barbashev near center ice, who while closely guarded by the Sharks' Burns, executed a perfect flip pass to Tarasenko, sending the Blues' star in on a clear breakaway. Burns desperately tried to catch Tarasenko and impede his progress and in the process tripped him from behind.

A penalty shot! Penalty shots are extremely rare, especially in the playoffs, and are only awarded when a player has a clear, unimpeded path to the goal and is hooked, tripped or improperly interfered with from behind. In fact, the Blues were awarded only one during the entire year, and this was the first and only penalty shot by or against the Blues in the playoffs. (While players take the same breakaway shot from center ice in a "shoot-out" during the regular season when a game is tied after a five-minute Overtime, that technically isn't a penalty shot which only occurs *during* the game in lieu of a two-minute penalty.)

The penalty shot is the most exciting play in hockey - not only because it occurs so infrequently, but also because it is a classic one-on-one battle between the shooter and the goalie, with tremendous skill, creativity and athleticism on display in a five-second window that can have significant repercussions for the outcome of the game. (The first penalty shot ever scored in NHL history was in 1934 by none other than Ralph "Scotty" Bowman (*not* the famous coach) of the St. Louis Eagles!) More importantly, in this case, it was an opportunity for the Blues to take a three-goal lead and put this game largely away.

Tarasenko was indisputably the best goal scorer and pure shooter on the Blues and undoubtedly in the top five - perhaps the top two behind that Ovechkin fellow - in the entire NHL. But that didn't mean he was likely to score. Being a great shooter doesn't always translate into excelling at penalty shots. Often players skate in and try to make several fancy moves and fake the goalie out - getting too close to the goal to get off a good shot or to lift the puck and sometimes losing the puck before they can even get off a shot. Also, unlike soccer where the shooter has the overwhelming advantage - the likelihood that a penalty shot results in a goal in soccer is about 75% (*I would have thought it was even higher*) - the odds in hockey strongly favors the goalie. A successful shootout percentage of 35% is generally considered pretty solid. Tarasenko's career percentage in shootouts in his career was in that range - decent but not special. But he had been 0 for 4 in shootouts during the 2018-2019 season. And he had never taken a penalty shot *during* the game before.

Thus, despite the score, the pressure seemed to be more on Tarasenko - if he didn't score (as was statistically far more likely) it would likely create a momentum surge for the Sharks. And as our superstar goal scorer, he was kind of expected to deliver. My hope was that the Tank would be sure to at least fire one - using his greatest weapon, his lethal shot, and not get too close or try to deke the goalie.

Tarasenko took the puck at center ice with the Blues and Sharks and nearly 18,000 in attendance and millions on TV watching his every movement (none more intently than me). Upon the referee's command, Tarasenko confidently gathered the puck at center ice; he weaved to the right and then back to the left in a steady but unrushed march toward the Sharks 'goalie. Jones moved out slightly from the goal to cut down the angle and also to see if he could force Tarasenko to give away his move or be distracted. Tarasenko didn't flinch and didn't try to deke Jones. Instead as he got in the midrange area, he quickly unleashed one of the most wicked wrist shots Martin had likely seen - it came flying off the stick with ferocity and uncanny accuracy and hit the top left corner of the twine glove-side before Jones even moved. No goalie in the world could have stopped that shot and the Blues now had the commanding 3-0 lead.

Binnington kept the Sharks off the scoreboard for the rest of the second period. Then, for the third time in three periods, the Blues scored an early goal - this one by Schwartz, his second of the game on a deflection off a bounce in front, almost like a drop kick with his stick, to go up 4-0. *When you're hot, you're hot.* And then Schwartzie added yet another one late in the third for good measure on a brilliant feed from Tarasenko. It was his second hat trick of the playoffs - something that hadn't been done in more than a decade! Binnington also had his first playoff shutout. And the Blues skated to a thoroughly dominating 5-0 victory, outshooting the Sharks 40-21. *There were actually moments during this game where I took time to relax and enjoy the moment! Call off the psychiatrists!*

Game 6 (Stanley Cup Finals Baby after 49 years!)

After Game 5, the Sharks looked beat-up and frustrated and a few of their key players were injured. Rumor was that Pavelski, Hertl and Karlsson would not be playing Game 6. *What a break that could be.*

And the Blues were returning to home where there would be a boisterous crowd ferociously cheering on every check and goal. Although the Blues hadn't played particularly well at home, it still had to be an advantage to have your fans behind your every movement encouraging you to give that extra ounce of effort when there was little oxygen in the tank.

But, at the same time, you can never take another team for granted - especially a veteran playoff team with talent and a guy named Couture. The Blues' fans had enough history of heartache and battle scars to avoid any premature celebrations. Hopefully, the players had also learned their lesson from the Stars' failure to put away the Blues in Game 6 at home.

It was essential for the Blues to kick the Sharks while they were down and never let them feel like they were back in the series. And we did just that. Naturally, the Blues scored the first goal and very early - Perron this time the hero deflecting a shot by Blais into the goal just one and a half minutes into the contest. Later in the period Tarasenko added a power play goal to make it 2-0 Blues after one period - another great top shelf goal, this one to the stick side. *Only forty minutes left to the Stanley Cup Final - but don't get ahead of yourself here Sophir.*

The Sharks scored one-third of the way into the second period, after the Blues had a three on one and couldn't convert and then got caught up ice. It broke a streak of seven straight goals by the Blues. More importantly, it cut the margin to one. *See I told you.* And then the Sharks came within a whisker of tying the game. Justin Braun took a wicked slap shot from the point which Binnington stopped but the puck was lying on the doorstep for Couture to put it in, when Parayko came to the rescue and quickly cleared it out.

Fortunately, Schenn helped keep me off the proverbial window ledge by scoring a power play goal - a rebound on a Pietrangelo shot - to extend the lead to 3-1 as the second period expired. *Twenty more minutes - is this really happening?*

The score stayed that way until seven minutes left in the game when on a slick give-and-go from O'Reilly to Bozak to Perron and back to Bozak the Blues took a commanding three-goal lead. *It was only matter of time now.* The Sharks desperately pulled their goalie with nearly five minutes left and Barbashev scored an empty netter to raise the score to 5-1.

The party was in full celebration and the crowd was going bonkers as the time went off the clock and the Blues were heading to the Stanley Cup Finals for the first time in 49 years. I sat down at my seat. I had been standing much of the game and for the entire last five minutes - and the emotion flowed. I was just ten years old when I had last seen my Blues on the national stage fighting for the Stanley Cup, albeit unsuccessfully. *Could we actually win this thing?*

After the game, Coach Berube congratulated his troops on a great series win but reminded them, just in case the team needed one heading into the freakin' Stanley Cup final, "We're not done yet Boys!"

Recap of San Jose Series

Against a talented and hungry Sharks team, the Blues avenged a couple of their most disheartening playoff losses in history. The Blues came back from being manhandled in Game 1 to win a tight Game 2, after having relinquished a two-goal lead. And as deflating as Game 3 was - first, giving up a terrible last-minute tying goal and second, getting a horrible call in Overtime to give the Sharks the game - the Blues did not fold. The boys hung on (barely) for a 2-1 win the next game. And then, as if given a fresh dose of oxygen and the blessing of a new heart, suffocated the Sharks the next two games winning handily by a combined score of 10-1!

The Blues had now survived three grueling and excruciatingly close series. We beat a tremendously talented offensive Winnipeg team in six games while trailing by two goals late in Game 5 of a 2-2 series. We beat a dynamic defensive Dallas team in a nerve-wracking seven game series after trailing three games to two, defeating Dallas in their building in Game 6 and winning Game 7 in Double Overtime at home. And we beat a veteran explosive San Jose Sharks team in six games after falling behind two games to one on a goal in Overtime that the NHL conceded should not have counted.

So alas and unbelievably it's off to the STANLEY CUP FINAL - 49 years in the waiting!

The Stanley Cup Final vs Boston
(Will the Blues get redemption?)

The 2019 Stanley Cup Final would feature the St. Louis Blues versus the Boston Bruins. *Of course, it would - it only made sense in this oddball mystical season.* The Blues had played the Bruins the last time we got this far - a mere 49 years ago - so it was about high time for a re-match.

Despite the lopsided nature of the 1970 Stanley Cup Final, it produced the most iconic moment in Bruins' history, the Orr Cup-clinching "flying through the air" final goal. Indeed, that moment has been cast in bronze and saved for immortality in a sculpture that serves as the signature monument outside of Boston's TD Garden. If that wasn't enough humiliation, the artwork was created by Harry Weber - a St. Louisan and the man who created sculptures of Stan the Man, Jack Buck, Ozzie Smith and Bob Gibson!

For further evidence of a possible cosmic connection, Neil Armstrong, the father of Blues General Manager Doug Armstrong, was a linesman during the 1970 Stanley Cup Final *(pretty impressive after having just walked on the moon only one year ago!)* If that weren't enough, David Backes - the long-time St. Louis Blues' captain and close friend to many Blues' players, now played for the Bruins. And the Blues' Zach Sanford grew up near Boston rooting for the Bruins and went to Boston College.

Beyond the hockey coincidences, St. Louis and Boston have had a sports rivalry like few others not in close proximity. The cities' beloved baseball teams, the Cardinals and the Red Sox, had played against each other in the World Series four times, with the Cardinals winning twice - in 1946 and 1967, and the Red Sox winning twice - in 2004 and 2013, the former their first World Series win in 86 years.

I was at the clincher for Boston at Busch Stadium on October 27, 2004 sitting next to a young boy, his father and his grandfather who had travelled from Boston to witness the dream and the moment that the elderly granddad never thought he would see. The Red Sox had twice lost to the Cardinals in the World Series. At the end of the game they were all in tears and while I couldn't quite go that far, I was very happy for them. Now the roles were reversed. The Blues had previously lost in the Final to Boston and I had been waiting for 52 years, virtually my entire lifetime, to have my team win the Stanley Cup - something that I wasn't sure that I would ever see in my lifetime.

In football, the St. Louis Rams (not to be confused with last year's Los Angeles version which some of us in the Lou refuse to acknowledge) played the New England Patriots in the 2002 Super Bowl. At the time the Bostonians and their young 24-year old quarterback Tom Brady were considered a longshot as a decided 14-point underdog to the "Greatest Show on Turf." But the Patriots pulled off the upset. Again, the roles were now reversed as the Bruins entered this series as the decided favorites at minus 170 according to the oddsmakers (meaning that to win $100 on Boston you would have to risk $170).

Even in basketball, the old St. Louis Hawks, who moved to Atlanta shortly after (and in part because) the Blues came to town, played the Boston Celtics for the NBA crown a rather astounding four times in five years (from 1957 through 1961). Unfortunately, the local squad only won once - in 1958 behind Bob Pettit's miraculous 50-point performance.

The 2019 Stanley Cup Final also presented a rivalry beyond the banks of the Mississippi and Boston Harbor: a rivalry between the United States and Canada (at least as far as Canada was concerned). The Blues happen to have the most Canadians on their squad of any team and the Bruins the most Americans (and one of the least numbers of Canadians). Needless to say, in hockey-proud Canada, and without a Canadian team in the Final for the eighth straight year (with the last Canadian Stanley Cup *winner* 26 years ago when Montreal took the crown coached by former Blues' Coach Jacques Demers), most Canadians would be rooting hard for the guys in blue.

But so apparently would be most Americans, according to polls that showed only a few of the fifty states had majorities of hockey fans who were pulling for the Bruins. *So much for*

America First. I'm sure a significant number of puck nuts were captivated by the Blues' underdog story and coming from last place at the start of January all the way to the Stanley Cup Final and also by the fact that the Blues had never won a Cup in 51 seasons and were the oldest team never to have won one.

But I suspect that many were also rooting for the Blues as a vote *against* Boston. Certainly, cities like New York and Montreal that have strong rivalries with Beantown might root for even Russia and North Korea over anything Boston. But folks from other cities were also likely tired of the arrogance and smugness of Boston's fans who had experienced more Championships recently than some felt any city deserved. Their self-imposed nickname as "the City of Champions" because the Red Sox and Patriots were current champions in their respective sports obviously did not serve to endear themselves to many folks outside New England. Not to be overlooked in the "I hate Boston" crowd was the Marchand factor - the talented and pesky winger who had crossed the line from aggressive to dirty on several occasions in his career and was therefore disdained by fans of any team he had utilized his questionable tactics against.

It never hurts to have the support of folks from across the nation; it feels good as a fan to have that national and even international backing and, who knows, it may even help the karma. Having the collective support of most also makes the lows just a hair more tolerable and the highs that much more rewarding. It's the difference between betting with the roller and the crowd at the crap table versus being the lone "don't pass" guy. Your odds don't improve but winning and losing somehow feels a little better. But the players still have to perform, and widespread fan support can't score and stop goals (at least as far as I know).

As clutch and resilient as the Blues had been in dispensing with three great teams in very close contests which tested their toughness and emotional mettle, their opponent in the Final might have been on a different level.

The Bruins had been initially tested by a terrific Toronto team, coming back from being down 3-2 in the series to the Maple Leafs to win Game 6 on the road in hockey's biggest market and then winning decisively at home in Game 7. The Bruins then defeated a sizzling hot Columbus team, which had remarkably swept the best team in the NHL all season long, Tampa Bay, in four straight. The Bruins came from behind in that series as well, winning the last three games. And then they drew a Carolina team that had been playing great and had defeated the reigning Stanley Cup Champions, the Ovechkin-led Washington Capitals. Indeed, the Bruins destroyed the Hurricanes in four straight games, by a combined score of 17 -5.

To say the Bruins were in the zone would be an understatement; they entered the Stanley Cup Final having won seven straight playoff games, dominating their opponent by the score of 28-9 in those games. And although they had two tough, bruising series with multiple Overtime games, they had a shorter lopsided one most recently, so they were now well rested.

Boston possessed the top power play in the playoffs as well as the alleged best line in hockey in Patrice Bergeron, David Pastrnak and Brad Marchand (so good, in fact, that they were labeled the "perfection line"). The trio combined for 106 goals during the regular season and 22 goals in the playoffs. And they were on fire. When they were on the ice at even strength in the Eastern Conference Final they scored 11 goals while yielding zero! The Bruins also had a world class goalie in Tuukka Rask and a goliath veteran 6-foot 9 defenseman in Zdeno Chara, to go along with speedy and skillful defensemen Torey Krug, Matt Grzelcyk and Charlie McAvoy. Further, the Bruins were deep, well-coached and experienced. *But at least they didn't have Bobby Orr this time around!*

In comparison with the Blues, the Bruins both scored more goals and gave up fewer goals per game in both the regular season and in the playoffs. They also had a much better power play percentage in both the regular season and playoffs and a better penalty killing percentage in the playoffs than the Blues.

Moreover, numerous Bruins had played in a Stanley Cup Final before and had won the Cup. Not a single member of the Blues had ever won a Stanley Cup, and only one player had ever even played in the Stanley Cup Final (David Perron last year for the Vegas Golden Knights, though he was a healthy scratch for some of the games.)

And the Bruins had home ice advantage to boot. The Bruins had been an outstanding home team throughout the year (29-9-3) and very solid in the playoffs to date as well (6-3).

Not surprisingly, the Bruins were a very confident team - some might say downright cocky. The media was talking about the Bruins as if they were the old Montreal Canadiens, Edmonton Oilers and New York Islanders in their hey days - essentially unbeatable. And Boston was drinking the cool aid.

Even Boston Coach Bruce Cassidy - from all accounts a savvy and calculating hockey coach - appeared to be a bit overconfident about his team. He was asked by a reporter at the pre-series media talk "Why do you think the Bruins have an edge in this series?" Most coaches would have completely dodged that kind of question, not buying into the premise and making his team feel too special or risk ticking off the opponent.

But Bruce could not resist. While initially qualifying his answer that he's "not trying to create bulletin board material here" (the phrase for the other team posting his comments and using them as a motivation tool), he explained that his team was more experienced than the Blues - that the Bruins had essentially been there and done that and that the Blues' players had not. While that may have been true it was probably not the wisest thing to say. *Why poke the bear in the cage before the first puck has even been dropped?*

And the Blues *were* a serious team to be reckoned with, having had the best record in the NHL for the last half of the season and having defeated three very solid teams to get to the

Final. And we had an arsenal of diversified players who were committed to one another, played extremely hard and bought into Coach Berube's system.

The Blues had a calm, determined and hot goalie in Binnington, a great face-off guy and smart two-way player in O'Reilly, a shutdown defensive pairing in the tall and skillful 6-foot 6 Parayko and the experienced and nearly as rangy 6-foot 4 Bouwmeester, a first-rate sharpshooter in Tarasenko, a scrappy, elusive puck-possessing monster in Schwartz, an experienced sniper in Perron, a tireless, highly-skilled offensive defenseman in Captain Pietrangelo, a hard-hitting winger who could score in Schenn, a solid experienced second center in Bozak, a highly underrated and speedy aggressive center in Sundqvist, and lots of tough "character" guys - young and old - who would crash into and block anything to bring home the Cup. There were the big defensemen Edmundson and Bortuzzo, the veterans Steen and Gunnarsson, the speedy and elusive youngster Thomas, the emerging stars Blais and Barbashev, and the local Big Rig, Patty Maroon. I only hoped that our most skilled defenseman in my view, Vince Dunn, could make it back for the Finals at some point after taking a puck to the choppers - gotta love hockey.

The Blues also had at least one statistical advantage over the Bruins - our defensemen had more offensive and scoring ability. Three Blues' defensemen (Pietrangelo, Dunn and Parayko) had double digit goals during the year; not a single Bruin defenseman had more than seven goals.

So, the Blues were clearly a credible opponent, but we still were a significant underdog according to the oddsmakers and most hockey "experts." While a few picked the Blues to win the series, the vast majority were pretty darn sure that the Bruins would win - most in 5 or 6 games.

Game 1 (A lost opportunity and a crushing hit)

The series that most expected Boston would win relatively easily could not have started better for the Blues. Coach Berube encouraged the squad in his pre-game remarks to "be physical and get after them." And the boys did precisely that. The Blues came out with tenacity and did not seem the least bit intimidated. And true to form throughout most of these very long playoffs, the Blues scored first, on a goal by Schenn midway through the first period. It was the 14th time in 20 playoff games that the Blues had scored first. And the Blues had gone on to win 10 of the first 13 - needless to say, a very encouraging development.

And then in the second period, again "right off the hop" (to quote a favorite expression of Blues' colorful announcer Darren Pang), the Blues doubled their lead only one minute into the second period when Schenn was literally handed a puck behind the Boston goal, quickly fed Tarasenko who stuck it into the net high on the stick side of Rask before he even knew it was in. *Wow! This couldn't be going any better as far as I and my fellow Blueliners were concerned.*

The Blues had played very well with the lead since the Binnington era - maintaining vigilant offensive zone pressure, employing sound defensive strategy all over the ice, making it hard for opponents to enter the Blues' zone, forcing opponents to the outside, eliminating many free shots in the middle and rebounds, and, especially, avoiding the "soft' goal. But, as the cliché goes, there was still a lot of hockey to be played.

No sooner had I allowed myself to revel in the Blues' wonderful start and good fortune when two minutes later the Bruins Conner Clifton tipped-in a pass from Sean Kuraly with Bortuzzo hanging all over him to cut the lead in half.

And then the Bruins jumped all over the Blues. A penalty by Sundqvist - the Blues' fourth straight penalty - would prove costly giving Boston's lethal power play yet another chance to tie the game. After going 0 for 3 on the first three attempts, and with the time for this power play winding down below thirty seconds, the Bruins finally capitalized and tied the game. Defenseman Charlie McAvoy was given far too much room to enter the Blues' zone, skating in essentially one man on three, and took a distant wrist shot apparently deflected by Pietrangelo that somehow found its way to the net. While I fully expected the Bruins to mount a surge and potentially tie the game, neither of the goals was of the type I would have expected or that frankly should have occurred.

With the game tied 2-2, the Bruins took their first lead five minutes into the third period on an "effort" goal by the Bruins' Kuraly who chipped away at a loose puck and stuck it past Binnington. It was a lead the Bruins refused to relinquish. With a late empty net goal, the Bruins skated away with the 4-2 victory, their eighth straight playoff victory and the Blues' 13th straight loss in the Stanley Cup Finals.

After the game, the most talked-about play was a hit delivered by Bruins' defenseman Torey Krug midway through the third period. Krug had gotten into a wrestling match with Perron in front of the Bruins net. Perron was clutching and grabbing and slashing Krug and making a general nuisance of himself, and at one point even ripped Krug's helmet off. Krug was not exactly being a choir boy either and was retaliating in kind. Penalties could have been called easily on Perron, or frankly both players, but were not.

When Perron was asked later what he was possibly thinking by his antics, with the Blues down a goal and wanting to avoid yet another Bruins power play, he explained that the Bruins had been given the vast majority of power plays in the game and felt that the Blues were "due" for one and was hoping he could draw a retaliation penalty or perhaps at least offsetting penalties to create a four on four and more ice space and chances for his team to score.

That Perron would unilaterally take on that questionable strategy that could have helped seal the game for the Bruins seemed short-sighted and not within his job description. And what followed as a result was not great for the Blues. Krug got up from the scrum helmetless and clearly very pissed off and then proceeded to skate the full length of the ice at high speed, looking for revenge and to hit something - anything - in blue. Unfortunately, he took out his venom on the 19-year-old Thomas, who was directly in his path and near the puck.

Just as Thomas got rid of the puck, and while stationary and with his head down, he was blindsided by a monstrous full speed hit by Krug who launched himself directly into the unsuspecting Thomas, knocking him flying through the air and landing awkwardly. The crowd erupted in glee, as hockey fans tend to do at such things. Thomas got to one knee when play later stopped and barely made his way back to the bench, never to appear in that game or for the next several games. Indeed, he next played in Game 6 and was a shell of himself.

After the game the hit by Krug was wildly celebrated in Boston and the National media as a huge momentum event (even though the Bruins already had the lead at the time and were, by then, dominating the game) and as a thing of beauty and wonderful thing by those in the hockey world who love a crushing hit. Indeed, Boston's Coach Cassidy excitedly praised the hit in his post-game locker room speech to his team, calling out Krug for his hit on Thomas with the odd compliment: "Torey Krug, you are ... a sexy tough son of a bitch."

To admittedly biased Blues' fans Krug's hit was a classic "charge" designed to injure a defenseless player. Krug skated full speed for 100 feet with no helmet and no attempt or desire to play the puck or do anything related to "hockey" other than to hit something hard. And when he saw the young Thomas, he sought to and did destroy him. Yet no penalty was called on the play, and the hit was widely defended as perfectly legal since Krug had technically broken his stride by turning slightly toward the boards before engaging Thomas (allegedly eliminating "charging"), Thomas just released the puck when he was leveled (eliminating "interference") and he did not have his face to the boards (eliminating "boarding"). The fact that Krug's motives appeared pretty darn clear after his tussle with Perron, or that he appeared to launch himself into Thomas was apparently discounted because, it was explained, the point of contact was more to the upper shoulder or neck rather than to the head.

But if that wasn't a penalty under the current rules (and I will accept the views of astute hockey folks who insist that it wasn't) then it sure as heck *should be* if the NHL is truly concerned about limiting concussive-type hits. It was also interesting how quickly the attitudes of the Bruins, national media and the NHL would change once a Bruins' player was on the receiving end of some questionable hits by the Blues' players in games to follow.

Blues' Coach Berube once again sought to distance himself from any controversy and to keep his players focused on the future and what they could control rather than any slights or bad calls against his team that they couldn't do a thing about. When asked about Krug's hit after the game, Berube boldly claimed that it had nothing to do with Thomas not taking another shift for the remainder of the game.

To most folks who saw the hit, and Thomas' stunned reaction afterwards, and the fact that by not playing, he left the team one player short (not to mention the fact that he never touched the ice again for the next four games), that statement seemed ludicrous. NHL coaches are notoriously some of the most secretive, and least honest, guys around when it comes to player injuries and will almost never disclose the true nature or severity of an injury for fear that the opponent will exploit the injury the next time the player steps on the ice. *Who said hockey players were such nice guys?*

(No doubt influenced by this hit, the rules for the 2019-2020 season have been commendably changed to preclude a player from continuing to play without his helmet which would

have prevented Krug's vicious hit. But too late for Robert Thomas. At the same time, the rules now also call for a penalty when a player rips off the opponent's helmet - Take note David.)

In any case, right call or not, momentum changer or not, the Bruins went on to win the game and were now up one game in the series. It was clearly a wasted opportunity for the Blues, who were up by two goals in the second period. And it put the Blues in the unenviable position of needing to win Game 2 or put themselves in an extremely difficult position: having to win four of the next five games.

Game 2 ("Just give me another chance!")

Game 2's are always huge games and strong indicators of what a series will look like. In this case, either the Bruins would be taking a commanding 2-0 lead in the series, one that historically would give them greater than an 80% chance of winning it, or the Blues would even the series and go back home tied, with three of the remaining possible five games in St. Louis. For that reason, Game 2 often answers the question: Is this going to be a series or not?

Boston had now won an impressive eight playoff games in a row, the third longest streak in their 94-year history. If the Blues couldn't beat the Bruins when we had a two-goal lead, it did not look especially promising. We would need another good start to this game, hopefully get the first goal, but this time hold the lead.

Unfortunately, the game did not start out well. Early on, Blais made a nice move and had a step on Boston defender Krug and was driving for the net. While being hounded and hooked by Krug, Blais knocked into or was pushed into the goalie (depending on your point of view). Rask fell backwards into his net from the contact. It seemed far less invasive than the collision initiated, for example, by Dallas' Alexander Radulov with Blues' goalie Binnington in Overtime of Game 7 when no penalty was called. But in the opinion of the only one who mattered, the referee in *this* game, Blais' contact was a penalty, giving Boston's top-rated power play an early opportunity. And worst of all, they cashed in on it - a rare weak goal through Binner's wickets by the Bruins' Bay Stater center Charlie Coyle.

But fortunately, Robert Bortuzzo, the sudden secret offensive weapon, tied the game with a shot from a highly unlikely angle along the boards that barely squeaked between the crouched Rask's head and the top of the net just under the crossbar. The big defenseman had exactly two goals for the entire season, and now suddenly had two large ones in the playoffs.

However, the Bruins' Joakim Norstrom wasted little time striking back to give Boston a 2-1 lead with less than half of the first period even gone. Once again, the Blues responded - this time on a goal from a far more likely candidate in Tarasenko. Four goals in fifteen minutes with two defensive-minded teams and top-notch goalies were an avalanche of goals. It seemed unlikely that there would be many more to follow.

And, indeed, there weren't. There was no scoring the rest of the first period or the entire second period, as the goalies matched each other save for save. But the game was full of heavy hits and heated exchanges. At one point great friends Pietrangelo and Backes were getting into it in front of the Blues' goal. Petro finally lassoed the rambunctious ex-Blues' captain and admonished him to "settle down buffalo head!"

The third period looked familiar to the second period: some decent chances on both sides but lots of forechecking and limited available space or rebounds. But as the final period wound down the Blues started applying the team's signature pressure. And in the waning moments, Blues' defenseman Gunnarsson took a pass skating in from the left point unimpeded and rifled a wicked rising slap shot that cleanly beat Rask up high and to his left. Unfortunately, it did not beat the goal post (or, as Panger likes to say, "the goalie's best friend."). The shot clanged loudly off the iron and came directly out. No careen off the goalie this time. It was a terrible break for the Blues who needed this game badly, as the game headed to Overtime.

The Blues' players did not hang their heads or show any dismay from their misfortune at the end of regulation; instead, they came out to start the Overtime with a vengeance. The boys controlled the play unlike they had for the previous six periods, dominating in every facet of the game. We were beating the Bruins to every puck, outskating, outhitting and out pressuring them. The Blues had the Bruins pinned in their zone for several minutes and the exhausted Bruins' players could not get off the ice. And then the Bruins took a penalty. But since we had possession, play continued with the Blues now having an extra player on the ice for the goalie.

The Blues continued to control the puck in the Boston zone circling around looking for a decent open shot when O'Reilly found that same man Gunnarsson alone at the point - this time on the right side. Gunnarsson decided to give it another college try – he sent a ferocious slap shot toward the net, though this time to the other side of Rask. It was another blast that beat Rask cleanly, but this time it found its way into the net just inside the post to Rask's right side. "Boom Boom Gunnarsson!" bellowed Blues' radio voice Chris Kerber excitedly.

The Blues' Barbashev had stationed himself in front of the net to provide a screen and conceded later that he had tried to tip the puck with his stick but had just missed it. It will likely go down as one of the greatest misses in Blues' history.

The Blues had won their first Stanley Cup Final game in the 52-year history, breaking a streak of 13 consecutive losses. More importantly, we had tied the series and were heading home to St. Louis with a chance to win our first *home* Stanley Cup Final game in history. Big smiles all around.

In the post-game talk with his team, the often publicly-serious Berube, couldn't help but grin widely as he told a story of "taking a leak" next to Gunnarsson after the third period.

Lamenting not scoring the game-winner in regulation by a fraction of an inch, Gunnarsson predicted to the coach standing next to him at the urinal that he would score in Overtime if he got another opportunity: "All I need is one more chance," he offered.

It was a bold statement from a guy who had not scored a single goal in the playoffs to that point and was not especially known for his goal scoring mastery: in fact, he had only scored three goals for the entire season. But on his very next shift in Overtime and his very next shot, the veteran Swede did precisely what he predicted he would do - Babe Ruth style!

The one buzzkill on the Blues' win was the NHL's decision the next day to suspend Blues' player Sundqvist for his Game 2 hit on Bruins' defenseman Matt Grzelcyk. Grzelcyk was injured by Sundqvist on a hit from behind into the boards late in the first period and received a two-minute boarding penalty. While clearly a penalty, the Bruins' defenseman contributed to it and his injury by awkwardly turning at an odd angle just as Sundqvist approached. The referees on the ice saw it as being worthy of a penalty, but a minor one. However, after the game the NHL Player Safety Committee decided it should have been a major penalty and issued a one-game suspension to Sundqvist, despite the strange movement by Grzelcyk, no apparent intent to injure and that Sundqvist had a "clean record" - having never been suspended before.

Blues' fans were outraged. One Blues' blog posted a side-by-side comparison of a hit by a Bruins' player on the Blues' Sammy Blais in the same game along the boards that was not even penalized. While there was a distinction - Blais was hit slightly more to the side than from behind - the hits were otherwise remarkably similar in the nature and the severity of contact. One could even argue that the hit on Blais was worse since Blais did not change his body angle, and was hit higher, and arguably with an elbow as well.

But Blais got up from his hit and continued to play and Grzelcyk did not. And the Bruins complained that they lost Game 2 in part, because they had to play with one less defenseman for a good portion of the game.

Game 3 (Power play perfection)

The excitement and build up for Game 3 in St. Louis - the first home Stanley Cup Final game in 49 years - was sheer madness. The town was on fire - if fire can be blue. Signs hung from office buildings, homes, fences, lampposts and dog houses. Churches all over town prayed for the Blues and their outdoor signs to parishioners paid clever homage to their quest for salvation. Television and radio stations talked nothing but the Blues; one radio station belted the song "Gloria" for 24 hours *non-stop*! Some crazy folks, like me, even carved "LGB!" (Let's Go Blues) into their lawns.

The players were fully aware of the excitement and the moment but also feeling the pressure. At the same time, the Bruins were not happy about losing Game 2 and especially how it ended, with being badly and uncharacteristically outplayed in the last few minutes of the game and all of the brief Overtime. They were determined to show what the Boston Bruins were all about and that Game 2 was a fluke. The testosterone on both sides was flowing uncontrollably.

The stage was set. The Enterprise Center was as loud as I'd heard it since back in the days at the Old Barn, with the lower roof and louder acoustics. I was privileged to be there as a guest of a great friend who grew up in the Lou and now lived in Berkeley, California who had flown in for the game. *Now that's some friend!*

Egged on by the atmosphere and contagious enthusiasm, the Blues came out smoking; playing fast and hard and hitting everything in sight. The Blues were first it seemed on every puck, giving the Bruins no space and pushing the puck deep into the Bruins' zone and making it difficult for them to exit. The Blues were creating chances and getting shots at Rask, but he was playing like the All-Star goalie he could be. It was clear that it would be very difficult to beat him this night.

As often happens in games where one team comes out flying and owning the play for long stretches but without scoring, there is often a counterpunch of some kind that completely changes the momentum - perhaps a penalty or one breakdown that leads to a goal.

And sure enough, after thoroughly dominating play for the first half of the first period, Perron took an ill-advised interference penalty with a little over ten minutes left in first period. And it took Boston's greatest weapon, Bergeron, all of 19 seconds to deflect a shot from the point to take the lead.

The Blues were determined to fight back and had some great chances at Rask but were unable to get the equalizer. And then with just a few minutes left in the first period, the Bruins Coyle scored on a 3 on 2; a wrist shot glove-side that seemed to catch Binnington by surprise. It was now 2-0 Bruins even though the Blues had been the better team for most of the period.

Still stinging from the disappointment and shock of finding themselves in a two-goal deficit in the biggest game of the season to this point, despite playing well, Binnington may have for the first time (aside from his stick swinging display at Ben Bishop) lost his composure and let frustration sink in. With only ten seconds left in the period, he gave up a "softie." The puck was caught in Nordstrom's skate as he entered the Blues' zone but was extracted by a trailing Kuraly who sent a relatively harmless shot toward the goal along the ice and it went in through Binnington's legs, probably the worst goal of his career.

Coach Berube decided to challenge the goal as being offsides. It looked like a highly doubtful challenge to my eyes, as I was sitting right on the Blues' blue line. The risk if he was wrong would be a delay of game penalty and yet another power play for Boston. But the prospect of being down 3-0 after one period sure seemed like too much of a deficit to overcome, especially against a team that protected leads so well and a guy named Rask in goal. So Berube took a chance... and lost.

The Bruins were now both up 3-0 and had the man advantage heading into the second period. And in the course of 41 seconds into the second period, the Bruins scored yet another power play goal - a brilliant backhanded shot by the Bruins' big scorer Pastrnak - to go up 4-0.

Thus, in the first home Stanley Cup Final home game in 49 years, the Blues were already, in effect, toast one minute into the second period. *How deflating was that to Blues' fans - some of whom had waited five decades for this moment and shelled out thousands to get a seat to the game? You don't want to know.*

The rest of the game was a mere exhibition - the Blues scored two goals, but that was answered by two more Bruins' power play goals, to make them a perfect four for four with the man advantage - and on only four shots! Boston skated off with a demoralizing 7-2 victory. It was the first time in Binnington's professional career that he had been pulled from a game. It was also indisputably the most disappointing loss in Blues' history, which is really saying something.

Yes, the Bruins were good. More accurately their power play was fabulous. It didn't help that one of the Blues' best penalty killers, Sundqvist, had been suspended for the game, but he could not likely have made up that large of a deficit. However, the Blues actually did not play as poorly as the score indicated. Indeed, we arguably outplayed the Bruins when they were not on the power play and we even had the higher "expected goals" differential for the game, according to the statistical gurus. But the play of Rask, and the cascade of first period goals were just way too much to overcome.

Game 4 (An early goal, a late goal and lots of Binner makes for a happy dinner)

If Game 2 was an important barometer of where this series was headed - whether it would even be a meaningful challenge - Game 4 represented that proposition on steroids. It is arguably the most important game in a 2-1 series as it means a team is either up 3-1 and has three chances to win a single game to win the series, or the series is tied.

The Blues, and in particular Binnington's ability, to bounce back from losses was becoming legendary. We had been able to score early in several of those bounce-back games to remove the stench of the prior game's loss and build early confidence and momentum.

The Bruins were well aware of this trend and were determined to stop it. Good luck with that! Just 43 seconds into the game, Blues' stud O'Reilly gathered a rebound on a shot by Dunn, who was finally back after missing several games with a shot to the mouth, drove quickly around the net and stuffed the puck in the left side of the goal before Rask or any of his comrades in black and gold could get there (There was no long-armed veteran Bouwmeester on the ice for the Bruins to prevent that from happening.) The Blues thankfully had the all-important first goal.

The Blues continued to play with passion and purpose. Even though we gave up a game-tying goal to Boston's Coyle on a rebound from a shot by Chara later in the first period, the Blues responded shortly thereafter. Pietrangelo, pressing forward from his defensive position as he did throughout this game, took a hard wrist shot which Rask blocked. But Tarasenko quickly gathered the rebound and fired it into the net to put the Blues up 2-1 at the end of the first period.

The Blues came out hard in the second period and had chance after chance against Rask, seeking the comfort of a two-goal cushion - at one time with nearly two consecutive minutes of time in the Boston zone. But Rask was being highly uncooperative, stopping every type of shot from every angle.

One shot taken by Schenn, however, did not make it to Rask. Rather, it was blocked by the stick of the Bruins' leader Chara and then the puck hit him squarely in the face, causing a cascade of blood to flow. The colossal Chara had to leave the game and did not return other than as a cheerleader for his team.

Finally, with about six minutes left in the second period, the Blues' sustained pressure led to a power play chance. Disheartened with the performance of the Blues' power play over the playoffs, their far better play five-on five, and the team's propensity to give up shorthanded chances and even goals, I facetiously asked my wife sitting next to me if the Blues could *decline* the penalty like in football?

That half-hearted joke turned out to be prophetic as the Blues not only failed to score on the power play and lost the momentum that we had been building, but inexplicably gave up a two-on-one resulting in a shorthanded goal for Boston that tied the game. Binnington had actually stopped the initial shot by Bergeron but the Bruins, with one less man on the ice, also managed to beat the Blues' players to the rebound, and Brandon Carlo, the most unlikely goal-scorer on the ice, deposited it into the open net vacated by the initial save. It was Carlo's first goal of the entire playoffs and only his third of the entire year.

Aside from the Yzerman goal in Game 7 of the 1996 playoffs, that may have been the single most painful goal in Blues' history. The Blues had a hammer on the Bruins and it appeared had the game in hand. To lose the lead and potentially the game and the series because of a goal scored against when you had more players on the ice than the opposition made every Blues' fan want to vomit profusely.

But unlike the Yzerman goal, the game was *not* over, and the Blues were still tied. So perhaps it was too early to have a total meltdown?

The second period ended soon thereafter with the teams tied. The score remained that way through the first half of the third period, as the most anxious of Blues' fans chewed through their nails, clothes and other gnawable items.

And then to the rescue came the bearded wonder acquired from Buffalo. Oh, Oh, O'Reilly scored on a rebound off of another effective shot by Pietrangelo (this one a high slap shot that Rask blocked but could not hold onto) to put the Blues ahead 3-2. The mantra of Coach Berube to "get pucks on net" (or as fans often complained when players passed the puck incessantly to "shoot the damn puck") had paid dividends and thankfully Petro was heeding that advice.

Al MacInnis, who was undoubtedly part of the team encouraging Pietrangelo to shoot the puck more to create rebounds, was sitting in a box next to Doug Armstrong. As the camera panned on him after the goal, he seemed as genuinely excited as if he was playing himself and had launched one of his own famous slap shot missiles.

The boys hung on for the last ten minutes and added an empty net goal. The Blues finally had their first home Stanley Cup win in history and had tied the series at two games apiece for now the fourth straight series. It was back to Boston for what was now a three-game series.

Game 5 (Gunner saves the day to "trip" up Bruins)

Any time a seven-game series is tied two games each Game 5 is monumental; at the most basic level, the winner of the game has two chances to win the series, the loser has to win two in a row. As noted, the historical odds for the losing team of this game to win the series are small – only about 21%. That said, both the Bruins and the Blues had overcome a Game 5 loss in a 2-2 series previously in these playoffs (the Bruins' win over Toronto in the first round, and the Blues' win over Dallas in the second round). But in both instances, they had home advantage in the series. Undoubtedly, it is easier to lose Game 5 and still win the series if you have home ice advantage in Game 7.

Thus, as important as it was for both teams to win Game 5, it was arguably even more incumbent for the Blues to do so. But to do that, the Blues would have to win back-to-back games, something that neither team had done to this point in the Final.

There was no doubt that Boston would be fired up. Adding to the pumped-up Boston crowd was that Chara was dressed in his Number 33 and planning to play despite a broken jaw and having his mouth wired shut - and he was naturally starting the game to attempt to further inspire the team and the Boston faithful in attendance.

Commensurate with expectations, the Bruins began with a flurry. Right off the bat Binnington was tested early and often. And there was no early goal for the Blues this time around. To make matters worse, six minutes into the game, the Blues once again got the dreaded delay of game penalty when Vince Dunn inadvertently shot the puck into the crowd. *There has got to be a change in this silly rule when there is clearly no intent, pressure or reason to clear the puck over the glass.*

Fortunately, the Blues were able to survive the Boston power play (after a few scary moments), but the Bruins were dominating and getting the better chances and far more shots. Late in the period the Blues got a rare power play - a slash from the guy that all hockey fans not from Boston love to hate, the mischievous Marchand. Often a cause for optimism, an opposing penalty was not exactly a reason to celebrate these days in St. Louis given the woefulness of the team's power play, and having already given up three shorthanded goals in each of the last three playoff series - to the Stars' Cogliano, the Sharks' Couture and the Bruins' Carlo. (The Blues almost gave up a shorthanded goal to Winnipeg as well but Binnington managed to stifle a shorthanded breakaway by Par Lindholm in Game 1). The Blues didn't score with the man advantage but at least we didn't allow

Boston to score this time around and two more minutes had ticked off the clock to essentially close the first period and give the good guys a chance for a breather and to regroup.

And the Blues did just that. Very early into the second period Zach Sanford gained possession of the puck behind the Boston goal on a Pietrangelo pass that had missed the mark. The 6-foot 4 winger, the team's lone Massachusettsan, was being pressured hard by Bruins' defenseman McAvoy on one side and Chara on the other. With seemingly nowhere to go, Sanford passed the puck backwards between his legs to the front of the net. (*It's a move that I had seen him make several times before, but I suspect the Bruins may not have; as essentially a 4th line guy who only played sporadically, Sanford was not likely much of a focus for the Bruins' coaching staff or video guys.*)

Sanford executed this pass beautifully, sliding the puck between defenders to a charging O'Reilly, who seemed to be anticipating "the move." O'Reilly took the pass right in front of the goal, moved swiftly to his backhand, and then flipped the puck beautifully into the top corner to beat a disgruntled and befuddled Rask. Just 55 seconds into the second period the Blues had the lead we so badly coveted.

Thereafter, the Bruins came in waves and took shot after shot, but Binnington was on his game and the Blues limited the quality of the chances and rebounds. There was no further scoring in the remaining 19 minutes of the second period or half way through the third.

And then the biggest controversy of the Stanley Cup Final occurred - at least as far as the folks from "Bah-ston" were concerned. With the Blues forechecking in the Bruins' zone and applying pressure, the Bruins' Noel Acciari was tripped by Bozak (or, fell over Bozak's stick if you bleed blue). Either way, Acciari went down. Bozak paused momentarily and flung his arms into the air as if to say, "I wasn't *trying* to trip him, he just fell over my stick. Please don't call a penalty on that." The national TV commentators interpreted Bozak's actions as a confession that he had committed the crime, should go directly to jail and not pass go.

The referees uncharacteristically kept their whistles in their pockets - perhaps agreeing it was inadvertent, perhaps influenced by their desire not to make EVERY game one where the Bruins had a disproportionate number of calls (the Bruins had already been given three power plays in this critical game to only one for the Blues, and the Bruins had been given far more power plays than the Blues in the series). Or perhaps Berube's rare but calculated criticism about the officiating after Game 3 had some effect. Boston Coach Cassidy later whined that it did.

But had the referees known the effect of their non-call they might have ruled differently. Following the trip, Perron gathered the loose puck, made some slick moves around two Bruins and then redirected a pass to Bozak who was now stationed alone on the other side of the net. Bozak, the perpetrator of the alleged felony, scored into the empty side to give the Blues a commanding two-goal lead with only ten minutes to play.

I will say for the record that Bozak's actions constituted a penalty, however inadvertent. But trips and slashes and holds occur frequently throughout a game and the referees often let them go, especially in critical times of critical games and, in particular, if it doesn't seem likely to effect the game and lead to a goal. (*In fact, this situation seemed similar to me to the non-call on a trip of Schenn by the Dallas Stars' Cogliano in the third period of Game 3 of that series when Cogliano later came down ice and scored a killer shorthanded goal to tie the game.*)

When Bozak tripped Acciari it did not seem like it was about to lead to much. But thanks to some great work by Perron, and Bozak's alertness, it did. NBC analyst Ed Olczyk went bonkers and didn't stop talking about it the rest of the game. Boston General Manager Cam Neely had a temper tantrum in a Boston Skybox taking an unknown object (perhaps a bowl of clam chowder) and heaving it with all of his might against the wall.

Those in Blues-land admittedly felt fortunate but also ticked that the media was going to dilute this Blues' victory on the basis of one missed call, when from our perspective; the Bruins had been getting the majority of calls throughout the entire series. Besides, the Blues were already ahead before this non-call. I was really hoping that we could maintain the two-goal cushion to make the whole issue moot - no one wants to win on a controversial goal.

But it was not to be. The Bruins responded to the Blues' goal, and the sense that they had been cheated, with a barrage of pressure. And with six and a half minutes left in the game Boston finally broke through against Binnington to cut the lead in half on a slap shot from Jake Debrusk. And then the Bruins really got their bear on - they continued to swarm and shoot pucks on net, as the Blues valiantly tried to hold them off.

With only about a minute left in the game, Boston's John Moore took a hard shot from straight away that Binnington struggled with. Although he blocked the shot, the puck slowly trickled through him and was heading into the goal for what appeared to be the game-tying goal. But the hero of Game 2, Carl Gunnarsson, saw what was happening and dove behind Binnington and just barely swept out the puck before it crossed the line. Ironically, he may have been assisted by the Bruins' Charlie McAvoy who also saw the puck trickling in and wanted to help it along. In racing to get to the net or perhaps prevent Gunnarsson from doing so, he pushed and slashed Gunnarsson which made him fall and may have actually accelerated Gunner's ability to get there just in time.

So, the best save of the entire night, in a game where Binnington brilliantly stopped 38 of 39 shots, belonged to Gunnarsson, arguably the Blues' sixth defenseman who was a healthy scratch at times during the playoffs. And now, the man from Orebro, Sweden had remarkably won the last two games for the Blues played in Boston - one if by offense and one if by defense. A regular Paul Revere! The Blues were heading back home with a chance to win the Stanley Cup - and on home ice!

Once again, though, the thrill of a Blues' victory was tempered to some extent by the League's decision to suspend a Blues' player, Ivan Barbashev, for a hit on the Bruins' Johansson. Unlike with Sundqvist, no penalty was even called at the time by either official. And, unlike with Sundqvist, Johansson was not hurt - he continued to play throughout the remainder of the game and was planning to play and did play in Game 6. Like Sundqvist, Barbashev had never been suspended before and was not known as a dirty player. Moreover, it looked like the kind of contact that happens relatively frequently when players joust for position near the face-off circle.

But when the TV announcers suggested that the NHL "might want to take a look at it" since, they claimed, Barbashev made contact with Johansson's head, I knew it wasn't going to go well. (*It sure looked to me like the contact was to the high shoulder/neck area just like Krug's hit on Thomas, but what do I know?*) Sure enough, the Player Safety Committee decided to once again suspend a Blues' player for the next game for an unwarranted hit "to the head" following the Blues' victory.

Although Barbashev was not as an important player to the team as Sundqvist, he had been playing great and was an integral part of the 4th line that was playing a lot of minutes and helping effectively shut down the Bruins' top line. I have no doubt that the NHL Player Safety Committee strives to be fair and get things right, and believe it serves an important role in deterring dangerous play and severe concussions. But it was hard for many to fathom that this hit would have resulted in a suspension during the regular season. Indeed, there were many folks who believed that it would not have been issued if the Bruins had won Game 5 or if there had not been a cataclysmic outcry from Boston and the media about the non-call on Bozak, though I'm sure the NHL would claim that such matters were completely unrelated and any connection preposterous.

In any case, the paranoia among Blues' fans had now reached a crescendo. First the hand pass goal, then the no-call on Krug, then the disproportionate number of power plays given to Boston in this series, then the Sundqvist suspension and now this one. It was enough for a paranoid person to feel well... paranoid.

Game 6 (An unlucky two-man advantage and the most disappointing loss in Blues' history)

The city was rocking like I had never seen it in anticipation of the possibility that Blues could really be Stanley Cup Champions after 52 years - and in this year of all years. You could take the buzz around town from Game 3 and multiply it by a factor of ten. The City was amped up and now cautiously optimistic that the Blues could actually do this - win the freakin' Stanley Cup! Very little actual work got done in town on June 9, 2019. Many of us were unable to think clearly - it was a day where likely the most passionate of Blues' faithful forgot to shave, take their meds, wear a seat belt, and/or feed the dog, cat or child. It was not a day that I would want to have surgery (as if there *ever* was such a day) - not only because you might miss the game, but because the doctor might be a bit distracted.

I didn't have a ticket to the game but naturally was dying to go. I couldn't imagine not being there if the Blues actually won the Stanley Cup! But, at the same time, the prices for even single tickets in the highest stratosphere of the building were in the several thousand-dollar range and hard for me to justify. But once again I was saved by the great generosity of a friend - this one also a family member through marriage who happened to own a piece of the team, have an extra ticket and knew how much this game meant to me. And I got to sit next to another family friend through the luck of marriage whose passion for the Blues rivals my own. I am one very lucky dude!

I was more pumped for this game than I had ever been for a sporting event - and I had been to several World Series clinching games, the Rams' Super Bowl win over Tennessee in Atlanta, and to the Rose Bowl to watch my beloved Texas Longhorns win the College Football National Championship Football over USC in thrilling fashion.

Some in the national media and most in Boston felt the Blues had been lucky to be up in the series and that the Bruins were the far superior team. But the numbers told another story. Through the first five games, the Blues had held the Bruins top two lines, including the line branded "the perfection line," to only a single point at even strength (excluding an empty net goal). Moreover, the Blues had outscored the Bruins 11-7 when both teams had the same number of skaters on the ice.

The vast majority of the Bruins' damage and superiority occurred only when they were on the power play and had an extra skater (or when the Blues did!). And thanks to the referees (if you are a Blues' fan) or the brutish ways of the Blues' players (if you are a Bruins' fan), the Bruins had received 20 power plays to only 14 for the Blues. (For those who thought the Blues were being too thuggish, the Bruins were the second most penalized team in the NHL during the season with nearly 175 more penalty minutes than the Blues, including nearly double the number of fights.) The Bruins had scored six power plays thus far and the Blues only one, and the Blues' lone power play goal had been nullified by the horrendous shorthanded goal we gave up in Game 4. Although the Blues naturally wanted to play their style of game we needed to stay out of the penalty box *(and perhaps avoid receiving any power plays of our own?)*.

The Blues had a great start to Game 6 - equally determined to achieve the players' lifelong dream of having their name permanently engraved on the Stanley Cup and to not let the City down. The boys applied significant pressure from the outset causing Boston to take an early penalty. We didn't score but had several excellent chances. And the Blues continued to press; we looked like the faster, more determined, and more confident team, but Rask was at his best. Maroon worked a nice give-and-go and just missed wide on a deflection. Dunn took a wicked slap shot from close range that Rask was able to block and Petro was able to beat several Bruins to the rebound and get off a crafty backhander that Rask barely got a piece of as the puck fluttered over his head toward the goal. But like a contortionist, Rask reached back with his glove hand high behind his back and somehow caught the puck. Things were going pretty well so far for the men in blue - well except for the "no goal" yet part. It was the exact reverse of Game 5.

In accordance with the plan, the Blues were hitting everything in black and gold to cause disruption, turnovers and wear them down - just as we had done so well late in the San Jose series. But there can be a fine line between being aggressive and banging the opponent and committing a penalty and the Blues were doing their level best to straddle that line within the letter of the law.

And then Schenn, who had been one of the leaders of the team and the hit brigade throughout the playoffs, made a foolish mistake. He saw the Bruins' Nordstrom along the side boards in the Blues' zone with his back turned and gave him a shove from behind. It didn't look like he hit him all that hard, but he fell forward into the glass and crumbled to the ice, arguably exaggerating the contact to ensure that Schenn received a penalty. He didn't need to embellish though - it was a clear penalty. It's widely understood that if a player is facing the boards and you can see the number on his back you don't hit him. It was completely unnecessary, as Nordstrom was hemmed in without any real opportunity to do much with the puck.

It was a huge momentum changer as the Blues were controlling the play and it allowed Boston's best weapon a chance to give them the lead and completely change the complexion of the game.

The penalty kill started off very promising and almost led to a Blues' shorthanded goal. O'Reilly, per usual, took the initial face-off in the Blues' zone against Bruins' star center Bergeron. The puck skirted to the boards where Marchand beat the Blues to it. But as he sought to reverse the puck back to the point to his teammate Krug, O'Reilly anticipated the pass perfectly and with an outstretched arm got his stick on it and deflected it skillfully past Krug just outside the blue line along the boards. O'Reilly then accelerated into another gear and raced after the loose puck beating Krug to it.

Then as Krug and the other Boston point man, Pastrnak, converged on him along the boards, O'Reilly deftly tipped the bouncing puck toward the center of the ice. At the same time, he cleverly maneuvered his body between Krug and Pastrnak, springing himself for a breakaway. It was a scintillating single-handed effort and series of moves against three of the best players in the world. If O'Reilly could manage to score this goal, it might go down as the greatest goal in Blues' history - not only because of the sheer genius of a play, but it would give the team the lead in a closing game and set the building on fire.

But alas it was not to be. As O'Reilly swept in on Rask at full speed ignoring the stick check *(or was that a slash?)* from behind by Krug, he cut from his forehand to his backhand to attempt to push the puck past Rask. It looked like it would work but at the last second, he lost control of the puck preventing even a shot on net. *So close (and yet, so far)!*

And now O'Reilly had expended a lot of effort, was caught deep in the Bruins' end and needed to get back to defend as the Bruins charged down the ice, effectively 5 on 3. On his rush back, O'Reilly astutely raced to the closest end of the Blues' bench allowing him to be replaced by a fresher skater and one on the other end of the bench closer to the Blues' goal. And, fortunately, the Blues quickly intercepted the Bruins effort and sent the puck down the ice, barely missing a pass for a two-on-one break. And then O'Reilly was somehow back on the ice - the shortest break on the fly I had ever seen in a hockey game.

Once again, the Blues stymied the Bruins' entry into their zone as Pietrangelo gained clean possession. But instead of clearing it down the ice or at least to center through the open middle of the ice, the Captain tried a sneaky clear along the boards. Unfortunately, the clever Marchand was there; he anticipated and blocked the pass before it left the Blues' zone and charged toward the Blues' goal with Pietrangelo in hot pursuit. Marchand then saw an open Bruin streaking down the center toward the goal alone and attempted to pass it to him. Pietrangelo appeared to deflect his pass and the always hustling back-checking O'Reilly intercepted it on his backhand. As Marchand hounded him, O'Reilly sought to quickly clear the puck out of the Blues' zone before his effort could be blocked. Unfortunately, the puck was not settled and with the angle of his body and his momentum toward the boards, he inadvertently and uncharacteristically flipped it over the glass and into the stands – yet another automatic delay of game penalty.

Penalties are never a good idea in a scoreless game in Game 6 of the Stanley Cup Finals when everyone knows the importance of that first score. This is especially true when your opponent has the best power play in the NHL. But giving them a two-man advantage is of a gift of a different order of magnitude. It turns a top power play unit, which is still only able to score less than three out of ten chances, into a 50-50 proposition.

As one of the smartest and cleanest players in the League, O'Reilly almost never got a penalty (he only took six penalties the entire year and this was his first in the Stanley Cup Final). And yet, ironically, he was the one taking perhaps the most damaging penalty in Blues' history - it wasn't from stupidity or carelessness or lack of effort, but because of bad puck luck and a stupid rule in my judgment (*though I wonder if the very short rest after a breakaway chance and his race to gain control of the puck contributed in some way?*).

So, the Bruins were about to have a 5 on 3 advantage, the first (and only) two-man advantage in the entire Stanley Cup Final, and it would be without our best face-off man and one of our best penalty killers, who was sitting in the penalty box. Needless to say, this felt like it could be the turning point of the game. And then Coach Berube, who had seemed to pull every right switch since he took over months ago, made what I thought at the time was a big tactical error: He sent out Steen to take the draw and be the lone forward on the penalty kill.

Steen was a veteran player and one of his regular penalty killers to be sure. But with no disrespect to the veteran he was not a center and was not good on draws - and winning the draw and control of the puck on a 5 on 3 advantage can be huge. Moreover, although Steen was a very experienced player who could block a shot (he had a nice kick save on a shot from the point in Game 5 as the game was winding down) he was 35, and now among the slowest players on the team. That can be a big problem when the other team has two more players on the ice and the lone forward has to race from one player to another to attempt to defuse the attack. *Where was Sundqvist or Bozak?*

Sure enough, Steen lost the draw. The Bruins surgically passed the puck around looking for the best shot and settled on a big slap shot from the top of the key from the big man known as "Pasta" with Steen attempting to get in the way but unable to do so. Binnington managed to block the shot but the puck came right out in front of the goal. The Blues and Bruins scrambled hard for the rebound and it landed briefly right on Steen's stick. But he was unable to corral it and shoot it down the ice, as the puck rolled off of his stick and Boston once again had control. The puck went back to Pastrnak who this time faked a shot, passed it to Marchand to the left side of Binnington and with a great one-timer buried the goal. The Bruins had the all-important first goal in Game 6 - their seventh power play goal of the series.

The Blues never recovered. The boys fought valiantly but could not get one behind Rask. The calamitous second goal and separation occurred early in the third period on the most unlikely of shots. It was a long wrist shot from the point from offensively-challenged Brandon Carlo that bounced half way toward the goal and then somehow skipped through Binnington - a terribly unlucky goal, especially at that juncture of the game. Boston scored again at the halfway point of the third period for the insurmountable 3-0 lead. The Bruins went on to win the game handily 5-1, with the lone Blues' goal by O'Reilly.

So, forget about what I said earlier about Game 3 being the most disappointing loss in Blues' history. Game 3 *was* very hard to swallow. But losing Game 6 with Lord Stanley's Cup actually in the building and polished and ready to be displayed in front of thousands of delirious fans inside, and thousands more outside (and perhaps hundreds of thousands about to descend upon the area for one of the greatest, if not THE greatest, sports moment in St. Louis history) was outright devastating.

The Blues had not only just lost their chance to win a Championship at home, and disappointed so many in the City who they so badly wanted to please, but their odds of winning the series and the Stanley Cup had markedly diminished. Though the team acted as if it was not worried, even the most ardent fan had to have serious concerns. Yes, anything could happen in Game 7 and yes, the Blues had played brilliantly on the road in these playoffs. But the Boston crowd would be electric (even though the Bruins had been around since 1924, they had never hosted a Game 7 in the Stanley Cup Final before), the Bruins now had the momentum (to the extent you buy into such things), they were clearly the more experienced team, and some might argue the better team.

Certainly, the oddsmakers in Vegas with millions at stake felt that Boston would win the game - they placed the odds at Boston "minus 180" - almost a 2-1 proposition and, remarkably, even higher than the line on the series at the outset, when most thought the series would only last five or six games.

Game 7 (Exhilaration, Euphoria and Ecstasy for the Men and Women who bleed Blue!)

On June 12, 2019, the 1,444th game in this NHL season would be played and would decide who would go down in history as the 2018-2019 Stanley Cup Champions.

Fifty-one and a half years ago on a Wednesday night in October 1967 the Blues were born and played their first game. Fifteen and a half years ago, on a Wednesday evening in October of 2004, Boston Red Sox fans descended upon enemy turf at Busch Stadium seeking their first World Series in their lifetimes. Now the Blues, the owners and a few fans who could afford such a venture, including lucky charm little Laila at the team's expense, were on enemy ice at Boston's TD Garden (naturally on a Wednesday) trying to capture our very first Stanley Cup.

To the most hard-core Blues' fans, June 12 started as a difficult day - many of us didn't sleep the night before, couldn't eat, and had difficulty concentrating, listening to others or even forming intelligent thoughts. We were nauseous, irritable, excited and nervous, trying to be optimistic about our chances given this team and Binnington's incredible ability to bounce back after tough losses. After all, Binnington had been 11-2 in his short career after a loss - having never lost back to back games during the regular season and only twice in the playoffs after a loss (Game 4 vs Winnipeg and Game 5 vs. Dallas).

But we also knew that the rookie goalie would have to be at his best. During the onslaught late in Game 6, Bruins' players could be overheard after their last goal encouraging their teammates to "shoot everything on this fu**ing kid." The Bruins were undoubtedly going to follow that same strategy in Game 7.

And logic, math and history suggested that the Bruins had a significant advantage playing this game at home. Sure, the Blues had been nothing short of outstanding on the road in the playoffs - and had already won two of the three games in this series in Boston. But the Bruins had been a great home team all year long and Game 7 was another animal. There was no doubt that a home team gets a special emotional lift in a game like this from the start. Indeed, only four other teams in NHL history had ever won Game 7 in the Stanley Cup Finals on the road.

The biggest issue for me going in was whether we could withstand the initial likely onslaught from the Bruins and somehow manage to register the first goal, as the Blues had a special knack for in the playoffs thus far. The Blues had scored first now in 16 of the 25 playoff games and had gone on to win 12 of those games. And in a remarkable number of games the Blues were able to score early: twelve in the first five minutes or so, eight of those in the first couple of minutes and four of them, incredibly, in just the first 45 seconds of the game!

In his pre-game speech to the team, Craig Berube implored the team to do what had gotten them there: to be aggressive and get on the puck, to pressure everywhere, to be physical and hammer them, and to support each other all over the ice in all three zones. He confidently told them (at least the G-rated version) that "We're here for a reason and we're going to come home with the Stanley Cup here tonight!" *I would have been fired up - put me in coach!* But there is a big difference in sports and life between words and actions, and the Boston Bruins were every bit as pumped up to win this thing in front of their rabid fan base.

As anticipated, the Bruins came out with a purpose and dominated early, even more than I suspected would be the case. In fact, there were early stretches where it looked like the Blues might actually be blown out of the building. How disappointing would that be after such an amazing season? At one point, the raging pessimist in me was just hoping to keep it close and make it a credible game. We could then at least talk about what a great series it had been.

There was a first-rate chance by the Bruins' Kuraly on a rebound where he one-timed a backhand which appeared to be heading toward an empty portion of the net, but Binnington slid masterfully over to prevent it from going in. And there was a dangerous screened shot from the point that got through but Binnington snared it and held on confidently. And then Boston's Johansson broke in all alone and had a backhanded effort that Binnington repelled as well.

The Blues were misfiring on passes, not clearing the zone and turning pucks over. We seemed to be skating at half the speed of the Bruins and not winning the all-important chase for the puck along the boards and elsewhere. And it certainly didn't help when Parayko misfired on a clearing pass and inadvertently sent the puck over the boards for yes, "delay of game," yet again! It was an early power play for the Bruins in a game where there figured to be few of them. Indeed, that was the only penalty that would be called for the entire night.

But throughout the early onslaught, Binnington stood tall, making save after save with a calm aplomb reminiscent of Glenn Hall and Jacques Plante (one undoubtedly watching on TV from his farm in Northern Canada and the other even further north - from the heavens above). Binner was determined to play the game of his life and he was doing it so far. But he couldn't score a goal himself and it wasn't clear the Blues would be able to help him much the way things were going.

As the Bruins' superior play continued but was not being rewarded on the scoreboard I had a sense, or perhaps it was just *hope*, that the Bruins may be getting a bit frustrated. Perhaps the tables would turn soon, and the Blues would finally get a good chance or two. And what if we actually converted? Rask had not yet been tested, and goalies often perform their worst in such situations. Or what if the Bruins started pressing a bit and gave up an odd-man rush?

For the Blues it was all about getting the first goal in my book. As the first period lingered on, and the Blues' play picked up somewhat, it looked increasingly like we might just survive the first period tied, which would give the guys a chance to settle down, regroup and realize that we were now only forty minutes from hockey immortality.

And then the unexpected happened: With just over three minutes left in the period, Bouwmeester took a rather innocent moderate speed slap shot from the point with several Boston players well-positioned in his way. The shot was likely heading wide of the goal. It was not even intended to be a credible shot at net, but rather to avoid the Bruins' forward seeking to block it and maintain zone time and pressure, with the opportunity for a potential deflection. And indeed Blues' savior O'Reilly (who was positioned in front of the net) got himself a piece of the puck with his crafty stick. His deflection changed the direction of the puck and took it on a different path - low and right down the middle of the goal. That's not normally the objective and typically results in a relatively easy save for the goalie. But Rask had stretched his pads to his right to block Bouwmeester's shot just in case it was on net, and in the process had opened up his legs ever so slightly, leaving a slither of space. And gloriously, that sweet magical puck found that small opening and snuck between Rask's pads and into the beautiful net!

    As is often the case with goals, the goal scorer and those providing the assists are the ones celebrated for the achievement. But sometimes there are others who played a major role in making the goal happen who are overlooked, and this was certainly the case here. The unsung hero of this goal was Sammy Blais. It was Blais who charged speedily into the Bruins zone, laid a heavy hit on Bruins' center Acciari along the left boards and stripped him of the puck. He then carried it forward and took a quick shot at Rask from a sharp angle. Although Rask blocked it, Sammy was able to regather the puck with the aid of O'Reilly, skated around the net and then made a crisp pass to Pietrangelo. Petro faked a shot and re-directed the puck to his fellow point-mate Bouwmeester who took the shot heard 'round the world - which produced the greatest goal in Blues history!

    I'm certainly not taking anything away from Bo or O'Reilly - it was a well-executed play and a decent deflection. But that play never happens if it wasn't for Blais. His name doesn't appear on the score sheet. Nor are his efforts captured in the edited highlights of the goal on the NHL's website. Blais' play that allowed this goal to occur is, in effect, permanently excised from the history log unless you watch the entire game.

But we Blues' fans should always remember his pivotal role in the Blues' biggest goal ever.

That's not to say that most of us thought that one goal would win this game with over forty minutes to play. We fully expected a big push-back, and to likely have to defend another power play or two before it was over. But scoring that first goal meant A LOT - it gave the team confidence, allowed the team to settle in, and made the Bruins feel uncomfortable and press knowing that they were likely in this game for the long haul. At minimum now, it would not likely be an easy win for them.

The objective at this point switched from surviving the first period tied at zero to making sure we held on to the one-goal lead until intermission. And it sure looked like that would be the case as the clock was winding down and as reliable Jaden Schwartz had possession of the puck at center ice and was moving into the Bruins' zone with less than fifteen seconds to play in the first period.

Schwartz had no real viable offensive chance as he entered Bruins' property essentially one man on three - with pesky Bruins' winger Marchand in his face and defensemen McAvoy and Grzelcyk also surrounding him. But rather than simply dump the puck behind the Bruins' net to kill more time and end the period, Schwartz decided to creatively pass the puck to himself off the side boards to buy some extra time and see if there was any additional play to be had. At that point, the normally defensively-reliable Marchand inexplicably left the ice for a replacement (a change that Bruins fans will never forget).

After beating McAvoy to the puck off the boards, Schwartz heard a fast charging Pietrangelo racing up from the defense to join the play and calling for the puck. Schwartz swung a reverse pass perfectly to Petro who had a largely free path to the net. McAvoy had stayed with Schwartz and Grzelcyk was covering the hustling Schenn who was streaking down the left side. With no one in front of him Petro charged toward the goal. McAvoy broke from his cover of Schwartz to try to interfere with his progress, but Petro eluded him by switching to his backhand and now had a free close-in shot on Rask.

The big Boston goalie came out of his net to reduce the available shooting space, but Petro lifted a perfect backhander into the top shelf of the goal with only 7.9 seconds left in the period! *Take that Robert Bortuzzo!* And just like that the Blues, incredibly, were ahead 2-0 in a game that we had been frankly outplayed to that point. *Forty minutes to nirvana!*

The importance of a second goal and two goal lead could not be overstated - it allowed the team to shift into a defense-first approach (hopefully without abandoning aggressiveness and still pressuring the puck in the O-zone), enabled the Blues to relax a bit and play their game (knowing that even one mistake would not relinquish the lead) and put the Bruins and their fans on edge. If O'Reilly's goal was Exhibit 1-A of the most important goal in Blues' history, Petro's goal was Exhibit 1-B. At the same time, the Blues had squandered a two-goal lead in Game 1 at Boston and needed to make sure that didn't happen again.

Blues' fans and the team knew that the Bruins were going to be a very desperate hockey team in the second period and for the rest of the game. And, as expected, the Bruins came out in the next period with a chip on their shoulder and fire in the belly. But unlike in Game 1 the Blues seemed undeterred and more confident with the lead - we were skating with the Bruins, pressuring the back end, limiting the space in the middle, forcing the Bruins in the Blues' defensive zone to the outside, and winning as many pucks as our counterparts.

The Bruins had a few good chances to get on the scoreboard but to no avail. At the end of two periods the Blues still had the precious two-goal lead. *How does one stay relaxed, composed and focused on the task when they are on the cusp of the greatest sports achievement in their entire lives? How could these twenty-somethings keep it all together when so many of us fifty-somethings, who were not even playing one shift, were having so much trouble?*

I certainly expected the Bruins to come out for the third period possessed and as determined as ever. If they could just score one goal, the Boston fans would go wild and the energy created by it easily could completely turn the game around. *Don't let these guys back in it I continually said to no one in particular inside my head.*

As the third period started, the Blues did a pretty good job of matching the Bruins' effort fully aware of the stakes and the impact of even a single goal. The Blues' players were giving every ounce of energy they could muster after 82 regular season games and 26 playoff games, knowing that they were exquisitely close to the finish line and the dream that many of them had since they were little boys growing up in Canada, Sweden, Russia, Massachusetts and St. Louis, Missouri.

But suddenly the Bruins had their golden opportunity. Noel Acciari took a quality shot from the right point to the left of Binnington. He was able to make the save, but there was a rebound which he couldn't hold. The Bruins' Johansson was inexplicably left unguarded right in front of the net with no defenseman in sight. As the puck skirted away from Binnington, he tried to push it away, but Johansson gathered it in his skates, and skillfully kicked it to his stick on his left-shooting forehand. With Binnington now down on the ice and out in front of the net, Johansson moved to his left, with the puck firmly in his grasp. It looked like he would be able to just jam it in the open side of the goal. But like a cheetah, Binnington sprung from his crouch, and quickly kicked his legs to his right, managing to block what seemed like a sure goal. It was the save of the game, the save of the series and the save of his goaltending life!

And then with less than ten minutes remaining in the game and with Boston feeling the pressure, the Blues pulled off a spectacular goal: Tarasenko used his speed and power to race down and control a puck that Schwartz had sent into the Boston corner to the right of Rask. The man known more for his goal scoring touch sent a perfect no-look pass right on to the stick of a fast-charging Schenn who without any hesitation one-timed a hard, low shot perfectly labeled for the corner of the goal to the left of Rask. It was bang-bang – the shot hit the inner goal post and went in the net before Rask and the Bruins knew what hit them, and the Blues had a 3-0 lead!

It was tempting to start celebrating - a three-goal lead with less than a half a period to play was a daunting obstacle even for the Russian All-Star team. But crazier things had happened. Just ask Vegas about their three-goal lead over San Jose in Game 7 of Round One with about ten minutes to play. With that as a guide, the Blues needed to be sure to stay out of the penalty box - and certainly no five-minute major penalties!

And then came the icing on the cake and a special symmetry to it all. Perron, the man who scored the Blues' first playoff goal months ago against Winnipeg, would be responsible for the Blues' last goal of the season as well. He won a battle for the puck deep in the Bruins' zone along the same boards where Tarasenko worked his magic only a few minutes before. He then dipsy-doodled between two frustrated Boston players to break in all alone on Rask. Rask came out to greet him but at the last minute, instead of shooting, Perron smartly directed a pass to Sanford who was sitting alone on the other side of the net. The Massachusetts' kid simply tapped it in for his first playoff goal against the team that he rooted mightily for as a kid. And it produced the shocking and seemingly insurmountable 4-0 lead with just four and a half minutes left.

The Bruins prevented Binnington from earning the shut-out with a little over two minutes left, when Bruins' defenseman Grzelcyk got the last goal of the 2018 -2019 season, but it was inconsequential. As the clocked ticked down, I couldn't help but scream over and over "I can't believe it." *Aside from my marriage and the birth of my kids, I had never been happier in my life.*

Postscripts

The Stanley Cup

We are often told that it's the journey in life that matters. Yes, the voyage is important, and we need to constantly remind ourselves to slow down and enjoy it. But don't let anyone tell you that winning the prize doesn't feel pretty darn awesome.

It certainly wasn't easy for our Blues, which probably made winning the Cup that much sweeter. It wasn't just that it took 51 seasons, after so many chances, and that so many great teams, players and coaches were unable to deliver one. Or that this year's march to the playoffs from last to first in only a few months was so unexpected, unrealistic and unprecedented. It was also the way the playoffs themselves unfolded, the teams the Blues played, and how incredibly close the Blues came to be heading home for the summer without the Cup.

There were many facts and figures that demonstrate how difficult this was. The Blues played 26 playoff games, the most *ever* for a winning team in the Stanley Cup. Ten of the team's sixteen playoff wins were by merely one goal. The Blues were tied after four games in each of the four series and were behind in games in three of the four series and at some point, in every playoff series (if you consider that in Game 5 vs Winnipeg with the series tied 2-2, the Blues trailed the Jets by two goals in the third period). The Blues only scored five more goals in the playoffs than their opposition - the lowest differential for any Stanley Cup Champion in history. And, perhaps most incredibly, the Blues scored only one power play goal in 17 chances and gave up seven power play goals on 25 chances in the Stanley Cup Final (and also gave up the only shorthanded goal).

In addition, the predicted outcome of the games based on advanced metrics like "expected goal rate" from Jeremy Rutherford of The Athletic suggested that the Blues should have (in theory) lost 13 of the 26 games, including the initial Winnipeg series (though for Bruins' fans who felt their team outplayed the Blues, the metrics show the Blues with the better expected goal rate in four of the seven games). And the Blues won despite losing a game in the Conference Final due to an illegal hand pass and losing two games in the Stanley Cup Final in which a critical player was suspended by the NHL. We also lost our top young player to injury (undoubtedly caused or contributed to by a brutal hit from the Bruins' Torey Krug).

But the team persevered and played insanely well on the road, winning three out of three in Winnipeg, two out of three in Dallas, two out of three in San Jose and three out of four in Boston, including the last three in a row! Mind you, these were all teams that excelled with home-cooking - a combined record of 103-46-15 during the regular season and 11-6 in the playoffs against teams not named the Blues.

And the Blues were the epitome of resiliency. The team bounced back from every disappointment, bad call, bad break, and unfortunate puck bounce... led by their rookie goalie. The Blues were 6-0 on the road after a loss. And with each series tied after four games, the Blues went 8-2 and outscored the opposition 30-16.

As for the Most Valuable Player, it was an extremely close race in my mind. Ryan O'Reilly, the winner, certainly deserved it. And it was nice seeing him win the award because he was clearly the team's best player during the regular season; the best player in the first half when the Blues were bad, and few players were playing up to their potential, and the best player in the second half when the team started playing well and the Blues were the best team in the NHL. He is also the consummate two-way player, who unselfishly took his defensive responsibilities as a forward every bit as seriously as offensive performance - not common among scorers. In short, he was a model of consistency.

O'Reilly was also our best face-off guy, played on the power play *and* the penalty kill and was extremely tough and durable, playing every game in the season - all 82 regular season games and all 26 playoff games. He finished with a plus/minus goal differential at five on five of plus 24.

In the playoffs, O'Reilly played well during the early rounds but did not seem to be quite his dominant self, especially on face-offs or defensive coverage. Naturally the quality of the competition and the sheer effort of opponents was higher. But I was personally convinced that he was injured. Sure enough, after the Cup was won, O'Reilly reluctantly conceded that he sustained "kind of a cracked rib" in the Dallas series. Last time I checked bones are not "kind of" broken (they either are or aren't). And it sure seems like a very painful injury to play hockey with and to perform at the highest level. But O-Rei knew that the team needed him and that he couldn't afford to miss a single shift, much less a game and he didn't. And, despite his injury he still managed to register 23 points in 26 games.

And when it came to the Final, O'Reilly was somehow recovered, and the best skater on the ice. His performance in the last four games in particular was off the charts; he was everywhere. He scored in each of the final four games, and often the most critical goals, becoming only the second player to score in four consecutive Stanley Cup Finals - the other naturally Gretzky (but even Wayne didn't do it in the *last* four games). And he played stellar defense against some pretty top-end talent on the other side. The play he made in Game 6 on the penalty kill, stealing the puck from Marchand and going around Krug and Pastrnak, was one of the best plays I saw all year, even though unfortunately he wasn't able to score. O'Reilly certainly did not let Blues General Manager Armstrong down and went to extraordinary lengths to help get Bobby Plager his parade, fulfilling his highly ambitious promises to both of them.

So, how could anyone but O'Reilly possibly be the MVP? Only because Jordan Binnington was equally important to winning the Cup. In a game where only a couple of goals, and very often only one, separates winning from losing there is tremendous pressure on the goaltender. A goalie is not only the last line of defense, he is on the ice for all sixty minutes of the game and all of the Overtime, not just twenty minutes or so.

And Binnington rose to the occasion time and time again. While the Blues generally played solid defense in front of him, there were other times when his teammates left him out on an island to hold down the fort. And almost every time when the game or series was on the line, he came through.

There were so many big saves and moments but the performances by Binner that stand out most for me include: the save on Mark Scheifele with 14 seconds left in Game 1 at Winnipeg that would have tied the game and could have dramatically changed the series; the many saves in Game 7 against Dallas to keep the score tied for hours - none more so than the save on Jamie Benn's wrap-around attempt in Overtime - until such time as the Blues could finally beat Bishop; his overall play in Game 3 vs. San Jose, stopping 29 of 30 shots with the Sharks holding a 2-1 series lead and again in the final two games of that series limiting the Sharks' potent attack to a single goal; the barrage of shots he stopped in the first ten minutes of Game 7 vs Boston to keep the game scoreless when the Blues looked like we might get blown out and, of course, the sprawling save on Joakim Nordstrom's rebound attempt in the third period of Game 7 with the Blues up 2-0 and the Bruins desperately trying to cut into the lead and shift the momentum.

Binnington set the tone early in most games and played with such calmness and confidence that it rubbed off on his teammates. And he was the epitome of resiliency, following up every loss with a stellar game. He became the first rookie goalie in NHL history to win all 16 playoff games. In short, the Blues would not have won the Cup without him.

So, I'm not sure how you distinguish between O'Reilly and Binnington; they equally deserve the award. Although awards are wholly inconsequential in the scheme of things, and completely secondary to winning the Cup, my vote would have been for co-MVPs.

That said, and as great as these guys were, it takes far more than two players to win a Stanley Cup - and truly every player to a man played a major contribution in making this happen and deserves to have their name stenciled in perpetuity on this wonderful piece of silver.

A Season to Remember in the Lou

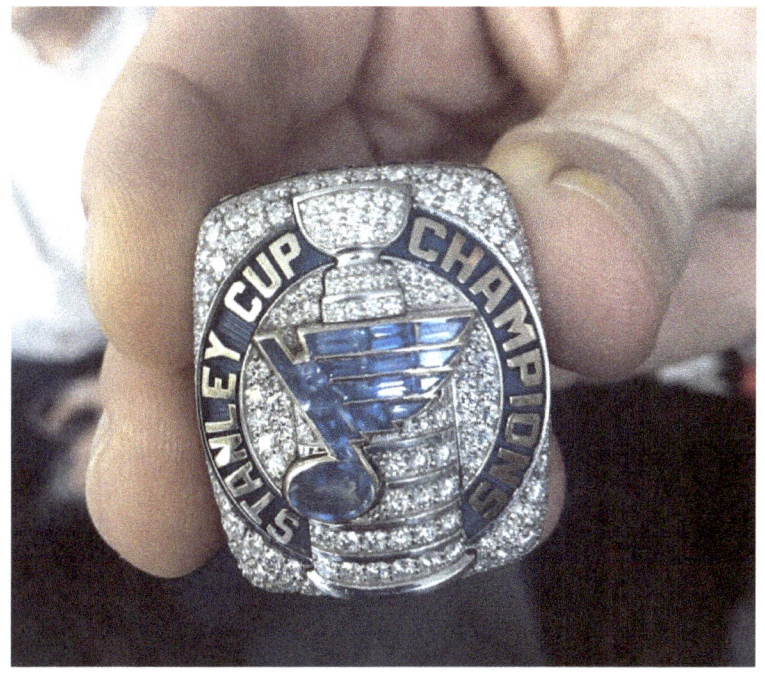

Despite all of the great play and herculean effort by so many guys, the Blues would not have won the Stanley Cup this year had not been for a series of circumstances, some fortuitous, some completely unexpected, and some even damaging and deleterious at the time. But looking back, there were so many critical moments and events that made the difference between the ecstasy of winning the Stanley Cup and the agony of falling short yet again for the 51st time:

If the Blues hadn't had such a woeful start (if the results had even been slightly above average), it's doubtful that management would have fired Mike Yeo or hired Craig Berube when they did, and thus the chances that we would have won the Cup this year would have been remote at best.

If entrenched starting goalie Jake Allen had not had such a poor start (not entirely his fault); and if the backup signed to fill in for Jake hadn't been awful; and if the third-string goalie Ville Husso hadn't been injured at the time; then Jordan Binnington undoubtedly doesn't get his chance to show his goalie mettle this year, and perhaps ever. The likelihood that the Blues would have won the Stanley Cup without Binnington is well, let's say, preposterous.

If left-handed Brayden Schenn doesn't happen to come off the ice in the waning moments of a critical Game 5 in Winnipeg with the series and the score tied to be replaced by right-handed Tyler Bozak who gets the puck in the right corner and immediately fires a mid-waist pass/shot in front of the net where Jayden Schwartz is standing closely guarded; and if Schwartzie doesn't just happen to get his stick on the flying puck in just the right way that it trickles by a 6-foot 3 defenseman glued to his butt and a 6-foot 4 goalie who has 90% of the net covered with 15 seconds remaining; then there was a greater than 50-50 chance that the Blues would have lost Game 5 and thus a high statistical probability that we never would have even made it out of the first round of the playoffs.

If Oskar Sundqvist doesn't elevate his play in the playoffs to a level that Blues' fans had not yet seen, showing tremendous speed, grit and skill often defending against the other's team's best players and making critical offensive contributions, none more so than his drive around Dustin Byfuglien in Game 5 vs. Winnipeg to help tie the game; then I doubt the Blues would have won the Stanley Cup in 2019.

If Jay Bouwmeester doesn't anticipate a wraparound attempt by Dallas' speedster Roope Hintz and use every bit of his hockey acumen and speed at age 35 and the long reach from his 6-foot 4 frame to deflect what was a sure backdoor goal in Game 7 vs. Dallas with less than a minute left in the game, the Blues would have lost that series, and there would have been no San Jose or Boston series to even talk about.

If Pat Maroon doesn't decide to forego a better contract for a longer term and more money to come play in his hometown and be with his young son at an important juncture in his life; and if he doesn't happen to be in a position in Game 7 in Double Overtime against Dallas to see a loose puck lying just behind Ben Bishop, after a great move and shot by Robert Thomas that glanced off the goalpost and then happens to hit Bishop's head; and if he hadn't pounced on the puck at that precise moment with his long reach; the Blues could just have easily lost that series (or might *still* be playing that game trying to score a goal).

If Robert Bortuzzo, the big lumbering defenseman with the big heart but not exactly known as a master stick-handler, shooter or offensive weapon hadn't picked not one but two times to go Bobby Orr on everyone, we likely wouldn't be talking about a parade in the Lou.

If budding star defenseman Vince Dunn doesn't come back after missing numerous games from taking a brutal puck to his mouth, unable to eat solid food or hardly talk, to start Game 4 of the Stanley Cup Final and rush the puck up the ice in the opening minute of the game and take a decent shot on goal that results in a rebound which O'Reilly collects and wraps around into the goal and past Tuukka Rask to seize the early momentum after a devastating Game 3 loss, then perhaps the Blues wouldn't have won their first (and still *only*) home Stanley Cup game in 51 seasons and, in such event, would undoubtedly not be hoisting the Cup in St. Louis this year.

If our best offensive player, Vladimir Andreyevich Tarasenko, doesn't score eleven goals in the playoffs, including several crucial goals and three in the Stanley Cup Final, and also commit to playing the best defense of his career, the Blues undoubtedly do not advance through four rounds of the playoffs.

If Craig Berube hadn't shown the foresight to see the value of Sammy Blais and hadn't inserted him into the line-up against Dallas in the potential elimination Game 6 after a lengthy absence, and kept him in thereafter, the result likely would have been different. Not only did Blais score a pivotal first goal in the first game he played, get two huge assists in other games as well as play a valuable role as a very heavy player throughout the rest of the playoffs, but he also deserves as much credit as anyone for the critical first goal in Game 7 of the Stanley Cup Final.

If Doug Armstrong doesn't trade for Ryan O'Reilly, and he doesn't prove to be the terrific two-way tactician and tireless hockey tsar that he was this year; and if O'Reilly doesn't score goals in each of the last four games, none more critical than the first goal in Game 7 after the Blues had been thoroughly outplayed, I'm pretty darn sure that there would be no championship to celebrate this year.

If the snake-bitten Jaden Schwartz didn't become the Jaden Schwartz we have come to know when it came playoff time - scoring the pivotal game-winning goal in Game 5 against Winnipeg, two hat tricks thereafter, and other key goals, along with his relentless forechecking; and if, in Game 7 of the Stanley Cup Final, he doesn't try to make an offensive play in the closing minutes of the first period despite being out-numbered by passing the puck off the boards to himself; and if Pietrangelo is not hustling hard and calling for the puck and Schwartz doesn't deliver a brilliant reverse pass to him; and if Schenn doesn't hustle and fill the other lane and occupy another Bruins defenseman; and if Petro doesn't cleverly deke Charlie McAvoy and then lift a perfect backhand shot over the all-world goalie Tuukka Rask, giving the Blues a hugely important two goal lead as the team skated off after 20 minutes; the Blues very well may not have been able to sustain the pressure of a Boston rally in Game 7 and could have easily lost the series.

If Carl Gunnarsson doesn't pick a great moment in his long career to unleash the best slap shot of his life in Overtime in Game 2 of the Stanley Cup Final and then block a sure goal from occurring in the waning moments of Game 5, then I would not likely be writing this book.

And on and on. There were so many plays that were game and series' definers - and if any one of them didn't happen, we are likely on to season 52 without the cherished Stanley Cup.

The Blues' historical connections to teams and places

A sports team's identity and character often derive as much from its rivals and enemies as it does from its friends and its fan base. How interesting would it be for Yankees/Red Sox, Cardinals/Cubs, and Longhorns/Sooners fans if it weren't for the other team that you love to despise? The Blues repeated and even bizarre connections to numerous cities and franchises over the past half-century are uncanny and merits mention.

First, there is naturally Chicago - the closest major city and a rival since the beginning of the 19th century when the cities competed for business, prominence and the 1904 World's Fair and the first U.S. hosted Olympics. The Cardinals and Cubs have been doing battle for over a century. The fact that the Blues owe their very existence to the Chicago Blackhawks is certainly compelling. The teams have also played in the same division since 1970 and competed against each other in the playoffs twelve times, with the Blackhawks unfortunately winning eight of those series. And the last three Stanley Cups won by the Blackhawks were coached by Coach Q, a guy who started his head coaching career with the Blues and is still *our* all-time winningest coach. And most miraculously, the Blues' greatest player of all time is the son of the Blackhawks' greatest player of all time. That's downright bizarre.

And then there are the Stars of Minnesota and Dallas. The Stars were born at the same time as the Blues on October 11, 1967 and the teams played their very first game against each other - naturally to a tie. The Stars were also the last team to play the Blues in the old Arena - nearly 27 years after the first game. This wasn't something that was planned or orchestrated; it just so happened to be the team the Blues were playing in the playoffs when the Blues were eliminated, and our season ended prematurely.

Over the years the Blues and Stars have competed against each other more in the playoffs than any other team - 14 times, with the Blues up 8-6 thanks to this year's miraculous seven game Double Overtime win. It was the fourth time the Blues and Stars have gone to seven games in a series and, incredibly, all four of those final games went to Overtime and two of them to Double Overtime! Fortunately, the Blues won three of those series, including both Double Overtime events (if you are going to suffer for five hours it is sure nice to win). Each team has won exactly one Stanley Cup now in 51 seasons - the Stars accomplished theirs with current Blues GM Armstrong as their Assistant GM, and with our greatest player in history scoring the biggest goal in their history.

Finally, the connections between the Blues and the Stars this year were Hollywood-like: with St. Louisan Pat Maroon scoring the game winning goal in Game 7 against his long-time St. Louis buddy Ben Bishop.

Not to be forgotten is the City of Brotherly Love. Philadelphia was also a fellow expansion team of the Blues in 1967. It became an instant rival when the teams squared off against each other in the teams' very first playoff series. The fact that the Blues won that series in seven games after having won only one out of ten games against the Flyers during the regular season solidified their rivalry.

Indeed, the Blues' greater physicality in the early days - led by the Plager brothers and Noel Picard - undoubtedly played a major role in Philly seeking to out-brawn the Blues and other teams in forming the biggest and toughest team around, which also proved (along with some talent to boot) to be a pretty effective way to win hockey games. So, Philly may actually have the Blues to thank for the Broad Street Bullies and their first and second Stanley Cups.

On a broader sports scale, Philadelphia is the city where St. Louis Cardinal Curt Flood famously refused to be traded to which sparked his challenge to the reserve clause in baseball and eventually precipitated the cataclysmic rise in salaries for athletes in every professional sport.

But nothing quite says rivalry like a team's coach being pelted with trash and beer and having his shirt ripped off by the opposing fans and then that team climbing into the stands, skates and all, to fight the fans in response. And then having 200 police officers join the fray swinging billy clubs at your players. And so hated were the Blues in Philly that the team went out of its way to make sure the Blues were not a welcome guest in the Spectrum - making life so difficult for the Blues there that we didn't win a game there for 16 years and 32 tries!

Thus, for hard core Flyer fans - at least those at Jacks - to embrace the Blues this year and adopt them as *their* team during the playoffs - even dressing in Blues' jerseys - defies any sense of logic. Then again, most of the fans were rooting for more goals from Red Berenson once he had scored six that glorious night in Philly in 1972. And Coach Berube began both his NHL playing and coaching career with Philadelphia.

Then there's the unlikely connection between St. Louis and Saskatchewan, the remote province in Canada thousands of miles apart. Saskatchewan is where the Blues' first superstar, Glenn Hall came from - the small town of Humboldt where there is a permanent Glenn Hall monument in Glenn Hall Park on Glenn Hall Drive. *That's some major hometown worship going on there.*

And the player who has played the most career games with the Blues (927 of his career 1000), had the most assists (721) and the most points (1073) in team history, Bernie Federko, also hails from this less populated region of the world. Indeed, Federko is actually from Saskatoon - the city that almost stole our Blues 36 years ago. Further, Doug Wickenheiser, a Blues' legend because of the Monday Night Miracle and an inspiration because of the "14 Fund" is from Saskatchewan as well.

And there were more Saskatchewanians (*what a great name!*) on the Blues' starting roster this year than any other team in the NHL: Jaden Schwartz, Brayden Schenn and Tyler Bozak. The three are also among the top seven career scorers from Saskatchewan currently active in the NHL today. So, although we were competing against Saskatchewan for our team's very existence, I'm pretty sure that the province was big Blues' country, once all the Canadian teams have been eliminated.

Another significant Canadian connection we have is to Calgary. Of course, there is the Monday Night Miracle - generally considered to be the greatest game in Blues' history until this year, even though we lost that series to the Flames sending them to their first Stanley Cup Final (which they lost). But Calgary was able to win a Stanley Cup a few years later in 1989 led by Al MacInnis, who won the Conn Smythe Trophy for Most Valuable Player. Al, of course, became one of the greatest Blues' players of all time as well. His number is retired in both Calgary and St. Louis, but he has a bronze statue outside the Enterprise Center in St. Louis, and he chose to live here - so there! The number of significant trades between these two franchises over the years - over twenty! - and the quality of players to change teams is mind-boggling, including: Brett Hull, Al MacInnis, Joey Mullen, Doug Gilmour, Phil Housely, Mark Hunter, Rob Ramage, Rick Wamsley, Yves Belanger, Craig Conroy, Cory Stillman, Gino Cavallini, Roman Turek, Grant Fuhr, Brian Elliott and Jay Bouwmeester.

Finally, there is the remarkable rivalry with the City of Boston. The cities have competed against each other in Championship Finals in every major professional sport and the competition has been spectacular. Prior to the Stanley Cup this year, both cities' teams have won World Series and NBA Championships against the other. While the Patriots own the only Super Bowl win between the two cities who knows how that very close game would have turned out absent the Patriots' filming of the Rams pregame walkthrough? And now (thankfully) each team has won a Stanley Cup against the other!

The Parade of all Parades

There is always unparalleled elation, along with at least a modicum of relief, any time your team reaches the pinnacle of its sport and wins a Championship. I think it's the tremendous satisfaction as a player and as a fan base in knowing that you are a Champion and that no one can ever take that away from you. And that feeling is even more special when you have never done it before and when the path to get there has been excruciatingly arduous.

I have witnessed numerous celebrations in every professional sport and they are all great. But there is something special and unique about hockey's tradition of allowing each player on the team - from MVP to important role player to back-up goalie - to thrust the thirty-four and a half pounds of silver into the air as confirmation of your contribution, however big or small, to this massive team achievement. I'm not overly sentimental but when I see these tough men who haven't shaved in months and who have persevered through so many aches and pains raise the Cup over their heads, and show their sheer joy, with the widest and most genuine smile imaginable, it gets me every time.

And when the thrusting and toothless smiling is from MY guys on MY team after a 52 YEAR WAIT, I am completely overcome with emotion, even though I didn't score a single goal, stop a single shot or absorb a single check.

I have to give it to the Blues' magnificent ownership group who did everything right in connection with the celebration. The team made sure to include everyone. The players who didn't get a chance to participate in the Stanley Cup Finals but who practiced with the team and supported them in any way they could, were allowed to dress in their uniforms and come on to the ice after the game and be part of the celebration and team photo. The large tremendous Blues' alumni base in St. Louis was also included in every possible way. And most importantly, the fans were made an integral interactive part of the celebration like no fan base ever has in the history of sports.

I have been fortunate to attend several World Series parades and one Super Bowl parade in St. Louis and have watched numerous World Series, Super Bowl, NBA Championship and Stanley Cup victory parades in other cities on TV. Taking nothing away from these celebrations, the Blues' Stanley Cup parade was unlike anything that has *ever* occurred in my experience.

I am not suggesting that folks in St. Louis were more excited about winning the Stanley Cup than other cities that have won a championship in hockey or other sports. Our level of exuberance was extremely high (I rode downtown in a jammed packed standing room only Metro link car with hundreds of fans dancing to the tune of Gloria). And I can't ever remember a time in my life where the City experienced more collective joy. But undoubtedly our euphoria has been matched by other cities who have won championships; especially if it is their first such Championship in the sport and the wait has been especially long.

But what made this parade so unique were the Blues' players themselves. To a man, instead of just waving and smiling from a distance, they got off of their separate trucks that they had been assigned and chose on their own to immerse themselves into the crowd, to high five and glad hand everyone, to take pictures with them, to ride mini-bikes up and down the street, to hold babies, to place those babies into the Stanley Cup, and, yes to drink and share a beer (or more) with perfect strangers. In this age of high security and greater separation of players from fans, and celebrity from the common man, the players chose to share their utter jubilation with the ebullient masses - it was a spontaneous and genuine love-fest and the most unique interaction between athletes and fans that I have ever witnessed in sport. It was magical.

Conclusion

Most of us are fortunate to have formed special relationships in our lives - perhaps with spouses and significant others, kids, parents, siblings, friends, old and new, and cherished work colleagues. But many of us also have another special relationship: with our favorite sports teams. We experience unvarnished joy and effusive pride at their success, but also often utter frustration and even anger at their failings. Indeed, when things are going badly for our team, the days do not seem as bright, we are less patient and tolerant and daily nuisances seem more annoying. But we stay with them through thick and thin - because to a rabid sports fan, the team is another member of the family. But oh, when our team is winning! We are much nicer people; we are more charitable and forgiving, we appreciate more and find it a lot easier to smile. And I and my fellow blue bleeders have been doing a LOT of smiling lately!

After more than five decades, I have the best memory a hockey fan and Blues' fan could possibly have - a sports memory that trumps all others. It's the story of a group of young men; two from Russia, two from Sweden, two Americans (ironically one from St. Louis and the other near Boston) and a very large contingency of Canadians (indeed, more Canadians than any other team), who came from the Ghetto to Gloria in a few short months (*a 300-1 proposition!*) with a 4th string rookie goalie to achieve the greatest trophy in sports.

I am a very lucky and elated man! I can die happy and in peace! And, yes, I will always bleed Blue!

www.ingramcontent.com/pod-product-compliance
Lightning Source LLC
Chambersburg PA
CBHW051350290426
44108CB00015B/1956